THE STORY OF

Cyrus and Susan Mills

THE STORY OF
Cyrus and Susan Mills

BY ELIAS OLAN JAMES, /879-

STANFORD UNIVERSITY PRESS

STANFORD, CALIFORNIA

Library of Congress Catalog Card Number: 53-5757

STANFORD UNIVERSITY PRESS, STANFORD, CALIFORNIA

PUBLISHED IN GREAT BRITAIN, INDIA, AND PAKISTAN

BY GEOFFREY CUMBERLEGE, OXFORD UNIVERSITY PRESS,

LONDON, BOMBAY, AND KARACHI

THE BAKER AND TAYLOR COMPANY, HILLSIDE, NEW JERSEY

HENRY M. SNYDER & COMPANY, 440 FOURTH AVENUE, NEW YORK 16

W. S. HALL & COMPANY, 457 MADISON AVENUE, NEW YORK 22

COPYRIGHT 1953 BY THE BOARD OF TRUSTEES OF THE
LELAND STANFORD JUNIOR UNIVERSITY

PRINTED AND BOUND IN THE UNITED STATES OF AMERICA
BY STANFORD UNIVERSITY PRESS

Preface

THIS STORY OF TWO OLD-FASHIONED TEACHERS, CYRUS AND SUSAN Mills, who graduated from small colleges and founded a small college, was not written for the purpose of arousing nostalgia, though men and women who attended little colleges may find something familiar in the tune. Many small colleges were born on the American frontier in the nineteenth century, had a precarious infancy and were prayed over as puny children, and were forever being snubbed or ignored by bigger institutions. I am not thinking of anemic state schools that looked to the legislature instead of heaven, nor of colleges that were mere bursts of civic enterprise, but of those brave little schools founded by teachers who had caught from their own small alma maters a burning faith in education—founders who knew the best verses in Isaiah by heart. Most large colleges and universities, starting from humble beginnings, have outgrown the faith of their founders. But the precarious infancy, the anxious prayers, the years when it was touch and go whether the bantling would live: these are more interesting than any later bigness. The Currier and Ives quaintness is only a circumstance; the faces in the daguerreotypes grow upon the observer; those pioneer founders had what it takes.

Big colleges snub or ignore or condescend to the little, and that is grand discipline for the little. For where will you find a more pugnacious loyalty than among small-college people? One story may serve. We had driven through a mountain pass down upon a high plateau of cattle ranches. It was May. In the pastures were clumps of *Iris longipetala*, their silvery-blue a shade darker than those on the San Bruno hills or at Monterey. How to persuade someone in the neighborhood to send us a few seed pods in July? The road book stated that there was a normal school in the next town. I parked in front of the main building and went in. A few students, shy and constrained even among themselves, were standing in the hall. When I stated my need a tall youth took me in hand. "I'll take you over to meet Professor Smedley. He's your man." As we crunched along the cinder path I asked the name of a bright-flowered shrub that was whipping in the mesa wind. "You've got me, mister. But I'll ask Professor Smedley. He'll know. He's about the finest botanist in the world." I made no comment; not for worlds would I

v

have lifted an eyebrow. But one could feel the struggle in the boy's mind: *had* he overstated the case? Then Truth prevailed. "I b'lieve they count him about the fourth best."

Tell us, Father Time, where in this huge Pentagon of Success is the Lost and Found Bureau? We have mislaid our capacity for absurd and beautiful loyalties—a mere keepsake of no value to anyone but ourselves.

No man who ever sat on the student's end of the log at Williams College surpassed Cyrus Mills in devotion to Mark Hopkins. Other men were more brilliant, none was more humbly grateful or made better use of his talents. And to the end of her long life Susan Tolman (Mrs. Mills) embodied the versatile energy and educational faith of Mary Lyon of Mount Holyoke— with a warm and colorful difference. That is why I have lingered more than a minute upon Williams and Mount Holyoke. Is there too much Dorchester in the story? But Susan Mills was nearer in faith to her four-times-great-grandfather, Captain Roger Clap of Dorchester, than she was to any person of our times. She was really the last Puritan. The interwoven genealogy of her Dorchester ancestors, though not unique, was so "controlled" an experiment as to justify some detail. (My former students used to enjoy that sort of interest.) And so with other sectors of their story: each has its place in the pattern.

There are few Big Names in the story—none in the center of the stage. That should be a relief. Half our troubles in the college world come from our straining for Who-ness. In his great age Captain Roger Clap remembered a passage from a sermon Master John Cotton preached to the colonists: "That a small running Stream was much better than a great Land Flood of Water, tho' the Flood maketh the greatest Noise." That is the way we small-college persons used to comfort ourselves forty years ago; and many of the teachers we remember from the days of our youth were, and still are, at least the fourth best in the world.

Contents

THE STORY OF
Cyrus and Susan Mills

one

FROM DORCHESTER TO LEOMINSTER

S USAN MILLS HAVING BEEN BORN A TOLMAN, WE SHOULD BEGIN
with her first American ancestor, and serve this chapter up on
a blue and white colonial picture-plate: the first Thomas Tolman, gun on
shoulder, his demurely pretty wife Sarah by his side, marching with grave
fellow townsfolk across a blue-cold landscape on their way to Dorchester
meeting house, which stands somewhere beyond the left rim of the china
picture. Conventionally romantic, once—but never true. There is a glaze
over the plate; the figures move forever in a remote world, and the imagining
child within us cannot easily pass through that glaze into the blue-cold world
and warm the somber folk into naturalness.

Or one might portray the Dorchester brethren with ruder strokes: domineering husbands, acquiescent wives worn with childbearing; the congregation
cupping their ears to lose no syllable of a young husband's required confession
that he had known his wife carnally before marriage, and demanding a more
audible repentance; the voice of Scripture turned rasping in angry sermons;
thrift on its deathbed counting pewter spoons; a dread of innovation and a
terrible distrust of beauty. The best man in the village consented that

3

Quakers be whipped out of town, and more than one brother was o'ertaken with rum at a godly funeral. But the rude strokes too easily become a caricature which ignores too much, guesses too much, and fails to tell us why so many of those Dorchester families—Mathers and Capens, Blakes and Athertons, Claps and Howes—gave to American life an impetus amounting to genius.

Or, in brisk picture fashion, one might show Thomas Tolman in leather apron in his shop in Dorchester, teaching his sons—Thomas and John—the wheelwright's trade. What with farm chores, and plenty of wheels to make or to mend, father and sons are busy, but not too busy to give civil greetings to Captain Humphrey Atherton when he reins up to speak of matters debated in General Court in Boston yesterday, he being our town deputy and newly come from that sitting. Thomas Bird, the tanner, brings the leather we need for mending our bellows, and allows the cost to offset our mortising the thills and hounds of his oxcart last haying season. Thomas Davenport, careful for town affairs, sounds our mind about this new-proposed fencing of the common and a just wage for the town ox-ward. Abraham Howe brings us a small mending chore that cries for speed: the felly of his daughter's flax wheel must have new dowels, and he—poor man—so beset to finish weaving the new woolen stuff for Master Mather's gown, and winter coming on and all, and his bee skeps not yet winter-thatched, and so busy he nigh forgets to leave the peck of russet apples we bespoke of him, seeing that the new grafted trees in our own orchard want two or three years of bearing. Captain Roger Clap brings warrant of mouth from the selectmen that we make stout wheels for the new saker gun that is to be mounted upon the Point looking across to Thompson's Island: a matter of the common-weal, this, to be entrusted to no piddling craftsman. Roger's cousin, Nicholas Clap, stays for an hour to question profitably whether, now that Master Mather's body is failing, it were well for the church to call as helper a young man who is but newly ordained and hath no store of learning beyond that of Harvard school on the Charles: "For if the trumpet give an uncertaine sound, who shall prepare himselfe to the battell?" Goodmen Richard Leeds and William Pond pass with word that three several neighbors, sailing nigh to Lynn yesterday, took great catches of mackerel and scrod—enough, salted, to store their casks against a hard winter. At the word "Lynn" our tall sons redden and make a great to-do setting a tire. Each of them is courting a Lynn girl. And while this romantic method pauses for breath—and in good time!—our five daughters, Sarah and Hannah and Rebecca and Mary and Ruth, will be popping their comely Puritan heads in at the shop door, on one pretext or another, whilst we contrive to name their sweethearts, from Henry Lead-better to Isaac Royall.

Still, there was method in that lushness. We were to begin with Susan Tolman's first American ancestor. Who was the first? Thomas Tolman and the eight other freemen of Dorchester who came to his shop were all nine, in equal degree, ancestors of Susan Tolman. Besides, a tenth ancestor so well concealed himself under the name of Smith as to defy further identification. Ten first American ancestors, with their wives, in one small village—and on the paternal side only. And the count is still deceptive; for Thomas Tolman was Susan's great-great-great-great-grandfather twice over, as was Roger Clap. Susan was, indeed, more Clap than Tolman, for Roger and Nicholas Clap were first cousins, and she was a seventh-generation descendant of each —and of Roger twice.

"A tangled chain: nothing impaired, but all disordered." If you are avid for compound fractions, glance at the charts on pages 6 and 7.

What does it all come to? Is there any assayable quantum in attenuated heredity? Did any one of those seventh-generation forefathers pass more or less than his theoretical one sixty-fourth of traits and qualities to Susan Tolman? Each quantum being so small, there is little in heredity, then? A plant breeder who has watched seven generations of controlled mating would not share that doubt. The cord of heredity has more strands than we usually reckon. Some strands are better than others; some strands—better or worse— are more prepotent. In any case—bluestocking or barefoot—this attenuated heredity is what we have. No American community will ever again furnish such a "controlled" experiment in the intermarriage of good English yeoman families as occurred in Dorchester through five generations. The control was only partly planned—the town excluded undesirable persons; but young men rarely courted beyond the town borders, and as late as 1800 very few strange surnames appear in the records. The flow was out, not in; and by the fifth generation the interwoven family strands were compact.*

---

* Experience, Desire, Increase, Thankfull, Submit: these baptismal names, sampler-stitched, overpossess the mind at first, but the ear is soon tuned to them. Here for good measure are a few more from Dorchester records: Watching Atherton, Relief Blake, Unite Mawdsley, Vigilance Fisher, Rest Leadbetter, Standfast Foster (and his sister Comfort), Purchase Capen, Silence and Submit Withington (twins who died young, poor lambs). And with these whole flocks of other Puritan virtues: Preserved, Dependence, Deliverance, Renewed, Returned, Recompense, Take-heed, Free-grace, and Free-love (surely to be understood with ascetic connotation). These sound of the putting on of the whole armor of God; but one girl's name has the happy accident of poetry: Waitawhile Makepeace—what a wife for a nervous man, soothing as the Shepherd's psalm.

THE TOLMAN LINE

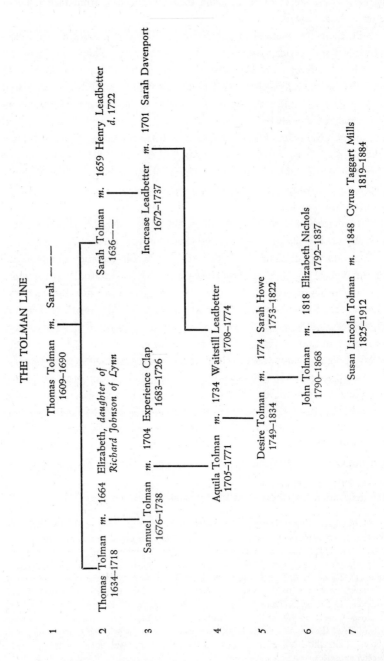

1   Thomas Tolman   m.   Sarah ————
     1609–1690

2   Thomas Tolman   m.   1664   Elizabeth, daughter of
     1634–1718   Richard Johnson of Lynn

     Sarah Tolman   m.   1659   Henry Leadbetter
     1636——   d. 1722

3   Samuel Tolman   m.   1704   Experience Clap
     1676–1738   1683–1726

     Increase Leadbetter   m.   1701   Sarah Davenport
     1672–1737

4   Aquila Tolman   m.   1734   Waitstill Leadbetter
     1705–1771   1708–1774

5   Desire Tolman   m.   1774   Sarah Howe
     1749–1834   1753–1822

6   John Tolman   m.   1818   Elizabeth Nichols
     1790–1868   1792–1837

7   Susan Lincoln Tolman   m.   1848   Cyrus Taggart Mills
     1825–1912   1819–1884

THE CLAP LINE

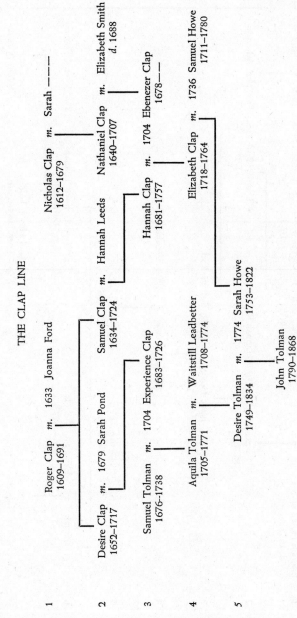

1   Roger Clap   *m.*   1633   Joanna Ford
     1609–1691

          Nicholas Clap   *m.*   Sarah ——
          1612–1679

2   Desire Clap   *m.*   1679   Sarah Pond
     1652–1717

          Samuel Clap
          1634–1724

          m.   Hannah Leeds

          Nathaniel Clap   *m.*   Elizabeth Smith
          1640–1707   *d.* 1688

3   Samuel Tolman   *m.*   1704   Experience Clap
     1676–1738   1683–1726

          Hannah Clap   *m.*   1704   Ebenezer Clap
          1681–1757   1678——

4   Aquila Tolman   *m.*   Waitstill Leadbetter
     1705–1771   1708–1774

          Elizabeth Clap   *m.*   1736   Samuel Howe
          1718–1764   1711–1780

5   Desire Tolman   *m.*   1774   Sarah Howe
     1749–1834   1753–1822

          John Tolman
          1790–1868

THE HOWE LINE

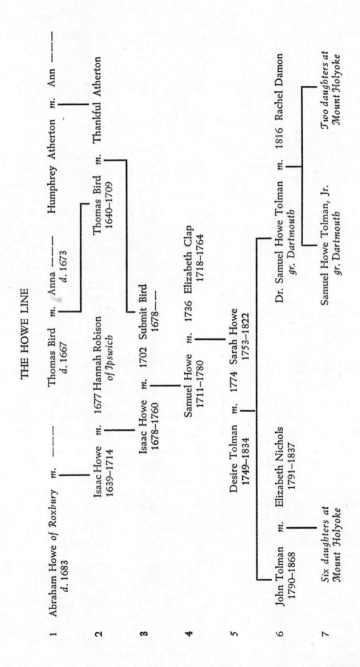

1   Abraham Howe of Roxbury   *m.*   ——————
    d. 1683

2   Isaac Howe   *m.*   1677   Hannah Robison
    1639–1714   *of Ipswich*

3   Isaac Howe   *m.*   1702   Submit Bird
    1678–1760   1678——

4   Samuel Howe   *m.*   1736   Elizabeth Clap
    1711–1780   1718–1764

5   Desire Tolman   *m.*   1774   Sarah Howe
    1749–1834   1753–1822

6   John Tolman   *m.*   Elizabeth Nichols
    1790–1868   1791–1837

7   *Six daughters at*
    Mount Holyoke

Thomas Bird   *m.*   Anna ——————
d. 1667   *d.* 1673

Humphrey Atherton   *m.*   Ann ——————

Thomas Bird   *m.*   Thankful Atherton
1640–1709

Dr. Samuel Howe Tolman   *m.*   1816   Rachel Damon
gr. Dartmouth

Samuel Howe Tolman, Jr.
gr. Dartmouth

Two daughters at
Mount Holyoke

James Blake, the town clerk and voluntary annalist of Dorchester two hundred years ago, did not like to see the younger generation forget the past. And being a wise old man, he knew that Time often throws bulky stuff away and keeps a little longer in his pack certain tiny kickshaws. In 1705 "the ould widow Wiat" of Dorchester died at the age of ninety-four. Later, Blake set down her humble record. She had helped more than eleven hundred babies into the world. She had observed intimately—we may say—most of the second and third generations, and a few of the fourth, and she knew the stock they came from. Is there a persisting family nose or chin or forehead, some brightness or shadow of mood or temper that throws back to a vanished great-grandmother? The "ould widow Wiat" knew what she knew—and we do not!

Let biological heredity be as it may, these Dorchester families developed another heritable estate: the healthy common sense of yeoman stock. Boston soon became—Boston. Cambridge had more leaven of book-learning. Some seafaring towns were bolder and tougher; some towns had a harder scrabble to make a living. Was it some inherent somberness in a few men that made Salem a wrestling place with dark angels? Dark angels and weird sisters avoided Dorchester. Whether by good luck or misfortune, Dorchester had none of those dramatic climaxes that demand bronze tablets. A few of her men became notables in the Colony—Humphrey Atherton* and Roger Clap particularly. Mr. Richard Mather and his sons and grandsons had throughout and beyond New England that quality which called for the old-style spelling —"preheminence." Four of his sons were to become notable preachers, one of them a president of Harvard.† But there were very few "Misters" in Dorchester, and the town continued long in the steady character of English yeoman stock—craftsmen whose feet were on the earth, and whose tools did not fly off the handle. Nearly all the first families of the village came from the southern shires of England. By methods which will appear, they kept their community relatively free from unwanted newcomers.

* Humphrey Atherton was one of Dorchester's deputies to the General Court, and an able soldier. He shared with Miles Standish and Captain John Mason the responsible leadership of the armed forces of the Colony. "Altho he be slow of speech, yet he is down right for the business, one of cheerful spirit, and intire for his country."

† Although Richard Mather's most famous grandson, Cotton Mather, cannot rightly be called a Dorchester boy, yet mayn't we suppose that young Cotton was, at the age of six, carried down from Boston to be edified at his grandfather's deathbed? And helped to make hay in that good minister's salt-marsh meadow? This hay-making hypothesis explains the uncompressed style of the *Magnalia*: balers had not been invented. And whatever grew upon the earth went into the windrow: flowers, weeds, thistles, plenty of mares' nests, along with salty marsh grass.

Dorchester was settled in June 1630 by a band of one hundred forty persons, most of them from Dorsetshire. Although they had felt the pressure of religious intolerance at home, they were not compelled from without but urged from within. They were to suffer hardships, but this was no wintry casting forth upon a stern and rockbound coast. They had an eye to husbandry in choosing their location.

They sailed on the *Mary and John*. (Socially, the *Mary and John* became to later Dorchestrians something of a password, mild and not too romantic. Though a larger ship than the *Mayflower*, she apparently carried fewer people.) They were to have landed on the grassy banks of the Charles, above where Cambridge now stands, but the squint perversity of one man thwarted them. The captain of the *Mary and John* is recorded as "a merciless man." His dark psychosis, begotten in Adam's sin, was hereditary with his name— Squeb.* This frustrated man put in, not at the mouth of the Charles, but close to the rocky point of Nantasket. The meadows of Mattapan, along the Neponset, looked good to sea-weary men and cattle, and so both men and cattle (as a chronicler puts it) "sat down."†

Town and church records show that here was a practical Christian democracy. Land was allotted to men in proportion to the size of their families and their ability to use the land well. "It is ordered that no man within the Plantation shall sell his house or lott to any man without the Plantation whom they shall dislike of." As early as 1633 Israel Stoughton was granted the right to build a mill, but with the proviso that he might not sell it without consent of the town, and that whatever fish he took at his dam be sold for a fair ceiling price. Land and forest were for the common-weal. Early and often the selectmen—"our most graue and moderate and prudent brethren" —granted or disallowed a freeman's request to fell trees from the common forest, or permitted a poor man to gather fallen timber. Citizenship was not an inherent right; a man had to win approbation to become a freeman, and church membership was a prerequisite. As in England, relief of the poor and

---

* R.L.S., he is yours by right. And for a proper enemy to Captain Squeb—a foeman grim as Calvin and firm as Euclid—let me nominate Mr. Andrew Quam.

† For orientation, the village of Dorchester was about ten miles south of Beacon Hill in Boston. Western readers should remember that "town" still means township in New England. In this sense, the town of Dorchester had the area of a modern county, a sweep of wilderness almost as far as Rhode Island. "The village was," for Boston has overspread and smothered it with untidy tenements and crowded streets where (it is said) racial and religious antipathies are worse than three hundred years ago, and are argued without citing Scriptures. The town meeting of old had its points, after all. Only in the old walled cemetery at Upham's Corner will you find the fading names: Wiswal and Tilestone and Capen, Tolman and Clap.

incompetent was the responsibility of the town where these belonged; the community knew better than some more remote governmental body the merits of the case. And the town was sharply watchful against being saddled with undesirable persons. In 1670, "Henery Leadbetter was Caled before the Select men to answer for his receauing Jonathan Birch into the towne contrary unto a towne order." On another day, "Ebenezer Hill came before the Select men and was aduertized Concerning Idleness." There is a teasing hint of mystery in another case: Thomas Makepeace "because of his novel disposition was informed we were weary of him unless he reform." He removed to Boston!

From January through July, school opened at seven and closed at five; during the other five months the hours were from eight to four. It was the master's duty to catechize the children and to instruct them "both in humane learning and good litterature, & likewise in pynt of good manners and dutifull behauiour towards all . . . the Rodd of Correction is an ordinance of God necessary sometymes to be dispensed vnto children." The masters were, at first, English university men; later, from Harvard. In 1652 the selectmen appointed three citizens to "take the volentary collection of the Inhabetance of Dorchester for the mayntenance of the President certayne Fellowes and poore scollers in Harvard Colledge." Throughout the years a decent quota of young men from Dorchester went to Harvard.

To our generation it may appear strange that a people so committed to self-government should accept from its ministers a degree of leadership far greater than our time allows. In a wilderness where all was rough-hewn and home-made, Richard Mather's scholarship in Hebrew, Greek, and Latin was regarded as a matter of course. There was mentality on both sides of the desk. Mentality, and Spartan rigor, too. If any soul in the congregation winced from the tortured verses of the Bay Psalm Book, the fact does not appear. That agglomeration of fractured granite was largely the work of Richard Mather; and—for whatever romantic association it may have—ten of "our" forefathers and (from over on the women's side) their ten wives lifted their voices—but how with one accord?—in singing:

> *The earth Jehovah's is*
> *and the fulness of it:*
> *the habitable world, & they*
> *that thereupon do sit.*

O grave and prudent brethren, O mothers in Israel, did not some small inner voice, timed to your pulse beat, tell you that the Authorized Version is better?

The earth is the Lord's and the fulness thereof, the world and they that dwell therein. Richard Mather's own voice was "loud and big, uttered with a deliberate Vehemency, it procured unto his Ministry an awful and very taking *Majesty*." Perhaps—but not in iambics.

> *O Lord our God in all the earth*
> *how's thy name wondrous great?*

A few Mills College women still remember Mrs. Mills' reading of the Ninety-first Psalm. "For He shall give His angels charge over thee, to keep thee in all thy ways. They shall bear thee up in their hands, lest thou dash thy foot against a stone. Thou shalt tread upon the lion and the adder; the young lion and the dragon thou shalt trample under foot."

> *They shall support thee in their hands:*
> *lest thou against a stone*
> *shouldst dash thy foot. Thou trample shalt*
> *on th'Adder, & Lion.*

Trample upon the wicked lion, Master Mather; but even a lion hath in the divine Bill of Rights *his* right not to have his accent wrenched for religious purposes.

And so they got on—miller and tanner, shipwright and wheelwright, blacksmith and cooper and weaver, and at least one "Biskett Maker." Also it was useful to know that neighbor John Eeles made beehives,* old-fashioned conical skeps of barley straw. Mere busywork for rainy days, the hands twisting the straw into a rope and coiling it, while the mind could dream a little of innocent pleasure domes in a wilderness. Everybody farmed; even Mr. Mather had his allotment of plow and meadow land. The men and women who had come in the *Mary and John* would long remember the hardships of the first years, but the earth was not unkind nor the wind always straight off Labrador, and these Dorset folk must have had green thumbs. Who among them brought the first seeds and slips of pretty things, along with wheat and rhubarb and parsnips?

In 1633 an English traveler, William Wood, was coming up the coast from Plymouth. His description of Dorchester has become a classic "quote":

> *Sixe miles further to the North, lieth Dorchester; which is the greatest Towne in New England; well wooded and watered; very good arable*

---

* The beehive maker was progenitor of a long line of ministers, some of whom were among the founders of Hamilton College; still later, another descendant was a Trustee of Mills College.

grounds, and Hay-ground, faire corn-fields, and pleasant Gardens, with Kitchin-gardens. In this plantation is a great many Cattle, as Kine, Goats, and Swine. This plantation hath a reasonable Harbour for ships: Here is no Alewife river, which is a great inconvenience. The inhabitants of this towne, were the first that Set upon the trade of fishing in the Bay, who received so much fruits of their labours, that they encouraged others to the same undertaking.

Forty years later, John Josselyn, coming by the same route (and maybe with Wood's book in pocket) saw Dorchester as it was when Thomas Tolman's grandchildren were young:

Sixe miles beyond Braintree lyeth Dorchester, a frontire Town pleasantly seated, and of large extent into the main land, well watered with two small Rivers, her body and wings filled somewhat thick with houses to the number of two hundred and more, beautiful with fair Orchards and Gardens, having also plenty of Cornland, and store of Cattle, counted the greatest Town heretofore in New England, but now gives way to Boston, it hath a Harbor to the North for Ships.

Josselyn moved on a mile or so to Roxbury, which links into our Dorchester story in two ways. John Eliot, apostle to the Indians, was the minister of Roxbury for sixty years. A close friend and collaborator of Richard Mather's, Eliot left a deep impress upon Dorchester minds. Roxbury had been settled mainly by men from Essex, two of these being Abraham Howe, the weaver, and his brother James. Though Abraham began as a Roxbury man he soon acquired holdings in Dorchester and figured often in the town records; and his descendants carried the family line down until Sarah Howe, of the fifth generation, became Susan Tolman's grandmother. A good line, these Howes. Four men descended from Abraham and three descended from James won places in the Dictionary of American Biography—and the count does not include Howe descendants who have other surnames. It appears that John Howe, of Sudbury and Marlboro, one of whose descendants built the Wayside Inn at Sudbury, was not related closely if at all to Abraham and James; yet James left a note referring to an ancestral coat of arms which resembles that of the Host of the Wayside—

> *He beareth gules upon his shield,*
> *A chevron argent in the field,*
> *With three wolf's heads . . .*

But fame had not yet come to the Howes of Dorchester. Isaac (2) was having a hard time when in 1677 and again in 1681 the selectmen remitted a part of his taxes. Slight as the importance is, this is the only instance in the town records where any ancestor of Susan Tolman needed aid. Isaac (3), a weaver as his grandfather had been, came up in the world. Dying intestate in 1760, he left a decent estate of 1,400 pounds, including six hives of bees, apples on the ground, his weaver's loom and tackle, and—for shame—some tobacco. The careful appraisers even added an amended list to their inventory in which they name one pair of silver-bowed spectacles and one grindstone. When two of this Isaac's sons applied for letters of probate they revealed a quirk of the changing social conditions of the time: son Joseph is still called "yeoman," but son Samuel ("our" ancestor) is called "Gentleman"—with a capital G.

And now let us go back to Thomas Tolman the wheelwright. It is not certain whether he came in the *Mary and John*, though family tradition—in this case from a singularly reliable source—holds that he did.* If so he was twenty-two when he came, and probably unmarried; and if he married in New England, the parents of his wife Sarah make still another couple of "first" American ancestors whose names we do not know. Thomas was a church member in 1636 when Richard Mather reorganized the church of Dorchester after half its members had removed to Windsor in Connecticut. He was a freeman by 1640, maybe a little earlier. In 1639 "It is ordered that Good[man] Tolmans howse be appoynted for Receauing any goods that shal be brought in whereof the owner is not knowen."

Thomas was never as prominent in office as Roger Clap, but he had a decent village dignity, beginning as fence-viewer, then constable, then super-visor of "the hie ways," and selectman. Meantime he and his sons figure in assessments on their land and payment for their work as wheelwrights. In 1653: "Item payd Thomas Tolman toward a pare of wheles for the Gunn," one pound. Again in 1670 he and John were paid for their "worke about wheels," and in 1673 "for worke about the Carridg." Thomas was no fire-eater, but in 1653 the town paid one pound "to Goodman Tollman for killing a woolfe." By your leave, good selectmen, a wolf with an *oo* and a final *e*— a wolf with his proper sound effects—should be worth five shillings extra. His very phonetics fill the Imaginacioun with an Horrour of great Darknesse.

One item in James Blake's *Annals* gives a nice picture of Thomas as an old man. Seats in the meeting house were assigned according to dignity. Blake recalls the "old" seating arrangement as it had been before 1690: Thomas Tolman senior sat with his son Thomas and his son-in-law Henry

* See Appendix A, Deacon Samuel Tolman's Hollow Cane.

Leadbetter, with nine or ten other men of esteem, around the table which stood in front of the minister's desk. First the men around the table, then the men in the first pew, and so on. But the best picture of all is the unconscious portrait in his will: he had earlier given land to his sons when they set up homes for themselves; he saw to it that his daughters were treated equitably; the one unthrifty son-in-law was not cast out but was expected still to make good. If the old man appears careful about pewter and tools, those tools had earned him whatever he had, and pewter and linen had cost patient labor.*

Both of Thomas' sons were wheelwrights, and both found their wives in Lynn. Perhaps trips on the fishing fleet had something to do with courtship. Thomas (2) left a larger estate than his father and seemed more concerned than his father had been about his possessions, and to apprehend envy among his children. One item in his bequest calls for comment: he left to his wife Elizabeth one Negro servant. We did not call them slaves in New England, yet they were bequeathed as property well down into the eighteenth century. (A case occurs in a Boutelle will in 1752.) As early as 1640 "Dorcas ye blackmore" was baptized in the church in Dorchester; and other Negro servants were baptized and married and buried as even Christians, and often by the family name of their masters, well down to Revolutionary times.

Two sons-in-law of Thomas the First deserve a word. Henry Leadbetter came late, probably around 1650, and apparently with no relatives. He worked his way up from laborer to selectman, though in the probating of his will (1722) he was still called "yeoman." One son was a cordwainer in Boston, one a carpenter in Dorchester; but a third son, Increase (ancestor of Susan Tolman), had gotten on so well that the probate records listed him as "Gentleman." Another son-in-law of Thomas the First, Isaac Royall, built the new meeting house, which stood for a century. His son Isaac built the house in Medford, famous in later times as the Royall Mansion.

Samuel Tolman (3) and Aquila (4) were blacksmiths. Aquila left a decent property and his will still voices the humble piety of his great-grandfather.

Desire Tolman (5), who married Sarah Howe (5) in 1774, was a minuteman on Lexington Day, and later served with militia on Castle Island. He continued a Dorchester man until, at some time between 1785 and 1789, he moved to Winchendon, a new town half way across the state westerly and near the New Hampshire line. Six of his and Sarah's nine children were born

---

* See Appendix B, Will of the First Thomas Tolman, and Appendix C, We Look at a Favorite of King Charles.

in Dorchester, the last three (including John Tolman, the father of Susan) in Winchendon. We shall see more of Deacon Desire Tolman later.

This much impress the Howes and Tolmans and Leadbetters left—a few facts, a few words, whereby we partly know them. But the clearest ancestor is Roger Clap; his public record is more complete, and he opened his heart and mind in a book. He wrote that little book with, apparently, no least thought that it would ever be printed or would even be read by anyone except his children and children's children. It was he who remembered that sentence from a sermon by John Cotton which sounded a theme in our Foreword: "That a small running Stream was much better than a great Land Flood of Water, tho' the Flood maketh the greatest Noise." This saying, which he knew by heart forty years after the words were spoken, is a key to his own nature.

Roger Clap came from Devonshire—not Dorset—and he came on the *Mary and John*—no doubt on that point; his own chronicle of that voyage and the first days of the town is a main source of information about it. In 1633 he married Joanna Ford, who was not quite seventeen. She bore Roger fourteen children and lived with him for fifty-seven years, and in his will he reveals toward her a tenderness that makes us wonder whether those grim Puritans were half as grim as our sophisticated age has supposed. A tenderness more than a little like that of the Old Shepherd in *A Winter's Tale*.

Roger Clap was, from the first, a man of affairs in Dorchester. He was early a selectman and elder, rose to be captain of the militia, and was long a deputy in the General Court (equivalent of the legislature) in Boston. Then in 1665 he was appointed Captain of Castle Island, most important defensive point for the central coast. (Castle Island became Fort Independence.) For twenty-one years he and his wife and their younger children made their home in the little brick fort. James Blake tells how the soldiers in the garrison attended family prayers, conducted by Captain Clap—"in which if he understood his Prolixity were disagreeable to any, he would be Troubled thereat." Then at the age of seventy-seven he resigned his post, not as awearied or unfit, but because his conscience could not approve certain dictatorial ways of the new royal governor, Edmund Andros. He and Joanna moved to Boston, where they spent the rest of their lives.

These things we learn from town and church records, and from James Blake; for in his *Memoirs* Roger Clap used an effortless self-effacement. He speaks of other public men—saints and a few rogues—but a reader would hardly suppose the author had been so much as a fence-viewer. Even of his appointment as Captain of the Castle he merely writes, apropos of the death of his predecessor: "the General Court . . . appointed another Captain in the Room of him that was slain." Few autobiographers are dull when telling of childhood and youth; few but lose some charm when they verge into *Who's Who.*

He wrote his *Memoirs* around 1676. In 1731 James Blake thought the manuscript too good to be lost, and saw it through the press. The book has been reprinted a few times, yet it would hardly be rated a classic. It is Puritanism with a difference. Richard Mather's journal of his voyage to New England breathes a strenuous faith that somehow leaves the reader as he was, unable to draw close to the austerity. And Cotton Mather's *Magnalia*, once terrifying, has long since been viewed as a hugeous unintentional caricature. Was the Puritan nature no kinder than this? Does the *Magnalia* speak for all hearts? The medicinal virtue of Roger Clap's little book lies in its simplicity; it is religious rather than theological. Note how he completes the remembered passage from John Cotton's sermon: "That a small running Stream was much better than a great Land Flood . . . So, saith he, A little constant Stream of Godly Sorrow, is better than great Horrour." In his young manhood Roger had felt troubled because the love of God had come to him quietly, in an unorthodox way, without tempest or whirlwind or angry fire. Afterward he had learned to trust the quietness. He is like a man that saith to his brother: Come and see.

Any brisk journalist could write the Captain's story for him and do it ever so much better—and leave us feeling not half so good. Time and again when he has started along some path of story, his eagerness for the well-being of the younger generation draws him off into conversational sermon, and yet the essential kindness of his heart saves him from officiousness:

In those Days great was the Tranquility & Peace of this poor Country: And there was a great Love one to another, very ready to help each other, not seeking their own, but every man another's Wealth . . . In those Days God did cause his People to trust in him, and to be contented with mean things. It was not accounted a strange thing in those Days to drink Water, and to eat Samp and Homine without Butter or Milk . . . After the first Winter, we were very Healthy, though some of us had no great Store of Corn . . . Frostfish, Muscles and Clams were a Relief to Many. If our Provision be better now than it was then, let us not, (and do you dear Children take heed that you do not) forget the Lord our God. You have better Food and Raiment than was in former Times, but have you better Hearts than your Fore-fathers had?

He had known Endicott; had long been, and was still, warm neighbor to
John Eliot; he recalled many a sermon preached under a spreading tree.
He had seen the colony in danger; and if he distrusted dissenters, he had
reason:

> *because God's People here, could not Worship the true and living God, as
> He hath appointed us in our publick Assemblies, without being disturbed
> by them.*

His kindness, then, is not the softness of timidity. He was a soldier. But
throughout his little book he speaks of love, not wrath.

> *To this very Day if I perceive or do but hear of a Man or Woman that
> feareth God, let him be Rich or Poor, English or Indian, Portugal or
> Negro, my very heart closeth with him.*

His mind was ripened with Scriptures. He had unaware that best of fortunes, the capacity to feel a welling excitement in passages that unify over
the centuries the deepest experience of men. In this respect there is no
cleavage between his generation and the persons among whom Susan Tolman
grew up. Whole pages of his *Memoirs* might be spread upon the diary and
the journal she wrote at Mount Holyoke, with no strangeness in spirit or
tone.

Blake wrote of the captain: "He was a hearty lover of his Country, a
well wisher to it, one that Prayed often for it . . . He was Buried in the
old Burying Place in Boston; the Military Officers going before the Corps;
and next to the Relations, the Governour and the whole General Court
following after; and the Guns firing at the Castle at the same time." The
"old Burying Place" is now King's Chapel Ground, where Beacon Street
descends to Tremont. Roger's and Joanna's gravestones are close side by
side under a low-spreading tree near the east side of the yard—one of those
islands of quiet which improvement has spared.

The captain's will would drive a careful attorney or title-abstract man
to distraction with its casual descriptions of real property: but why be fussy
about facts that every neighbor knows? Besides, if there be any doubt,
why, all is set down orderly "in my little Forril booke." One notes his
double gratitude toward his oldest son, Samuel, of whom the church clerk
wrote: "a very holy, wise, able, upright, faithfull, humble, usefull servant
of ye Lord all his Days." In a word, an Elder emeritus.

Tenuous as the long strand of heredity may be, *is* there something in it?
The record of the Howes and the Claps sets the thoughtful mind awonder-

ing about this strange force, this carry-over of power in individuals. Desire Tolman (5) was descended from Captain Roger's youngest son, Desire Clap. Sarah Howe (5) was descended from the captain's oldest son, Samuel. Argue what it may, Susan Tolman was in her youth, and considerably to the end of her life, nearer to the character of Puritan Dorchester than we are to the thought and feeling of, say, 1865.

Through her maternal grandmother, Susan Tolman was of the eighth generation of the Boutelles, who settled in Lynn and Reading in the 1630's. After a century her line of the family moved by a sickle-shaped course down through Sudbury and then northwesterly through Lancaster to Leominster, a new town about twelve miles south of the New Hampshire line. As the family of her maternal grandfather, Levi Nichols, followed the same course from Lancaster (and perhaps all the way from Reading), the topographical mind may visualize one of the many small currents whereby the coastal settlements populated the interior of Massachusetts. Those currents were slow and they flowed but a short way; one could now make the trip in three hours by automobile, with easy time to enjoy the vista of orchards, little rivers with their meadow ground, rocky hill pastures, and the succession of green and white villages.

There is less to tell of these Boutelle and Nichols ancestors than of the Dorchester families. There were no Roger Claps and James Blakes to set the story down while it was fresh, and not even a homespun deacon with a hollow cane. However, after the Boutelle and Nichols families reached Leominster (around 1750) their members became more distinct than the corresponding generations of the Tolmans.

The spelling of the Boutelle name was catch-as-catch-can for church and town clerks, and for members of the family, too: Boutal, Boutaille, Boutel, Boutill, Boutle, Boutwell, Bowtell—and otherwise as you like it. It is said that the name began in England as *de Boutville*, and that the first of the clan there helped William of Normandy defeat the Saxons (including the Tolmans!) at Hastings. Be that as it may, James Boutelle I, who was settled in Lynn by 1636, was of plain yeoman stock. He was a freeman and a landholder by 1638. So far as is known, all later Boutelles in America were descended from him.

The records do not show just when James Boutelle II and his brother John moved into the adjacent town of Reading. James II was a housewright and farmer. His wife Rebecca was a daughter of Deacon Thomas and Rebecca Kendall, who were of Reading's best russet-apple stock, prolific and with grand keeping qualities. Their eight daughters, marrying capably, carried the Kendall blood over into Eatons and Boutelles and Bryants and Parkers and Duntons and Nicholses and Goodwins and Parsons, until the town historian allowed that a good half of the families in Reading were of Kendall stock. Aunt Rebecca Kendall, dying in 1703 at the age of eighty-five, counted one hundred seventy-five grand- and great-grandchildren of her own, and had been all-round nurse, baby-receptionist, and home-remedy doctor to as broad a neighborhood as could be reached by sidesaddle.

James Boutelle II is listed as having his allotment of town lands, and as rate-payer for the church; and various entries show him as thrifty above the average. His death record names him lieutenant—and the times did not cherish honorary degrees. His will (1716) is voluminous with household details, and written in a transitional hand, blended of Elizabethan and Italianate script. His three older daughters could only make their marks on the probate papers, though their husbands signed; and the two youngest girls signed a fair hand. The will is homely with casks and firkins of winter stores, barrels of cider, and the like; and it provides that one or more of the brothers should furnish the unmarried sisters with a stipend of shillings and so many bushels of apples each fall.

James Boutelle III died before his father. In the death records his name is prefixed by *Cler;* this may have meant clergyman, but no other evidence of his being a minister has come to hand. With young James Boutelle IV our branch of the family moved to Sudbury. His wife, Judith Poole, was a great-granddaughter of that John Poole who was a man of affairs in Lynn in the early 1630's; and Judith herself stands tall in the Boutelle family story. By the late 1740's, James IV and Judith had moved on to Leominster, then a very new town. James IV, dying in 1752, left his three grown sons well stocked with land, and provided well for his wife and younger children.

By the 1770's the families of James Boutelle V and his brothers—William and Kendall and Timothy—were making Leominster another of those concentrations of family energy that were characteristic of early New England. The four brothers had twenty-nine children, most of whom continued to regard Genesis 9:1 as the will of the Lord. Timothy Boutelle rose to be a major in the Revolution, and was later commissioned colonel in putting down Shays' Rebellion. He represented Leominster in General Court, and bore well the distinction of the small-town man who has had a hand in state affairs. Two of Colonel Timothy's sons graduated from Harvard—the first Boutelles to attend college, so far as the records show. Among the older cousins of the two college boys was Eleanor Boutelle, youngest daughter of

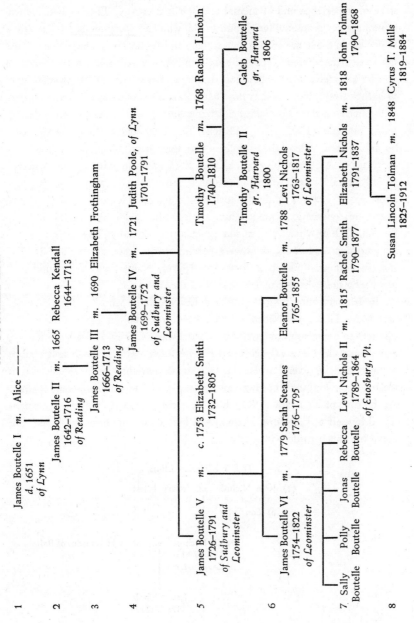

THE BOUTELLE LINE

1   James Boutelle I   *m.*   Alice ———
        d. 1651
        of Lynn

2   James Boutelle II   *m.*   1665   Rebecca Kendall
        1642–1716   1644–1713
        of Reading

3   James Boutelle III   *m.*   1690   Elizabeth Frothingham
        1666–1713
        of Reading

4   James Boutelle IV   *m.*   1721   Judith Poole, *of Lynn*
        1699–1752   1701–1791
        of Sudbury and
        Leominster

5   James Boutelle V   *m.*   *c.* 1753   Elizabeth Smith
        1726–1791   1732–1805
        of Sudbury and
        Leominster

6   James Boutelle VI   *m.*   1779   Sarah Stearnes
        1754–1822   1756–1795
        of Leominster

7   Sally   Polly   Jonas   Rebecca
   Boutelle   Boutelle   Boutelle   Boutelle

Eleanor Boutelle   *m.*   1788   Levi Nichols
1765–1855   1763–1817
        of Leominster

Levi Nichols II   *m.*   1815   Rachel Smith
1789–1864   1790–1877
of Enosburg, Vt.

Timothy Boutelle   *m.*   1768   Rachel Lincoln
1740–1810

Timothy Boutelle II
gr. Harvard
1800

Caleb Boutelle
gr. Harvard
1806

Elizabeth Nichols   *m.*   1818   John Tolman
1791–1837   1790–1868

8   Susan Lincoln Tolman   *m.*   1848   Cyrus T. Mills
        1825–1912   1819–1884

James V, who was leavened with eagerness. She, more than any other person of the older generation, poured into her granddaughter, Susan Tolman, a store of experience and of mental and spiritual energy. Eleanor had known intimately her grandmother, Judith Poole, who had spent the last forty years of her life in the home of Eleanor's father; and Judith Poole, though she could not have remembered Aunt Rebecca Kendall, was still not too far removed in time to catch the neighborhood tradition of that remarkable woman, and to gather from older persons how Mrs. Kendall would say: "In 1632 when we came from the Old Country, I remember . . ." Three women—Judith Poole Boutelle (1701–1791), Eleanor Boutelle Nichols (1763–1855), and Susan Tolman Mills (1825–1912)—and their overlapping lives cover two centuries of American history. Eleanor lived much in John Tolman's home, or only a mile away, when Susan was a child; she still put a deep impress upon Susan's nature while the girl was at Mount Holyoke; and she lived to see this energetic granddaughter return, broken but not defeated, from Ceylon. When Mrs. Mills in her great age spoke to college girls with an admonishing tenderness, they were hearing voices from a past more remote than they knew. (This is a story, not of Great Names, but of the unknown great who link the best of the past with the present.)

In 1788 Eleanor Boutelle married Levi Nichols, whose parents, Daniel and Mary Houghton Nichols, had moved from Bolton (in the Lancaster district) to Leominster about 1760. Daniel was a farmer, had a large family, and placed chief dependence upon his son Levi. And in town and church records, and in several wills, the fact stands out that Levi Nichols was a trusted man. He was a cordwainer—a dresser of fine (or Cordovan) leather. At the time of his death (1817) his oldest child, Levi II, had already established himself at Enosburg, Vermont—a long move for those days; and that move has much to do with our story.

THE NICHOLS LINE

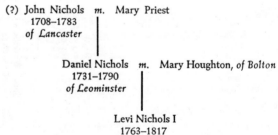

(?) John Nichols   *m.*   Mary Priest
1708–1783
of Lancaster

Daniel Nichols   *m.*   Mary Houghton, *of Bolton*
1731–1790
of Leominster

Levi Nichols I
1763–1817

In April 1796 Ephraim Adams and three other young men who lived in

New Ipswich, New Hampshire, some twenty-odd miles north of Leominster, bought a tract of land near what is now Bakersfield, Vermont, near the Canadian line, built a cabin, cleared some ground, planted a small crop of winter wheat, and in the fall packed back again to New Ipswich, where Ephraim taught school. North again in the spring, the wheat harvested by cradle and threshed by flail, another crop fall-seeded, and home again to New Ipswich. In 1799 Ephraim married Sally Boutelle, oldest daughter of James VI, and of course took her to the wilderness. "Her father . . . fitted out his daughter with a set of pewter crockery and other necessaries . . . and also a library of valuable books." A few years later "They visited her father, each on horseback, a journey of two hundred miles, carrying a baby in their arms." Sally Boutelle Adams dying in 1814, Ephraim married her sister Polly; and the Adams children became a power in northern Vermont. Soon after 1800 young Jonas Boutelle joined the Adamses, bought a farm near Enosburg; and in 1810 young Levi Nichols II joined his cousins in the north, and married a northern girl. Levi II is said to have been a teacher at first, but he turned farmer, and the farm he settled in 1812 is still managed by one of his descendants, whose Jersey cattle and maple sugar are (I am told) of the best. And so Enosburg, with its church and its leaven of learning and good traditions, became a northern outpost where other kinsmen would come. At some time before June 1814 young Levi Nichols' sister Elizabeth came from Leominster to Enosburg, probably to keep house for her brother. After his marriage she returned to Leominster; and at her father's death in 1817 she was one of the executors of his estate. A spirited girl of twenty-five, with a passionate earnestness, strong as her mother's; and, like her mother, a directing power in her family.

two

FROM WINCHENDON AND
LEOMINSTER TO WARE

IN THE LATE 1780'S WHEN DESIRE TOLMAN AND HIS WIFE
Sarah (Howe) brought their family from Dorchester to Winchendon, that town was comparatively new. Desire bought the Colonel Berry
farm on what is now the Gardner road, east of the village, near the block-
house that had been a shelter during the Indian wars. He fell into step
as a good Dorchester man was bound to do; he became deacon and selectman, was moderator of town meetings, and was a committeeman to smooth
out difficulties — one being a heated disagreement between the town and
the minister in 1799. The town was strongly Federalist and the minister
a tenacious Republican — old-style, long before the party of Lincoln. The
Republican lost, of course, enabling the majority to treat him with Christian
forbearance. Again, in 1818, "The Church tarried after divine service and
voted to petition the General Court for some amendment in the Sabbath Day
laws." Deacon Tolman was on the committee appointed to draw up the petition, but the tantalizing minutes give no hint whether Winchendon wanted
the Sabbath laws tightened, or liberalized, say, to allow a devout heart to
walk home from church by roundabout paths, when May at last arrived, or

when autumn leaves were (as a young poet has said) good for rustling purposes.

We have seen how the leaven of higher education began to work in one of the Boutelle families; note its beginning in Deacon Tolman's family. His fourth son, Samuel Howe Tolman (1781–1856) graduated from Dartmouth in 1806, taught in Dorchester and Charlestown, then graduated in medicine from Dartmouth in 1812, then was ordained a Congregational minister and served during the rest of his life in churches in Massachusetts and New Hampshire. He married Rachel Damon; of their five children who reached maturity, three went to college; their son Samuel Howe Tolman, Jr., graduated from Dartmouth in 1848 with a Phi Beta Kappa key, graduated from Andover Theological Seminary in 1852, and was a minister. Two of his sisters attended Mount Holyoke.

Deacon Desire Tolman's seventh child, Elizabeth, married Job Hyde; their grandson, William De Witt Hyde, born in Winchendon, was president of Bowdoin College from 1885 until 1917. The country knew him for the communicable vitality of his mind and character, a quality like that which endeared William James to a host of laymen. And Deacon Desire's eighth child, John Tolman, had six daughters who attended Mount Holyoke, three of them graduating and becoming teachers, and one of the three a college president. It is improbable that Susan Tolman ever saw this grandfather; but the influence which he began to work upon his family in his own time reached nine of his grandchildren in the 1840's. Considering the times and all, Deacon Tolman and his wife did not do so badly.

(Besides producing a college president, Winchendon became the capital of a charmed kingdom which may yet save the world when diplomacy confesses its failure: for Winchendon leads in the making of wooden toys. William De Witt Hyde, of Bowdoin, liked to recall that his father, Joel Hyde, was both farmer and maker of woodenware. The Puritans brought no fairies from England; but after awhile some farmer like Joel Hyde, turning out wooden bowls of a winter evening—bowls that would become fragrant with relish and piccalilli and mincemeat—had a visitation of fancy and tried his drawknife on a wooden horse shod with spools, or a duck that ducked and bowed when you pulled the string. And so Puck evaded the immigration authorities. Arthur Rackham should have lived to paint a street scene in Winchendon, an academic procession of wooden toys: wooden dish and wooden spoon for marshals; a stately gander [speaker of the day], splendid in Aberdonian hood and gown; spotted horses, pragmatic elephants, giraffes of vision, and files of young waterfowl that look like domestic Pekins but

may—who knows?—turn into swans [for which there is always a great vocational demand]; while from the curb two college presidents nod and chuckle,
and bend over now and then to free a too-stiff wheel or adjust a starry young
unicorn whose horn is snarled in a psychosis.)

John Tolman (1790–1868) was the second of his father's sons to leave
Winchendon. In 1816 he moved to New Ipswich, New Hampshire, and
leased or bought the Prichard tannery, which had been built in 1787. It
stood on the bank of Patch's Brook, a very little stream that flows into Kid-
der Brook, which in turn enters the Souhegan River not far from the village.
The rough-built stone dam that impounded water for the overshot wheel of
the tannery still stands, but the spillway is broken and the forest has taken
the site of the building and the hill around it. Twelve miles to the northwest, Monadnock looks down upon the chain of little lakes and wooded
hills. Monadnock makes it an Emerson country. Longfellow's wife belonged
to a New Ipswich family. And the Souhegan is, in a minor way, a Thoreau
river; he passed the mouth of the Souhegan or "Crooked" River on Tuesday
in his *Week*, and gave it a casual line or two.

It is not known how John Tolman met Elizabeth Nichols—probably
through business dealings with her father, tanner to cordwainer. They were
married in Leominster in March 1818, and their first four children were born
during the seven years they lived in New Ipswich: Elizabeth, named for her
mother, and John for his father, and Emily for her mother's sister who had
died a few years before, and Sarah Desire for the Tolman grandparents.
The New Ipswich church records tell most of the little we know about the
young family up until April 1825, when the parents received letters of dismissal to the church in Enosburg, Vermont.

The move to Enosburg was, for Elizabeth Nichols Tolman, a return to
familiar country and to her Boutelle and Adams cousins and her older brother,
Levi Nichols II. Her mother, too, had moved to Enosburg and was living in
the home of her oldest son by 1825. John Tolman built a new tannery on
one of the brooks that feed Tyler's Branch, a sizable stream that flows into
the Missiquoi below the falls. In New England fashion, the name of the
town has been portioned out—East Enosburg, West Enosburg, North Enosburg, and Enosburg Falls. The village that John Tolman knew is now called
Enosburg Center; his tannery was about two miles south of this.

And there, on November 18, 1825, another daughter, Susan Lincoln,
was born to the Tolmans. Her name harks back to a friendship in Leominster. Ephraim Lincoln and Levi Nichols were of an age, both married

in 1788; and Ephraim's Susan and Levi's first son were born in 1789. Little Susan Lincoln must have put a spell upon the neighbors, for the name Susan with its variants soon began to sprinkle the Leominster birth records. And Eleanor Boutelle Nichols kept the warmth we feel toward children who played with our own and whom we tended before baby sitters were thought of; and so Eleanor's new granddaughter in Enosburg was named for the maiden lady in Leominster. It is not known whether Miss Lincoln ever met her namesake; but Susan Tolman, when at Mount Holyoke, wrote Susan Lincoln's name in a special list in her diary. The older woman died in 1862, leaving part of a tidy estate to foreign missions and a tract society—the impersonal Cause rather than the personal missionary.

When he was an old man one of Susan Tolman's older cousins, Thomas Brainard Nichols, a son of Levi Nichols II, wrote a page or two about his memories of her when she was a small girl. His family had noticed how strongly Susan resembled her grandmother Eleanor; they had "the same snapping black eyes and full head of black hair." And the boy had marked with no apparent envy how fond the two were of each other. He recalled Susan's quickness of mind and body—"spry as a cricket" and afraid of nothing but the cattle in Squire Barnum's rock pasture, which lay between the Nichols and Tolman farms. To this cousin fell the big-boy responsibility of guarding Susan and his sisters home from a visit to their grandmother; and Barnum's bull pretended at least to respect the boy's skill at throwing stones. And so, having learned the hymn which grandmother assigned for memorizing, and having dared an ogre by the way, we got safely back to the Old Post Road, and home in time to learn by heart our verses for Sunday school tomorrow.

In her old age Susan remembered a certain Sabbath, and her missionary penny: an old-fashioned honest penny, big as a modern quarter, and it would buy more. She had earned it by some highly responsible chore. Once I would have guessed by saying a new psalm for Grandmother Nichols—but no, it would not be right to give or to accept money for that. An apple, if you insist, or a crisket of maple sugar, but no money. This penny is to bring light to the heathen who, poor things, do not have Bibles or ministers or grandmothers to teach them *He that abideth in the secret place of the Most High*. Only last Sunday our minister prayed for our faithful missionary Dr. John Scudder, who is in Heathen Climes, and if we all give our pennies, all we Tolmans and all of Uncle Levi Nichols' children, that will make how many pennies? Count them. And the captain of a ship will take them to

Sandwich-Ceylon-Islands and give them to Dr. John Scudder, and it is very exciting, and—our enormous penny falls, crashing the Sabbath decorum and starts to roll, and rolls like a wheelwright's tire across wide floor boards which are foreign shores, and everybody is too well mannered to titter in the Lord's House, but that penny rolls on and around until at last it comes back to us and wabbles down with the noise of cymbals and an instrument-of-ten-strings-selah. And is given to bring light to them that sit in darkness. Not clean and beautiful like Vermont.

It *was* a beautiful world for a child. Off to the north, in Canada, Pinnacle Mountain overlooks the Missiquoi; to the south Mount Mansfield and to the east Jay Peak point the sky line; while nearer, to the southeast, the Cold Hollow Range feeds Cold Hollow Brook, which joins Tyler's, and so into the Missiquoi and Lake Champlain. The summer green is fresher, cleaner than in our somber western forests, and autumn, unafraid of emotion, repeats herself like poems men never tire of hearing.

When she was eighty, Susan wrote six pages about her school days in Enosburg. "How proud I was when allowed to draw, bound, and describe Vermont." That "allowed" is worth reflecting upon. And a Vermont eager to be drawn and bounded and described. A present generation, seeing the world from the air and choosing like connoisseurs, may wonder why children and their elders once felt such passionate dearness in the home county, the little valley, or the sweep of prairie. Be patient with those who still do. "Hence it comes that our land, the earth underfoot, is holy ground."* She remembered Cold Hollow Brook, and that she was sent home from school three times "in a hurry" because she slipped and got a ducking. The teachers were men, fresh from some academy—serious boys earning their way through Dartmouth or Amherst or Williams. The teacher boarded around, a week for each school child in the family, and the Tolmans, being numerous, "rejoiced that we could keep him so long." Susan remembered the northern winters best: "The big family sleigh, crowded to overflowing with us children and those of our neighbors—the big lunch basket"—which always came home empty.

She remembered the spelling class: "toes on the crack, hands at our sides, all of us looking longingly toward the head where stood the bearer of the silver medal, a half-dollar piece . . . the definitions . . . how we were drilled until we had every one by heart. . . . There was Geography, begin-

* From *The Interpreters*, by Æ, with permission of the publishers, The Macmillan Company.

ning, 'The world we live upon is round as an apple.' " There being no factory-made globe, how did the grave boy-teacher—this coming judge or editor or senator—manage the object lesson in hemispheres? Naturally "by cutting open an apple, and threads marked . . . Latitude and Longitude." (A maiden's-blush apple would make a rare fragrance through the universe. A russet, though somewhat o'erflattened at the poles, would connote a sturdier world — a rind with no esthetic frills — durable against extremes of weather.) Turn the little world more slowly in your quick hands, child with the racing mind. That fleck of coral near the equator is an island; on the other side of the little world, green pin points—other islands; between them a coast of mottled green and dusky gold. Next year you will be allowed to recite their names, while your mind takes strange excitement from those words. Places ever so much farther than Mount Mansfield. But first we must draw and bound Vermont.

"The books were simple and rude, but treasured always, and used with greatest care . . . the little Peter Parley History my Father brought us from New York." (The first Peter Parley book—*The Tales of Peter Parley about America*—came out when Susan was only two; there were several more by the time she started to school.)

But the grammar story is the best. And how can a modernist who was promoted from room to room, one grade in a room, understand the spill of riches that fell to an alert child who heard, half the day, older children recite the lessons he himself would have next year? The method sounds distracting, but it had its points. This grammar story concerns the first day of a term and a new teacher, and Susan's class was having a first go at the sacred elements of syntax. The young teacher asked Susan, "What is your name?"

"Greatly moved by being allowed to recite, I began: 'It's a noun because it is a name; first person because it's spoken of; feminine gender because I am a girl; nominative case because it is the subject of the verb *runs!*' " Mere exhibitionism? Let the scoffer say so: a nicer ear hears an undertone of a whole life, in the words: "Greatly moved at being allowed to recite." She might have added that the verb *runs* was likely to be transitive when Susan was the subject.

Girls went to school, and did sums, and were strangely excited by poor little books, but, being of the feminine gender, they had no part in the Friday afternoon speaking exercises. "Once a week we girls sewed patchwork while the boys declaimed; and we girls wished we could go onto the little platform and say: 'On the Grampian hills my father feeds his flocks.'* We knew we could do it better than the boys, but we were girls only."

Two hundred years had passed since the selectmen of Dorchester had prescribed that the teacher should instruct children "in pynt of good manners and dutifull behavior toward all." And still in the 1830's the teachers at Enosburg did not slur that duty. "Let loose from school, we made our manners to all persons by lining up beside the road. We curtsied, while the boys doffed their caps so politely." Are all our changes improvements?

Three more children were born to John and Elizabeth Tolman at Enosburg: twins—James and Julia—in 1829, and Jane Cordelia in 1831. The little boy died in his third year. The precise date of the family's removal to Ware, Massachusetts, is not known; but in July 1836 the parents and one daughter (Sarah Desire) were granted letters of dismissal to the church in Ware. John Tolman had done well in the north, and was ready now for a larger enterprise. His younger brother, James, may have already settled in Ware; if not, he moved there about the same time as John, for both brothers figure in certain auxiliary church records in 1836. Local tradition faintly holds that the two were partners in running a tannery, first outside, then later in the village. A building near the bend of the river in Ware was still known as Tolman's Tannery well down toward the end of the last century; but it is clear that John Tolman became a jobber in leather goods, and by 1848 James and his son advertised as dealers in fur robes and clothing.

Ware is on the west slope of the hills that divide the watershed of the lower Merrimack—Nashua and Concord rivers—from the Connecticut Valley. The village was nearly a century old when the Tolmans moved there, and though compared with New Ipswich and Enosburg it had a big-town importance, it was still small enough for the mind to compass all its people, a Puritan town, its factory employees still of New England stock. The original village, now known as Ware Center, had been a farmers' town; by 1825 the growth of factories east of the Center had created what was really a new town with, presently, a new church. By 1837 there were two cotton mills, two woolen mills, and other smaller factories—one, intriguing to the imagination, being an augur factory. Business, like much else in life, was entering a com-

---

* Susan forgot the first half-line of this declamation. It began:

> My name is Norval: on the Grampian hills
> My father feeds his flocks; a frugal swain . . .

It came from John Home's play, *Douglas*; and it seems to have been a favorite passage in old school readers. One gentlewoman to whom my inquiry came was able to recite the passage "right off."

plete transition: the craftsman who personally managed his own shop, taught his apprentices and workmen, and sold directly to his customers was soon to give way to the large factory with its mass production and its mass of immigrant employees. But the new trend did not affect John Tolman; the town was still Ware Village; John became Deacon Tolman and had his friendships, his recognized dignity, among the best men of the town; and the unspoiled country was still within five minutes' walk for John's most active daughter.

Long after she was settled in California, Mrs. Mills continued to think of Ware as her home town. It had a beauty unlike that of Vermont. To the east, rough hills make late mornings, even in summer. The Ware River comes tumbling down from the north, makes a sharp bend and runs deeper through the village, then falls away to the west over rocky shelves, through pastures where the cattle pick their way over ledges and among boulders, until the river meanders through better farmland and reaches the Connecticut. The main street, with small reminiscent bends, parallels the westerly course of the river, and on three sides the hills shut out the world. From Pleasant Street, where the Tolman brothers built their homes, you look south across the town and hear in these days a noise of factories and of traffic from Main Street and the walled river, where in Susan's day the low sound of water wheels would have been pointed a very little, once a day, when the eastbound stage climbed the shelving road on its way to Worcester, or the westbound clattered on toward Pittsfield and the northwest (to Pittsfield and North Adams when Hawthorne rode it in 1837).

Susan's memories of the town were close-woven with old-fashioned friendships. Though only she and her two younger sisters outlived their father (who died in 1868), certain families in Ware—notably the Sages and Hydes—still kept a strong hold upon her affections long after the Tolmans were gone. These memories were not without sorrow; in March 1837 her mother died, and in 1845 one sister and the one surviving brother. Trying at this distance to know that mother as she was, one feels the earnest force of Elizabeth Nichols Tolman's nature. Surely she had heard Mary Lyon: the vitalizing ideal which that energetic woman passed on to the mother could hardly have come by hearsay. In 1836 and through the winter into 1837 Mary Lyon was traveling everywhere in Massachusetts and some way into the bordering states, talking earnestly to responsible persons—ministers, doctors, lawyers, teachers, businessmen, and formal and informal groups of women—about her consuming faith in the higher education of women. She faced some ridicule—most of it from persons who had never heard her, and an amount of sober opposition from men who doubted the practicability of her plan. But to a host of others, plain middle-class people like the Tolmans, she brought an exciting hope. Surely, somewhere—and probably in Ware—Elizabeth Tolman heard Mary Lyon, and knew that her own girls might now have the privilege which the times and conditions had denied to her mother and herself. Our generation, used to window-shopping for a college, and choosing as if conferring a favor on the institution, can hardly understand the hunger of youth a century ago. Here was a tangible chance, not for social prestige nor for mere vocational betterment; the new seminary then a-building at South Hadley offered unlooked-for spiritual opportunity. True, there were a few other schools for girls, but none with such compelling invitation. As she neared death Elizabeth Tolman enjoined upon her husband that their daughters should go to Mary Lyon's school. John Tolman kept that promise, not as a burden. His brother, Samuel Howe, had proved what college could do for a young man; his own nature was ready for this departure from tradition for his daughters.

Emily, the oldest girl, was eighteen when her mother died; Susan was eleven, and the baby—Jane Cordelia—was five. The next year the father married Submit Nash (1797–1873). Some of us remember hearing Mrs. Mills say that the word stepmother was not used in her home. The discipline and respect the children had learned from their own mother were met by the sensible goodness of the new mother.

FAMILY OF JOHN AND ELIZABETH NICHOLS TOLMAN

John Tolman (1790–1868)   *m.*   (1) Elizabeth Nichols (1792–1837)
(2) Submit Nash (1797–1873)

Their Children:

1) Emily Nichols Tolman   *m.*   John L. Condron
1819–1856

2) John Howe Tolman   *m.*   Mary Ann Wright
1820–1845

3) Elizabeth Tolman   *m.*   William De Witt
1821–1845

4) Sarah Desire Tolman   *m.*   Freeman L. Foster
1823–1852

5) Susan Lincoln Tolman   *m.*   Cyrus Taggart Mills
1825–1912   1819–1884

6) Julia Maria Tolman   *m.*   Lucius Alden Tolman
1829–1871   1823–1871

7) James Mallory Tolman (*twin with Julia*)
1829–1831

8) Jane Cordelia Tolman
1831–1912

The minister of East Church when the Tolmans came was Cyrus Yale (Williams, 1811), who had been pastor in East Hartford for twenty years. It speaks well for him that upon leaving Ware in 1837, after two years of service, he returned to his first charge at East Hartford and remained there the rest of his life. He was author of several modest publications, but should be remembered for a less prosaic quality: he braved New England conservatism to install a string quartet in the church. No more dependence upon pitch pipe and the singing-clerk's fallible calculation of the key, but a voice of instruments to coax the congregation toward one accord. And since no villager could reasonably invest hard wages in a bull fiddle for his own delight, the church bought the double bass at a cost of sixty dollars and (no doubt) many hours of insomnia on the part of tuneless old men who, rigid on their pillows at two, vehemently whispered to the darkness that things had come to a pretty pass. "And I, even I, only am left!" Indignant old chins, stabbing the dark with hurt percussion. But the double bass and cello and treble strings played on, and the congregation must have liked them, for in time they sanctioned a flute also and, by the middle '50's, a melodeon.*

Cyrus Yale was succeeded as minister by Jonathan E. Woodbridge (Williams, 1822),† who was one of the more than three hundred youths prepared for college by that remarkable man, the Reverend Moses Hallock, of Plainfield—a man to remember. Jonathan Woodbridge won a Phi Beta Kappa key at Williams, and was tutor there for three years, taught for a time in academies, then graduated from Princeton Theological Seminary, and had preached at Worcester before coming to Ware in 1838. With precarious health he retired from preaching in 1840 and was for many years joint editor of the *New England Puritan* and the Boston *Recorder*. Minor items: but fifteen years after he left Ware, when Mr. and Mrs. Mills, having returned from Ceylon, needed to voice their dissent from certain policies of the Mission Board, Mr. Woodbridge's papers gave them a hearing.

The third minister of East Church in Susan's time, and quite the most scholarly and distinguished, was Nahum Gale (Amherst, 1837). He had been principal of Amherst Academy for two years, then studied divinity at East Hartford and began his ministry at Ware, being ordained there in 1842.

---

* Thank you, Mr. Cyrus Yale (of Williams, 1811). Our college library should extend itself to find a copy of your published *Thanksgiving Sermon at Ware, 1835.*

† I am fairly certain that Jonathan Woodbridge was related to Sylvester Woodbridge, Jr., who helped establish the Benicia (California) Seminary in 1852. The Woodbridge family were prodigal of ministers, some of whom were Williams and Princeton men, but I have not verified the relationship.

He and his wife appealed to that faculty of hero worship which was a lifelong quality of Susan Tolman. They saw youth through youth's own eyes; their words were to make something of an aura around the figure of the beautiful Abby Allen, Susan's dearest friend at Mount Holyoke. Incidental to Mr. Gale's service at Ware, Susan wrote to a friend in 1846 when she was at home on vacation from her teaching at the Seminary: "We are having our church remodelled, so we have to meet in the lecture room on Sabbath . . . Mr. Gale has been unwell for a week or two, and last Sabbath could not speak loud, so my Father & Deacon Hyde were the ministers." Deacon William Hyde was also a Williams College man (1826), a Phi Beta Kappa, and one of John Tolman's closest friends in Ware, where he became head of the bank. He also was later a trustee of Williams College, as was Nahum Gale.

In the meantime the Tolman brothers had built their homes, side by side, on Pleasant Street, a block farther up the slope and paralleling Main Street. Their next-door neighbor, Dr. Minor, helped tutor the girls in turn for college. In the fall of 1840 Emily, Elizabeth, and Sarah Desire all entered Mount Holyoke as juniors—equivalent to freshmen in our modern terms, for the new seminary gave only a three-year course, and the classes were reckoned junior, middle, and senior. The Spartan conditions at South Hadley were too stern for many a girl; of one hundred seven who entered school with the class of 1843, only sixteen graduated. The three older Tolman sisters attended during only one year. Elizabeth and Sarah Desire were already trying to see where duty lay as between a second year of Seminary (with Marsh's Ecclesiastical History, Smellie's Philosophy of Natural History, Newman's Rhetoric) and the growing appeal of young William De Witt and young Freeman Foster; and Shakespeare could easily have told Marsh and Smellie: "Age, thou hast lost thy labor."

Very well for these older sisters, but Sixteen has a way of growing deeply excited by an idea, a hope; and Sixteen was always tenacious. As October '42 draws near, Susan spends hours with good Dr. Minor next door, drilling and reviewing to make sure that she has—as the catalogue specifies—

> *an acquaintance with the general principles of English Grammar, a good knowledge of Modern Geography, History of the United States, Watts on the Mind, Coburn's First Lessons, and the whole of Adams' New Arithmetic.*

For the twentieth time one or another member of the family rereads:

> *It is expected of all who are admitted to the Seminary . . . that they*

furnish their own towels, one pair of sheets and pillow cases and one blanket to be used on their own bed; also one table or dessert spoon, and one tea-spoon to be used in the family.

That every article of clothing be distinctly marked with the whole name.

Deacon John, usually phlegmatic, asks son John for the third time and for the third time is respectfully assured that the wheels of the two-horse shay have been well greased, all five wheels, Sir. (For this vehicle has five wheels, yet the fifth is not a spare.) Was ever luggage so wonderful? And are we in danger of forgetting anything? Each young lady should bring

A Bible, an English Dictionary, a Modern Atlas, Murray's Grammar and Exercises, Watts' Psalms and Hymns, Village Hymns, the Carmina Sacra and the Odeon . . . and books containing selections for improvement in reading, and standard poetical works.

Very many things to remember: square root, and the dates of all the presidents including Mr. Tyler, and the boundaries of India, and the rule of *shall* and *will*, and when one is confused it is well to steady the mind with a verse: *Wisdom is the principal thing, therefore get Wisdom, and with all thy getting, get understanding;* and are the spoons in the old leather-bound trunk or in the new portmanteau—unless the roads are very bad we should reach South Hadley by noon, and we shall need our spoons for dinner, which is served promptly at twelve. The shay is ready, and Father himself led the team to the blacksmith's only yesterday to have their shoes well calked, for the first three or four miles, dipping down into the valley, are stony; and yes, every article is distinctly marked with the full name: Susan Lincoln Tolman. Of Ware Village. It is a bright October morning, and Susan is going to college.

three

MOUNT HOLYOKE

IN THIS CHAPTER AND THE NEXT SUSAN TOLMAN'S SIX YEARS at Mount Holyoke Seminary will not be geared closely to the calendar. She took the regular three-year course in stride, graduated in 1845, had the coveted honor of being one of four members of her class chosen by Mary Lyon to continue as teacher, and taught until the spring of 1848. She developed, but with no dramatic crises, and these six years remained throughout her life a remembered unity.

Then, too, the elements of the story came to me without regard to the time pattern. In 1909 it was her long-used custom to have the nonresident teachers at Mills College as midday guests in her private dining room. That table-talk with its unprogrammed ease is good to remember. She herself was the best of listeners; there was no need to groove the conversation to her reminiscences. Yet, when she spoke, one sector of the past reappeared fairly often; one person towered in her memory—the figure of Mary Lyon. Her listeners found no repetitiousness; even her best story was not retold oftener than once a year. Nor did her memories of Mount Holyoke sound the minor key of nostalgia. Rather, there was ripened appraisal; she now saw Mary

Lyon as a recent writer has seen her, "shrewd, humorous, great-hearted," and possessed by an almost incredible energy. There had been an uncommon degree of rightness in Mary Lyon, and that rightness had not diminished in sixty-odd years.

In 1944 I came upon a small notebook which, during her last two years as teacher at Mount Holyoke, had been Susan Tolman's meager diary and reminder of duties. Here was Mary Lyon, viewed not in perspective but with a young devotee's consuming self-surrender. The lack of critical perception, the girl's complete subordination, were like an incoherent poem, eloquent only of the young writer's excited intent. Considered alone, the greater part of the notebook, charged with Mary Lyon's terrifying theology and Susan's acceptance of it, gave a picture of the two women as flat as a primitive mural of chilly saints. To humanize the picture I needed to remember the table-talk in the little dining room.

But along with the austere self-searching, that notebook had a seedbed of story: the names of thirty-six persons for whom Susan prayed. Twelve of these were relatives—her immediate family, her in-laws, "my dear Grandmother." But who were the other twenty-four? Most of them (I guessed) were fellow students or teachers; but what about them? The faded pages bore no comment.

Still later I found the voluble missionary journal which, through 1846–48, Susan composed as a sort of Mount Holyoke alumnae newsletter. Though devoted mainly to religious and missionary zeal in the seminary, it turned often to such tangible things as washday, Mountain Day, the two-way fever of vacations, a missionary bride's trousseau, the headache of finals, intimations of romance, and the fact that even in those Spartan days college girls were interested in food. Those friendships possessed the mind until one had to find out, if possible, where Abby Allen lived, and who the senior was who rode the elephant, and at what hour Emily Dickinson's section of the choir rehearsed, and where nice old Mr. Condit went to college. He was the minister in South Hadley, and we shall never know just how he pronounced *Israel*, but to Susan and her readers in remote mission fields that diction was memorable for beauty. At one point or another in this no-sequence appeared letters by Susan and her friends, some written in student days, some as long as sixty years after; and diary and journal and letters and table-talk all make one pattern.

The first twelve years of Mount Holyoke, ending with Mary Lyon's death in 1849, appear as a preoccupied golden age. The Seminary had a waiting list, the educational experiment was new and exciting, and with so

many absorbing things to do nobody had the time or the inclination to consider whether the undertaking would look impressive to future generations.
Everybody knew everybody; Susan knew the girls in six successive classes,
and practically all her teachers were Mount Holyoke alumnae, only a little
older than herself. A golden age: its regimen severe enough to test the fiber
of character and to be remembered with triumph. A naïve and youthful joy.
Disciplined conscience was animated and colored by something of mental
richness; science, the subjects that men studied, something to put the teeth
into. Even esthetic beauty might hope to emerge from disrepute. And though
the great missionary movement had begun in American colleges three decades
earlier, its tide came full in the 1840's, and in Mount Holyoke as in the men's
colleges the fierce introspectiveness of the Puritan soul turned outward to the
dream of evangelizing the world—the whole world. A golden age—and
Susan Tolman's six years were of one piece with all of it. Which should be
reason enough for disregarding the time scheme. Besides, I shall want to
reach forward through the years and tell at once what became of some of
Susan's friends; otherwise there will be too many threads to identify again
in later chapters.

When we are told that an institution is the lengthened shadow of one person, we reach for the salt shaker. Our generation suspects artificial lighting,
a trick of mirrors. Excluding the charlatan and the mere publicity expert,
the saying implies a domineering ego. We suspect the dangerous gift of self-
dramatization in the leader and an emotional sacrifice of common sense in
the devotees. Mount Holyoke was, and is, the lengthened shadow of Mary
Lyon, but rarely has a colorful personality made so little conscious use of its
color. Her power lay in a surge of enthusiasm, strenuous indeed but so
healthy that the student, swept far by it, was apt to develop an original energy
of her own. A great organizer, bristling with realism, she had the genius to
persuade a considerable sector of New England families to do what they were
already eager to do. A reformer without shrillness or militancy, she had not
a sliver of "anti" in her nature. And though she overworked herself and
others and, when too tired, enjoyed a good cry (and had the humor to ac-
knowledge it), she had no touch of the martyr complex. The best proof of
her greatness is that her ideas worked; after her death they still motivated a
a legion of teachers and largely determined the quality and direction of
women's education for half a century. Particularly they affected Susan
Tolman and the school which she founded. In afteryears the disciple developed self-reliance, the knack of adaptation, but her working faith and
practical habits never lost the impress of Mary Lyon.

No other American woman of her time, nor any man west of Concord, coined as many aphorisms as Mary Lyon did. They were hardly composed at all, the by-products of a mind too busy to be concerned with the turn of a sentence. She was too hearty to prize wit as an object, and she never thought of herself as an oracle, but many of her sayings fixed themselves upon her not-too-small world and became campus and household classics:

> *It is very important a teacher should not be schoolified.*
> *The intellectual miser is an object of contempt.*
> *Make the dull ones think once a day; make their eyes sparkle once a day.*
> *One teacher I shall always remember. He taught me education was to fit one to do good.*
> *Teaching is a sacred, not a mercenary employment.*
> *Go where no one else is willing to go; do what no one else is willing to do.*
> *The cultivation of the ornamental branches without a thorough education is like trying to polish cork or sponge.*

So much for teaching; and these, in variety, for her shrewd perception of life:

> *My soul is pained with this empty gentility, this genteel nothingness.*
> *Learn to sit with energy.*
> *I don't want artificial fire.*
> *It is one of the nicest of mental operations to distinguish between what is very difficult and what is impossible.*
> *There were more strong characters among us fifty years ago than now, because knowledge and reflection were better balanced.*
> *Remember there is no kindness you can show a poor person like helping him do for himself to the extent of his ability.*
> *I consider bread-making of so much consequence that, in giving attention to it, I am confident that I am serving God.*
> *Choose the society of such gentlemen as will converse without even once seeming to think that you are a lady.*
> *Humility consists not so much in thinking meanly of one's self, as in feeling one's dependence upon a higher power for success.*

In 1817 when Mary Lyon entered Ashfield Academy to get her first schooling beyond the country schools, she was grandly eager to learn but was oblivious to the fact that her linsey-woolsey dress had no style. Spinning and weaving flax and wool—these she understood; from there on she used no art at all. But during twenty years of going about, her quick eye and common sense taught her that homespun may be made to fit the wearer and

even have a becomingness. In her Mount Holyoke days she dressed well;
only, with a hundred things to attend to, from the Rumford oven to the
newest homesick student—well, sometimes she forgot. "Now, Miss Tolman,"
she enjoined Susan when they were roommates, "please don't let me go to
breakfast without my collar. I must set a good example."

*Many ladies are made most miserable by trying to be fashionable, because
they have no character.*

Makers of fashion are not usually educated persons.

These, as mere opinions, are not likely to detonate much protest. But the
following proverb, gleaned from a student's notes in the Mount Holyoke
archives and apparently overlooked or rejected by previous quoters, was
uttered as fact:

It takes very little money to support a female of good taste. Really now,
Miss Lyon! True, you allowed yourself a salary of only $200 a year, and
gave half of that to missions. Your girlhood mastery of spinning and weaving
made you a good judge of fabrics. You had your green marino and your
wool-colored delaine made over; and your lilac silk, which all New England
knew was your best dress, looked well year after year. Money bought more
in your time, ever so much more than it does now; but money was harder to
come by, and so the riddle remains. Generally you confined your expressions
of opinion to subjects that you knew—a remarkable trait in any public person. But this . . . this more than obiter dictum, this statement as of a
universal truth: *It takes very little money* . . . Accepted as a major premise
it compels a forthright syllogism which men of kindly nature would rather
avoid. As the great falcon said in T. H. White's *The Sword in the Stone*,
"Gentlemen, you may converse."*

The impetuous informality of her own education goes far toward explain-
ing Mary Lyon's bold departure from conventional routine. How could her
schooling have been other than informal, the persistent reach of a hungry
mind that had to go hither and yon to find capable and willing mentors?
Something needed to be learned, something not provided in the best academies for girls. Who could and would teach it to a young woman who was
already almost an old-maid schoolma'am? She would find that teacher. At
twenty, coming late to the opportunity, she had memorized the Latin grammar between Friday evening and Monday morning. Later she could prove
her worth to teachers of men at Amherst and Troy, and cram into a vacation

* By permission of Mr. White's publishers, G. P. Putnam's Sons (copyright 1939).

whole terms of chemistry and physics and geology—subjects which corseted convention held unsuitable for the female mind. She used her mind; she could inspire other women to use theirs.

From a modern point of view her practice of appointing her own graduates to her faculty looks like mental inbreeding. By 1841–42—the fifth year of the new Seminary—seven of the ten teachers were Mount Holyoke alumnae, and the other three, listed as "assistant pupils," were undergraduates. What else could Mary Lyon have done? Perhaps she could have found women teachers long experienced in the academies and presumably better qualified to teach in this new school which was to be more than an academy; but the best of such women already had their own schools, and it is doubtful whether many of them had that hearty appetite for new learning which Mary Lyon prized. By ransacking America she could have filled her roster once — but hardly twice — with women of superior culture, of solitary genius; but could they teach, and would they? Particularly, would they have shared her passionate conviction that education was to fit one to do good? For better or for worse, she wanted women of her own educational faith. She knew her young teachers and they knew her; the less need, then, of temperamental readjustments. Like any pioneer, she made her own tools, knew the grain of the wood, the temper of the iron. To intimate that her teachers were merely marking time until they could marry missionaries or other ministers is unjust. They had more than a little of her own perennial delight in helping youth to discover itself. In the long run her system might become unhealthy; but one of its best effects was that it produced enough women to carry the institution on after her death. From the outset she had fixed her heart upon this. She had seen small schools, each dependent upon the genius of one person, perish with that person. She wanted to create something permanent. She probably overestimated the immediate ability of her young women, but her daughters became proverbial in America and halfway around the world for their ability to do things well.

It provoked some protest, mostly at a distance, when Mary Lyon required her students to do all the domestic work of the big household, share and share alike. She did not propose to teach domestic labor; their mothers could do that better:

> Some may inquire, "What then can be the design of this arrangement?" It may be replied, that the family work must be performed—that it is difficult to find hired domestics, and to retain them any considerable time when they are found—and that young ladies engaged in study suffer much . . . for the want of exercise.

I think she had a deeper reason and was too wise to reveal it. By requiring all to do their share she made possible the incredibly low fee of $60 a year— board, tuition, practically everything—and thereby achieved a practicable democracy. Better than preaching the dignity of labor, she maneuvered her young women to practice it without ostent. She had worked with her own hands, and so had many of her students; this was her canny way of weeding out latent snobbery. She positively did not want an industrial school, but equally she did not want to cater to pained gentility. This rule excluded a few overnice daughters of pride, but mainly it worked happily. In one year the two girls who had to get up at three on Monday mornings to start the fires under the wash boilers were thankful for so grand an opportunity to study in the quiet. If their testimony savors of conscious virtue, they had earned the right. I like the authentic story of a genteel newcomer who, arriving just be- fore supper and feeling fatigued and sorry for herself, ordered that the meal be served in her room. Presently the tray was brought and the food served with simple courtesy—by Miss Lyon herself. The lesson was perfect.

There was another value in her all-round versatility, her knack of keeping the wheels oiled. Her daughters would go far, to the rough west, to distant lands; many of them, alone or with their husbands, would have to run other schools. Knowing how to bake good bread in school-sized batches was really a way of serving the Lord. Do you remember the first evening in Hawthorne's *The Blithedale Romance*? The utopians are sitting in a half circle before the fire; outside, a spring blizzard is howling. The new brethren dream, each after his own pattern, of the somehow miraculous society that is soon to be— of mental and economic freedom won by a few hours of simple work. The weather is foul, but tomorrow . . . Then Silas Foster, their hired foreman, remarks that they will need livestock. There is to be an auction at a neigh- boring farm tomorrow. "Which man among you," quoth he, "is the best judge of swine?" The doom of Brook Farm was in the question. Mary Lyon was no utopian. If the bread was not good, she herself could determine whether the fault lay with the oven or at the mixing table or farther back in the flour and yeast. The practical hand and mind, the Yankee knack of making things run—these take on a beauty.

One wishes that her environment and education had allowed her to know the wealth that lay hidden in that vast body of literature which she distrusted as "secular." When she was a strapping girl a neighbor had heard her "laugh half a mile away, from one hill to another." A pity that her hearty nature missed the answer from that other hill. The poetry she never knew would have surprised her with joy. But she had what she had: an exceptional gift of teaching what her students could comprehend; and though she was a Puritan, her goodness was not negative. She could bend her own rules, and fudge to save a student from penalty. Once when more literal-minded teachers demurred, "You are spoiling that child," she answered, "Well, she is young and far from her mother, and I am sorry for her, and I don't believe it will hurt her." When it came to the personal case her heart was often wiser than her theory. The final touch in her portrait is a very little thing. Writing of her mother's farm and the hills around it, she remembered the neighbors saying, "Nothing ever died in the widow Lyon's garden." Nowhere else had she ever seen wild strawberries so plentiful and tasty, and "nowhere else were rareripes so large and yellow."

What nutriment was in that curriculum? And how good was the teaching? Here is the course of study for 1844–45:

STUDIES OF THE JUNIOR CLASS

English Grammar, Ancient Geography, Ancient and Modern History:— Text Books, Worcester's Elements, Goldsmith's Greece, Rome, and England, and Grimshaw's France. Introductory Lessons in Botany, Day's Algebra, Playfair's Euclid, (old edition) begun.

STUDIES OF THE MIDDLE CLASS

Marsh's Ecclesiastical History, Smellie's Philosophy of Natural History, Gray's Chemistry, Hitchcock's Geology, Olmsted's Natural Philosophy, Wilkins' Astronomy, Beck's Botany, Lee's Physiology, Newman's Rhetoric, Alexander's Evidences of Christianity.

STUDIES OF THE SENIOR CLASS

Playfair's Euclid finished, Beck's Botany continued, Paley's Natural Theology, Upham's Mental Philosophy in two volumes, Whateley's Logic, Wayland's Moral Philosophy, Wayland's Political Economy, Butler's Analogy, Milton's Paradise Lost.

All the members of the school attend regularly to composition, reading and calisthenics. Instruction is given in vocal music, and in linear and perspective drawing. Those who have atttended to instrumental music can have the use of a piano a few hours in a week.

By 1848 four books of Virgil were prerequisite to senior standing, and many seniors had read twelve, but Mount Holyoke avoided the top-heavy program of the classics then prevalent in the men's colleges. Bible study was a matter of course for all students, but except for the incidental beauty of the Authorized Version, English literature was limited to Milton and (by 1847) a supplementary serving of Pope. The science courses sound like mere textbook formulas, but there was some laboratory work, meager by modern standards but probably equal to that in most of the men's colleges. In January 1847 Susan Tolman wrote:

> *I have just returned from the chemical room where Miss Whitman and myself have been engaged most of the forenoon in preparing for experiments upon Galvanism. Contrary to the custom in former years we have our experiments in the afternoon, rather than in the evening; the classes are able to see the experiments, and are more interested.*

> *We have quite an addition to our chemical apparatus, & Miss Whitman really gives very interesting lectures. She calls it talking. She became more discouraged today with the Galvanic Battery, & said she believed it was not for a lady to manage. There are about 70 in the chemistry classes. Miss Whitman has half & I the other.*

Botany fared better; those young teachers, especially Susan, approached it with more confidence. Long afterward she wrote to a young teacher at Mount Holyoke:

> *I taught Botany myself for two years and I had a delightful class. The students were required to collect, press and classify three hundred specimens. All the country about paid tribute to our wants. We gathered too many specimens and finally I remember that Miss Lyon talked to us about our wastefulness in that line. There were some choice plants in the Connecticut Valley and she told us that we were in danger of exterminating them . . .*

But even as in the men's colleges, most of the courses were textbook courses. A teacher taught Whateley or Upham; a class was examined in Paley or Butler. Miss Lyon had a mighty faith in drill and review. Attentive reading, concentration upon the author's statement—these may not have plowed the broadcast field, but the energetic principal saw to it that the soil was pulverized. And let no modernist suppose those textbooks were easy. *Natural Theology, or Evidences of the Existence and Attributes of the Deity collected from the Appearances of Nature*: this was Archdeacon Paley's book, forty years seasoned when Susan Tolman studied it. For all its limitations, and quite beyond the author's intent, that little book was preparing many minds for the idea of evolution. *Analogy of Religion, Natural and Revealed, to the Constitution and Course of Nature*: this was Bishop Butler's granite opus, logic-solid as Blackstone; it had taken many a fall from studious youth for more than a hundred years, and continued to throw them for half a century longer. As late as 1890 Butler was still required in at least one small college.

Twice a year classes were examined orally before the entire school and such visitors as chose to attend. The journal of young William Gardiner Hammond, an Amherst student who drove or walked to South Hadley in 1847, sparking a Seminary girl, is breezily refreshing upon this point. No one can indict him of reverence, even toward his Amherst professors. At first he came to scoff at everything except, of course, his young lady, Nellie Holman. He was sophomorically certain that Miss Lyon was a she-dragon, and this New England nunnery an easy target. By his third or fourth visit, still bantering, he had to admit that the Seminary wasn't altogether a joke. In August he, with his father, attended the finals.

A class in Virgil were on the floor when I came in and the little I could catch was highly creditable to their scholarship. Then the first four books of Euclid: very well done: the teachers gave out captions, and the girls drew their own figures and demonstrated them without the use of letters. Then a class in Botany, of which Nellie formed a part, very interesting to me and honorable to herself, then History and one or two other things of the kind, very good and very dull . . . then five compositions: very good indeed, though rather for style than ideas: even in the style it was often easy to detect traces of some popular author.*

Three villages had wanted the Seminary; South Hadley, most generous with subscriptions, was chosen. Beauty of landscape may have been only incidental in that choice; if so, the incidental now seems reason enough. A mere campus is not enough; a college needs a horizon, too. Four miles north of the village the Mount Holyoke Range makes a wooded barrier across the east half of the valley. The Connecticut, coming down from the north, finds a way between the western shoulder of that range and Mount Tom. Eastward are shaggy hills and rolling farmland; to the west, beyond the river, Mount Tom. A green world, cool-washed and clean, with white farm houses in just the right places, enough fertility near the river, self-respecting tidiness, and not too much of any one thing. And trees—trees with room enough to be themselves. Some of the elms and maples on the campus were there in Susan Tolman's time; some of them may have been planted under her direction when she and Miss Whitman were given charge of the landscaping.

Very early in the life of the Seminary somebody invented Mountain Day.

* Quoted with permission of Professor George F. Whicher, editor of *Remembrance of Amherst, an Undergraduate's Diary, 1846–1848* (Columbia University Press, 1946).

It was not fixed in the calendar; at some time in June or July a sudden feeling came of perfect weather and a forested world simply too big for even Paley to comprehend. And when that feeling came, the domestic "circle" outdid themselves filling the lunch baskets, and morning prayers left some details to the Imagination of Deity, and everybody set off early. They followed the old stage road that angles northwest from the village and skirts the river on the way toward Old Hadley. And at the right place the knowing ones led off up the winding mountain trail through the forest, and after a climb of nearly a thousand feet they reached the summit, from which, if the day was bright, they could see Monadnock (to the northeast) and the Catskills. They still have Mountain Day. Does it continue to get better? In 1847 (as Susan records) Daddy Hawkes, trustee and fiscal agent and general chaperon, allowed that that Mountain Day was the happiest he had ever seen. On their way down they visited the Columns. Nature study, a ten-mile hike for the day. Serious walkers could follow a trail along the top of the range to Mount Norwottuck, but the pestiferous Amherst students had a way of finding out the plan and coming to the same spot, they too having a bent for nature study. Mount Norwottuck was half Amherst's by right, for had not President Hitchcock, in dedication, scattered over the summit stones from India and Persia and China and the Holy Land—specimens sent back by Amherst missionaries—thus integrating geology with religion? A green world in summer; and when frost has tried a few experimental touches and then lets himself go with a free hand, they say that only an old-fashioned poet can tell of that glory. "Vital feelings of delight" might serve; or, as another poet who had seen those hills every year, wrote in a letter: "High in a crimson tree a belated bird is singing . . . You will find the blue hills, Austin, with the autumnal shadows sleeping on them, and there will be a glory lingering round the day."*

Of this glory the early catalogues breathe not a word; they were not selling scenery. Plain little catalogues, severe as a homemade linsey-woolsey dress: as who should say, "Come on the appointed day in October; young ladies will mind their gerundives," and then chuckle, keeping the real October under a bushel. No scenery, no salesmanship at all: one terse item about transportation.

STAGES

The Brattleboro' and Hartford Stage passes South Hadley daily, also one connecting Northampton with the railroad at Wilbraham. Young ladies

---

* By permission, from *Letters of Emily Dickinson*, edited by Mabel Loomis Todd (Harper & Brothers, 1931). See Appendix D, Emily Dickinson at Mount Holyoke.

coming from Brattleboro' or Hartford will arrive about noon, and those from Boston early in the afternoon.

This was in 1842; by 1845 progress was hurtling; one train of cars managed to come within whistling distance of South Hadley, but on the other side of the river; and then the road between ferry and village was trudged by arriving and departing students. Susan writes with a young teacher's grave responsibility:

> *We rose at 4 o'clock so as to have [the students] take the early train of cars. Most of those who went early walked to the ferry, provision being made to get their baggage there. It is now nine o'clock & all but seven who are to leave are on their way. I have had charge of getting them off & am now ready to go myself.*

South Hadley is still echoes-distant from the railway. Its seasoned quiet has vintage flavor. Very early of a summer morning the green-shadowed river road appears empty; but a century is nothing, and when the mind is peopled with old stories you may see the girls whom Susan liked best—the Foote sisters from Cayuga, and petite Harriet Niles, and Abby Allen herself, walking from the old ferry to the village.

It would savor too much of the modern to call the class of 1845 the Wonder Class. But it were strange if, before the end of October 1842, Miss Lyon did not remark to Miss Mary Whitman and Miss Abigail Moore, her vice-principals, that those new juniors looked very promising—very; or if Miss Susan Reed failed to report in faculty meeting on her "section" of those same juniors as being nice and eager young ones. Six years later when Susan Reed (by that time Mrs. Howland) was serving as a missionary in Ceylon, Susan Tolman, learning that she herself would be assigned to that mission, wrote with delight "that I may be associated with dear Mrs. Howland, my first section teacher."

Certainly the class of 1845 began early to stand on tiptoe and reach for good things. They broke all previous records for size—one hundred fifty-four intrants—and all records for staying power: fifty-one of them graduated. Forty-one of the fifty-one became teachers, and not all as merely marking time till marriage—though marriage, from the Mount Holyoke point of view, was not an evasion of responsibility. Two of them founded colleges. As academy principals, teachers in village schools, wives of ministers and doctors and judges and businessmen far and wide over the country, their leaven was potent.

Twenty-eight of the fifty-one came from Massachusetts, the others mostly from New Hampshire, Vermont, Connecticut, and New York. One intrant gave the catalogue a blob of color by registering from "Milwaukie, Ws. Ter." And what parent or brother or sister, poring over the catalogue at home, could affect indifference when reading: *Persis G. Thurston, Kailua, S.J.?* Why, mother, that must be the Reverend Asa Thurston's daughter—he that went to the Islands away back in '19 in the First Company. Our minister knew him at Yale, remember? And to think, his daughter's in our Mary's class. A good five-months voyage it must be, and around the Horn. Mary will have great things to tell when she comes home.

And so they found their way about the newish big four-story building and had their memories stamped forever with the feeling and air of certain rooms: the odor of cordwood and of the Franklin stove, and the thick yellow dimness of a whale-oil lamp of a winter morning, and the view of the mountain on a high clear day, and all the weather changes of feeling and the surprise of new ideas, and the impact of teachers. That plain four-story building looks severe in old pictures, but its interior won a certain respect from an amusedly objective mocker—young Hammond of Amherst.

> *We saw all that was to be seen, the pleasant recitation rooms: the pleasanter chapel, or what corresponds to such: the little library and reading room where all but the religious periodicals are carefully put away from Saturday till Monday: the huge dining room with its all but score of tables, and huge kitchen . . . We went through the long space-ways meeting any number of plain young ladies, and catching sly peeps into their little boxes of sleeping rooms: said "beautiful" at every eligible window . . .*

Those little boxes were each eighteen feet by ten; modern students have lived in smaller. And did any alumna ever forget the room she had lived in? In 1880, while visiting the old hall, Susan Tolman Mills wrote to her own students in California, and put a feeling deeper than words into the heading of the note: "Miss Lyon's Room."

If they learned "section" duties under a nice Susan Reed they had little dread of that semipublic Puritan confessional. They fitted into the gear of "circle" duties.* But let one of their own number tell it. These are parts of two letters written by Abby Allen, one to her father, the other to her younger sisters:

* There were three terms in the year: the first from early October until mid-January; the second until early May; the third ending in August; no Christmas vacation, but a fortnight's vacation after the first and second terms. "Sections," sometimes called "divisions," were group meetings for morale and discipline. "Circles" were groups assigned to a regular chore in household work.

My lesson in Algebra is recited in the room adjoining that containing the piano, where a young lady practices the same hour, and you will not doubt, dear Father, that it requires all my power of abstraction to shut my ears to the music, & attend to my lesson . . . everything is done by rule. It is as much against the rules to study out of study hours, as it is binding upon us to study in study hours.

We have specific hours given us in which to perform every duty except rising in the morning, every young lady is expected to be ready for breakfast at six. I prefer to rise at the first bell, which rings at a quarter before five. Morning devotions are attended in the Seminary Hall at ½ past 8 . . . At ¼ before 8 I recite in Gen. History, and at ½ past 9 in Algebra . . .

After that I have ¾ of an hour for study & then at eleven I go to the domestic hall (or kitchen) to assist in getting dinner, which I do not find quite so slight an affair as I used to at home. I often think, what would Maria or Emma say, could they see Abby attending 2 or 3 chaldrons of pudding & as many more of meat & as many more of potatoes, though the food is cooked in chaldrons it is done in the nicest possible manner.
We dine at ¼ past 12 immediately after which we walk 2 miles according to the rule . . . We have tea at 5. From 6 til ½ past seven and from ¼ past 8 to ¼ past 9 are silent study hours. At ½ past nine every one must have her lamp extinguished.

One of Susan's closest friends was Persis Thurston. Hardly a girl in the Seminary but had heard of the Thurstons and Binghams and Whitneys, who had sailed on the brig *Thaddeus* in 1819 and founded the first mission in the Sandwich Islands. Susan's parents and her grandmother had prayed for them and given money; and the dutiful little *Missionary Herald* had made the names of these veterans and the others who followed—Bishop and Andrews, Gulick and Judd—household names through the northeastern states. The girls at Mount Holyoke would expect something of the exotic in this girl from the Islands. The small-exotic had a place in their conception of missions; a missionary home from Burma preached a good enough sermon but thrilled them more by singing "From Greenland's Icy Mountains" in the Burmese tongue. Persis could, on occasion, cater to this hunger for the picturesque. "Miss Thurston made her appearance dressed in the Sandwich Island's costume. This as usual excited great interest." But she had not been brought up to think of missionary life as a travelogue. She had known from babyhood the hard conditions of life in a far outpost, and had absorbed much of her father's and mother's deep power to carry on through difficulties. She was

(I believe) the second girl born in a mission field to graduate from Mount Holyoke, and certainly the first with whom Susan Tolman had an intimate friendship. She and Susan were among the four members of their class chosen by Mary Lyon to continue as teachers. She endeared herself to the school; long after she had left, teachers and alumnae still spoke of her as "the beloved Persis," thus proving they had read St. Paul. She taught drawing; the old Currier print of Seminary Hall was her work. In 1847 when Persis was getting ready to be married and to sail with her missionary husband, Susan wrote: "She has had a mantua-maker from Springfield to fit & sew for her, while the young ladies have lent much aid." Twenty years later the two classmates and their classmate husbands were to be near neighbors in California—but that must wait.

In the class of 1845 were Mary Humphrey, daughter of the retiring president of Amherst, and Catherine Hitchcock, daughter of his successor. Mount Holyoke had much help from these and other Amherst faculty men—lectures on science, help in choosing apparatus, and always—when needed—sermons. Another classmate was Roxana Tenney, who became first principal of Willoughby Academy, which later grew into Lake Erie College. Helen Peabody, first principal of the school that grew into Western College, at Oxford, Ohio, was a student of Susan's. One intrant who did not graduate was Louisa Torrey; how close a friendship there was in student days between her and Susan Tolman does not appear. Louisa was a frank critic of Mount Holyoke rules, but in 1908 when Louisa's son was a candidate for President of the United States, the spirit of '45 aroused Mrs. Mills to electioneer for Mr. Taft. You just can't fail a classmate.

Another friendship teases the curiosity. There was no love lost between Congregationalists and Catholics. Accordingly, the public gasped and the newspapers were vociferous when, soon after her graduation, Mary P. Thompson of '45 entered a convent. "The New England Nun"—a headline made to order. The Seminary was shocked. Had not '45 devoted its compositions through half a year to Popery? Susan was hurt; everybody was hurt. But the context of Susan's missionary journal makes it clear that the estranged girl chose her as sole confidante among her former Mount Holyoke friends. Susan kept hearing from her, and a year later she reported to the alumnae that Mary Thompson had left the convent.

How did a generation uninstructed in vitamins put so much longevity into the chaldrons that Abby Allen and the kitchen circle tended? Of the fifty-one graduates in Susan's class, sixteen lived to their sixtieth class anniversary, ten to their sixty-fifth; and one, Miss Mary Hooker, lived until 1920.

No wonder: she was descended from the Reverend Thomas Hooker. But even this is no record at Mount Holyoke. Miss Emily S. Wilson, of '61, who taught for many years at Mills Seminary, lived until the eightieth anniversary of her graduation. At South Hadley, mere children who have been out of college only fifty years wait until their elders have spoken.

That little seminary was refreshingly unaware of its own potential greatness. There was plenty of work for educated women to do, and no time to waste upon mere niceties of exquisite personality. Few, if any, girls were drawn to South Hadley by any sense of social snobbery or any shrewd calculation of assuring successful careers for themselves. The country imposed upon Mary Lyon the office of appointment secretary in general; each year she had many more calls than she could supply: teachers in new academies in Ohio and Illinois and the nearer West, teachers in one-room schools in Iowa and in home mission schools in the Southwest. Mount Holyoke counts three colleges as daughters: Mills, Lake Erie College, and Western College; besides other colleges in whose making Mount Holyoke contemporaries of Susan Tolman were to have a hand as teachers or faculty wives: Illinois College, Knox, Beloit, Western Reserve, Lake Charles, and other schools as far west as Oregon. To know these women before they foresaw their own future, to be one of them, and then—as the years brought accelerating returns—to know that you were still one of them, would create a confidence in yourself and in the rightness of Mary Lyon's ideals.

When assigned to remain as teacher in the Seminary, Susan was not puffed up. She had been called home in January 1845 by the death of her sister, Elizabeth De Witt, and again shortly after by critical illness of her father. Then in June her only remaining brother, John, had died suddenly. Even in a happier mood she could not foresee how completely her friendships were to be interknit for life with the Seminary.

During its first thirty years, until 1867, Mount Holyoke was under the successive leadership of four principals; all four were Susan's teachers and colleagues. Of the first seven vice-principals, three were her teachers and colleagues and three more her students. Her sister Julia taught in the Seminary from 1851 until 1860, being vice-principal during two years; and her sister Jane taught there from 1858 until 1864. Besides the six daughters of Deacon John Tolman, three other Tolman cousins were students in the 1840's. With her lively and tenacious friendships, no wonder that Susan never outgrew her college loyalty.

What subjects did she teach? Chemistry and botany, as have been noted; physiology—at least during the autumn of 1847; and in the winter term of

1848 she had classes in Paley (Natural Theology) and Alexander (Evidences of Christianity). In afteryears she considered that her best work had been in botany.

But besides these serious subjects, every young teacher had to double in brass, and Susan had her share of calisthenics. Young Hammond of Amherst had called calisthenics "a species of orthodox dancing in which they perambulate a smooth floor in various figures, with a sort of sliding stage step." The girls in the class he saw wore white dresses and green wreaths, and looked so fetching that he was plumb vexed because Nellie Holman wasn't in it. Other witnesses recorded that the young ladies "maneuvered through their various figures with double, triple, and quadruple springs and other steps, and worked out the patterns of stars, crescents, wreaths, and crosses, and finally achieved the intricacies of the Star Promenade, the Promenade Wreath, the Heart and the cross . . . many similarities to contemporary dance forms." So similar that the Reverend Lyman Beecher, commencement speaker in 1843, was shocked: "This must be orthodox dancing!" Tut me no tuts, Dr. Beecher.

In addition to her share in this almost but not quite orthodox dancing, Susan had charge of the choir in 1847–48. "All who can sing belong," she wrote—whether in triumph or apology. A year earlier she had confided, after a small section prayer meeting: "There are only five of us who sing at all & none of us very independently." Her duty did not pertain to the village church, which teachers and students attended in a body. The South Hadley church went ambitiously beyond the church at Ware. South Hadley had "six violins, three bass viols, beside a whole brass band. The Chorister rising gives three taps with his fiddle bow, then the rest rise, then he commences *do*, then they all take the pitch and sing"—but still not very well.

Calisthenics, choir, *and* the old-time literary program. Susan recorded the subjects of the compositions which were read as between-course tidbits during the three-day ordeal of final examinations:

The Unforgiven
The House of God made a house of merchandise—in blank verse
The Etruscan Bards, by Miss Currier
Tears, by L. H. Hinsdale
Death of Henry 6
*Mary at the Sepulchre—"a very good piece of poetry written by a young
    lady from Long Island"*
*The Relations of the Educated and the Uneducated Classes, by Miss Rob-
    ertson of Canada*

MEMOIRS
OF
Capt. *Roger Clap*.

Relating some of GOD's Remarkable
Providences to *Him*, in bringing
him into *New-England* ; and some
of the Straits and Afflictions, the
Good People met with here in
their Beginnings.

AND

Instructing, Counselling, Directing
and Commanding his*Children* and
Childrens Children, and Houshold,
to serve the LORD in their Generations to the latest Posterity.

Heb. xi. 4. ---*He being dead, yet speaketh.*

BOSTON in *New-England* :
Printed by *B. Green*, 1 7 3 1.

---

14   *Capt.* Clap's *Memoirs.*

In our beginning many were in great Straits,
for want of Provision for themselves and their little Ones. Oh the *Hunger* that many suffered,
and saw no hope in an Eye of Reason to be sup-
plyed, only by *Clams*, and *Muscles*, and Fish. We
did quickly build Boats, and some went a Fishing :
But *Bread* was with many a very scarce thing :
and *Flesh* of all kind as scarce. And in those Days,
in our Straits, though I cannot say God sent a
Raven to feed us, as He did the Prophet *Elijah* ;
yet this I can say to the Praise of God's Glory,
that He sent not only poor *ravenous Indians*,
which came with their Baskets of Corn on their
Backs, to Trade with us, which was a good Supply unto many ; but also sent *Ships* from *Holland*
and from *Ireland* with Provisions, and Indian Corn
from *Virginia*, to supply the Wants of his dear
Servants in this Wilderness, both for Food and
Rayment. And when Peoples Wants were great,
not only in one Town but in divers Towns ; such
was the godly Wisdom, Care and Prudence (not
Selfishness but Self-Denial) of our Governour
Winthrop and his *Assistants*, that when a Ship
came laden with Provisions, they did Order that
the whole Cargo should be bought for a *general
Stock* : And so accordingly, it was, and Distribution was made to every Town, and to every *Person* in each Town, as every Man had need. Thus
God was pleased to care for his People in Times of
Straits, and to fill his Servants with Food & Glad-
ness : Then did all the Servants of God bless his
holy Name, and love one another with pure Hearts
fervently.

Before I proceed any further, I will inform you
that God stirred up his poor Servants to use Means
in

Capt. Clap's *Memoirs.*

in their beginning for their Preservation ; though
a low and weak People, yet a willing People to
lay out their Estates for the Defence of themselves
and others. They having Friends in divers Places
who thought it best for our safety to build a *Fort*
upon the Island now called *Castle-Island* ; at
first they built a *Castle* with *Mud-Walls*, which
stood divers Years : First Capt. *Simpkins* was
Commander thereof, and after him, Lieut. *Monish*,
for a little space. When the *Mud-Walls* failed, it
was built again with *Pine Trees and Earth* ; and
Capt. *Davenport* was Commander. When that
decayed, which was within a little Time, there
was a small Castle built with *Brick Walls*, and
had *three Rooms* in it ; a dwelling Room below,
a lodging Room over it, the Gun Room over
that, wherein stood *Six* very good *Saker Guns*,
and over it upon the Top *Three lesser Guns*. All
the Time of our Weakness, God was pleased to
give us Peace, until the Wars with the *Dutch* in
Charles the II's Time. At that Time our Works
were very weak, and Intelligence came to us that
Durother || a Dutch Commander of a Squadron of
Ships, was in the *West-Indies*, and did intend to
visit us ; whereupon our *Battery* also was repaired,
wherein are *Seven* good *Guns*. But in the very
Time of this Report in *July* 1665, God was pleased to send a grievous Storm of Thunder & Light-
ning, which did some hurt at *Boston*, and struck
dead here at the *Castle-Island*, that worthy, renowned Captain *Richard Davenport* ; upon which
the *General Court* in *Aug.* 30th following, appointed *another* * *Captain* in the Room of him

---

|| Or, DE RUITHER, a famous Dutch Admiral.
* It was Capt. CLAP Himself.

that

*Frontispiece and two
pages from the Memoirs
of Capt. Roger Clap.
(From a copy in the
Missionary Archives of
the Houghton Library,
Harvard University.)*

A Currier print of Mount Holyoke Female Seminary, first published during the 1840's, from a drawing made by Persis Thurston. (From a copy at Porter Hall, Mount Holyoke College.)

Eleanor Boutelle Nichols, maternal grandmother of Susan Mills.

PUPILS.

SENIOR CLASS.

NAMES.	RESIDENCE.
Harriette Allen,	*Lebanon, N. H.*
Susan M. Allen,	*Manchester.*
Caroline Avery,	*Conway.*
Jane F. Bagg,	*West Springfield.*
Lydia G. Bailey,	*Hopkinton, N. H.*
Lydia R. Baldwin,	*Southampton.*
Susan Frances Bates,	*North Brookfield.*
Mary H. Bissell,	*Norwalk, Ct.*
Sarah D. Clarke,	*Rowe.*
Esther H. Cook,	*Manchester, Ct.*
Sarah E. Everett,	*Benson, Vt.*
Mary A. Ellis,	*Boston.*
Sarah E. Foote,	*Cayuga, N. Y.*
Cynthia Fowler,	*Westfield.*
Susan H. Fowler,	*Greenfield, N. H.*
Hannah Green,	*Auburn.*
Mary S. Green,	*Lowell.*
Sarah Ellen Green,	*Lowell.*
Julia A. Hayes,	*South Hadley.*
Catharine Hitchcock,	*Amherst.*
Ann Maria Hollister,	*Manchester, Vt.*
Mary Hooker,	*Longmeadow.*
Mary Hopkins,	*Miller's Place, L. I.*
Mary E. Humphrey,	*Amherst.*
Elizabeth King,	*Vernon, Ct.*
R. Augusta Lane,	*Boston.*
Frances S. Leach,	*Pittsford, Vt.*
Diantha C. Lee,	*Northampton.*
Clementine M. Locke,	*Hinsdale, N. H.*
Sarah Loomis,	*Bennington, Vt.*
Freelove P. McIntyre,	*Charlton.*
Harriet S. Niles,	*Spencertown, N. Y.*
Mary P. Oliphant,	*Haverhill.*
Anna Maria Olmsted,	*East Hartford, Ct.*

Sampler worked by
Susan Mills' mother.
(Courtesy of the Estate
of Fannie A. Madison.)

5

Sarah H. Osgood,	Springfield.
Mary E. Parsons,	Newbury, (Belleville.)
Mary C. Pease,	Blandford.
Rhoda K. Perkins,	Braintree.
Elisabeth Pitkin,	East Hartford, Ct.
Mary A. Pond,	West Medway.
Lois W. Rice,	Conway.
Martha C. Scott,	North Hadley.
Julia W. Schuyler,	Ovid, N. Y.
Eveline A. Sherwood,	Jamesville, N. Y.
Helen M. G. Stevens,	Springfield.
Emma L. Taylor,	Derry, N. H.
Roxena B. Tenny,	Orwell, Vt.
Mary P. Thompson,	Durham, N. H.
Susan L. Tolman,	Ware Village.
Persis G. Thurston,	Kailua, Sandwich Islands.
Cornelia Youngs,	Farmington, Ct.

MIDDLE CLASS.

NAMES.	RESIDENCE.
Lydia E. M. Abbott,	Gilsum, N. H.
Abby M. Ainslie,	Onondaga Hollow, N. Y.
Emily L. Bailey,	Hartford, Vt.
Mary E. Barker,	Amenia, N. Y.
Ellen C. Barrett,	Rutland, Vt.
Lydia Bates,	Springfield, Vt.
Harriet L. Bissell,	Norwalk, Ct.
Lucy H. Brigham,	Framingham.
Mary M. Brinsmade,	Washington, Ct.
Eliza C. Hovey Brown,	Hampton, Ct.
Mary J. Brown,	Buffalo, N. Y.
Lydia P. Chase,	Millbury.
Sarah E. Clarke,	Montpelier, Vt.
Wealthy Clarke,	Williamstown, Vt.
Hannah Maria Condit,	Oswego, N. Y.

5

Faculty.

REV. MARK HOPKINS, D. D., PRESIDENT,
and Professor of Intellectual and Moral Philosophy.

EBENEZER KELLOGG, M. A.,
Professor of Languages, and Librarian.

EBENEZER EMMONS, M. A., M. D.
Professor of Natural History.

ALBERT HOPKINS, M. A.,
Professor of Natural Philosophy and Astronomy.

REV. JOSEPH ALDEN, D. D.,
Professor of Rhetoric and Political Economy.

EDWARD LASELL, M. A.,
Professor of Chemistry.

JOHN TATLOCK, M. A.,
Professor of Mathematics.

JAMES H. COFFIN, M. A.,
Tutor.

Page from the Williams College cat-
alogue for 1842, listing the faculty
of Cyrus Mills' student days.

Pages from the Mount Holyoke Female
Seminary catalogue for 1844–45, list-
ing Susan Tolman's senior classmates.

Batticotta Seminary compound. (Pen and ink drawing in the Missionary Archives, the Houghton Library.)

Samuel Bacon and Abby Allen Fairbank.
(A daguerreotype made in 1847.)

Cyrus Mills. (A daguerreotype
made in Honolulu about 1863.)

Rev. C. F. Mills

The three
Tolman sisters—
Julia, Jane, and Susan—
in San Francisco, about 1871.

David Hewes

Judge M. H. Myrick

The unplanted campus. Above: In 1871, near the site of Kapiolani.
The large detached building, left foreground, was the gymnasium.
"Pine Top" is treeless except for small oaks on the steep hill.
Below: About 1873, from the slope of Pine Top, above the modern
warehouse. A few apricot trees from the little orchard still survive.
The building with mansard roof, joined to the gymnasium since 1871,
contained recitation rooms and a studio. The spire of Divinity
Church, later known as the Tolman Cottage, shows in the distance
at the left of Mills Hall.

Susan Tolman Mills,
shortly after her
husband's death.

I. E. Dwinell

Warren Olney

Novels and Novel Readers

A Dream of Ancient Rome. "*This was* very *well read.* Most *have spoken very low.*"

Cotton, by a Southern Lady

Coming Events cast their shadows before, or a scene in 1948, by Miss Robertson of Canada

There may have been two Miss Robertsons. One became the mother of Ralph Conner, the novelist. But the prophecy of 1948, which should be a collector's item, was the work of Margaret M. Robertson, who later wrote children's books.

At the beginning of the autumn term in 1846 Susan and another young teacher were given charge of the sickroom, with the help of a student nurse. A year later, Susan was made supervisor of Wash Day. At three on Monday mornings the fires were started, and at three-thirty the first relay was busy at the washboards. Each student washed her own clothes, the laundry circle having the duty of keeping the fires going, the kettles refilled, and the successive relays moving, while a special detail—well shawled and mittened in icy weather—attended to the line work. After breakfast, while the last relays were at the tubs, the others turned to with mops and pails and scrubbed recitation rooms and hallways and stairs, and roommates scoured their own rooms, while other squads brought dried clothes in and assorted them by name tapes; and by noon everything smelt clean and everybody was ready for food. After this, they wrote compositions, and were then free to write letters and take long walks. Lights out at nine-forty-five.

And no grumbling—at least not from Miss Tolman. Even so, have some mercy, Miss Lyon. But no, Miss Tolman is also appointed to co-operate with Miss Whitman in working out a better plan for landscape gardening. Hitherto each young lady has spaded and planted after the imagination of her own heart; now we are to have an eye toward future effects. Some teachers broke down under the strain, and Miss Lyon's own health was beginning to concern her colleagues. Was she, then, a slave driver? Her teachers did not think so; their adoration for her is reflected over and again in Susan's journal. And surely their adoration had no sliver of the mercenary; the poor dears counted themselves passing rich at salaries of from $125 to $200 a year. A rare principal, to pay some of her teachers as much as she allowed herself. Besides, how many Prominent Educators ever had the gustatory heartiness to bring a basket of luscious peaches to a faculty meeting? Our oldest napkins, colleagues, and lean over well, for peaches stain.

And so the earnest pages of Susan's missionary journal have their marginal posies of word about weather and season: a late spring blizzard, a day when Mount Holyoke and Mount Tom were crystal-clear, the orchards in bloom, and the Connecticut bank-full from snows in northern Vermont; reports of big snows, when sleighs came in relays to take the girls riding; reports of May weather when they were allowed to walk after supper—until half past seven; reports of walks after breakfast, when Susan (as a young teacher) led fifty new students each morning in a lively half-hour hike; reports of the first green peas of the season. "The Aurora Borealis is now visible, lighting up the whole sky almost like day. I never saw it so finely exhibited as now." "Tomorrow evening after close of the examinations we are to have a social party. About fifty of the town's people are invited . . . We have had nothing of the kind this year & think the young ladies will enjoy it." The young ladies did. "At 9 o'clock we repaired to Sem Hall where we had refreshments, calisthenics, music, etc." Neighborhood news, too, one item of which utters itself with shocked voice: the father of one of the students has "died a Universalist."

The following demure item might be only a petal on the stream, but some of Susan's alumnae readers would catch the intimation. "I have not told you that Mr. E. T. Smith is soon to become our nearest neighbor, having bought Dr. Belden's place . . . His son Byron is, I believe, to keep the old farm while Miss Nancy Dwight is to become his help-meet." Mr. Erastus T. Smith owned a considerable part of what is now Mount Holyoke campus; he ran a paper mill at Lower Lake, and had been a generous donor to the school. All of which is humdrum. But read the mute italics in the final sentence quoted: "His son Byron . . . while Miss Nancy Dwight is to become his help-meet." Innocence! For Byron Smith had been one of Susan's beaus, and Miss Nancy Dwight one of her pupils. This mild item is but a telegraphing of the eye from woman to women: Miss Tolman's plans extend farther than the old farm in the Notch.

But Mr. Erastus Smith and his son Byron deserve a *brasse éternelle* in the academic theater; the father invented and the son made firm the office of academic marshal. It needed a retired farmer and herdsman to see the need. He "would announce in a commanding voice the order of procedure to the Meeting House and wave his cane with authority and gently prod the orator into place at the head of the procession, and see to it that visiting dignitaries and parents and 'intended' young men got into the right pews." In due time Byron Smith took over; many living alumnae remember seeing him wave *his* cane commandingly and behave with proper pomp and circumstance. And for a comely ending to his by-page, many years later when Mrs. Mills paid visits to South Hadley she was often a guest in the home of Byron Smith, who had of course moved down from the old farm in the Notch and become a village dignitary.

Venerable Mr. Joseph Condit, minister of the village church, died a week before the opening of the autumn term in 1847. He was a very dear old man, and Susan had written many an item about his sermons. Then for seven months the church listened to a series of "supplies," whose varying merits are indicated by whether Susan quotes their texts. At last in April young Mr. Laurie, returned from a mission in Persia, won the not-too-easy approval of the congregation. "He waits," wrote Susan, "until the house is perfectly still before be commences. He begins in a low voice . . . He pronounces the word *Israel* just as Mr. Condit used to."

Susan does not mention this next story, but it belongs here. In the autumn of 1847 word went round that a circus was coming to the village. Students prepared to make a virtue of staying away; Miss Lyon would never allow them to attend, but they misjudged that resourceful woman. She had already bargained with the Yankee manager to admit her students at half rates. (A pity that that circus man did not publish his journal.) The great day came. The caravan paraded the one village street shortly before noon, stopping for fifteen minutes in front of the Seminary. Dinner went un-Fletcherized; Puritan wardrobes furnished the equivalent of afternoon sportswear. Daddy Hawkes waited in the parlor to chaperone them. It was really one's duty to go; one might not again have the opportunity to see elephants, at least one tiger, and ever so many other living illustrations of Nature's methodology. Paley in motion, Paley in Technicolor. *But* — and this was soberly impressed upon them—*but*, while the menagerie was educational, the rest of the circus was not. They were to observe the animals studiously, and when they saw their teachers leave they were to rise and follow. Not that the clowns and the acrobats and the trick donkey were wicked—these were amusing enough, no doubt, to the vulgar mind—but not, not seriously educational.

So they were told; and so they did. And not one student, not the dutifullest little prissy, saw any teacher leave. Did the teachers miss their cue? Or did they, being real ladies, leave so unobtrusively that no one marked their going? At any rate, here came the elephants around the ring, massive and alien ideas from impenitent India, yet friendly as if heathendom could be old and wise and comical. The leader bore a howdah. Halt. The ringmaster, a proper man, admirably at ease, inquired: Would any young lady student of Miss Lyon's widely renowned institution of higher learning like to have the thrilling experience of riding this colossal beast, the behemoth of Scripture, oft referred to in classic lore? Every girl wanted to; none dared. One's parents. One's minister. One's example to others. Where was Daddy Hawkes? And then a senior, daughter (it is said) of a missionary, stepped down from the benches and, holding her skirts carefully, climbed the stepladder and seated herself in the howdah; and Ibn Suliman, a twinkle in his knowing eye, moved slow and stately around the ring, the assistant and acting-assistant and graduate-reader elephants following. Perfect poise and dignity. In a howdah a lady is still a lady. And in South Hadley an elephant is still a gentleman. Then the trained tiger came on and did his fiercely theatrical act; and the tumblers and the trained bear and the clowns. My goodness, two hours have gone, and we shall have to hurry to get back to section meetings, and how to sound the right note of educational opportunity in our letters home, and *we* saw no teachers leave, and what will Miss Lyon say? And wise Mary Lyon said nothing at all.

In December 1847 a strolling daguerreotypist set up shop across the street from the Seminary. Now one could have a portrait without traveling all the way to Mr. Samuel F. B. Morse. Contagion was swift. Have you had yours taken? It is very simple. You sit perfectly still for not more than two minutes. And really not expensive. Is it worldly? But Miss Lyon has had hers taken in Boston, to give to Susan Reed Howland when Mrs. Howland sailed for Ceylon, so it must be allowable. It was allowable; but Miss Lyon reminded them in chapel that they should not spend on these portraits money that should go to missions, nor should they waste time from regular duties. Particularly, it was a waste of time for friends to accompany one to the sitting. And so they went singly; the pictures in their glazed wooden cases were thrilled over, then laughed at, then lost beyond identification; and worth more now, if we had them, than the wandering Daguerrean ever dreamed.

Before the weather changes let us hear of the Yale man's grace before meat. By one of those Conrad shifts of time we are back in the little dining room in Mills Hall, and it is at once 1909 and 1847. The old voice telling the story chuckles with comical asides, building the approach. On a Saturday of bitter weather this Yale man had skated up the river to call on his sweetheart at the Seminary. Saturday was not the regular day for callers, but Miss Lyon waived that rule: after all, he was young and more than half frozen; he had suffered greatly for love. So his young lady was excused from other duties, and at noon he was conducted into the big dining room and stationed by Miss Lyon's side. Now it was not proper for a lady—even an authoritative Miss Lyon—to say grace or lead in prayer if a gentleman was present. And so she directed him to ask the blessing—poor young man, with his heart numb and his knees shaking—with his sweetheart and all those two hundred fifty strange young ladies and all the teachers—and even if their eyes were properly downcast, he could feel all their minds focused on him. A terrible ordeal. Yale depended upon him. All the blessings he could remember spilled over his mind and ran off the edges. "And so, he cleared his throat and girded up his loins and said: 'O Lord, bless this food to our use and—and these girls to our service!' "

Long ago a faithful alumna gathered the impressions of older Mount Holyoke women over whose minds the memory of Abby Allen still exercised a spell. One of them wrote:

> *She was slender and lady-like in person, with fine eyes, high-minded and ambitious. Miss Lyon delegated her to see to it that dinner was served promptly, and gave her supervision of food for the sick. Miss Susan Tolman was her most intimate girl friend. Abby was musical, nice about her dress, orderly and rather aristocratic in her tastes, as well as sweet-spirited.*

In her senior year she withdrew from the Seminary and taught; she was pledged to go as a missionary, and needed money for her outfit. In 1846 she married Samuel Bacon Fairbank. The Fairbanks were numerous around Oakham and in the country west of Leominster. By a strange quirk of pioneering his father had moved to a farm near Jacksonville, Illinois, and the young man graduated from the new college there in 1842, but came back to Oakham to marry Abby Allen. He was designated to the Ahmednugger Mission in western India; and in May 1846, while he and his bride were preparing to sail to Bombay, Susan Tolman, then at home in Ware, wrote a long and tender letter to Abby Fairbank. To careless eyes the letter might seem morbid with premonition, but these two friends knew that going to a mission post in India was no pleasure jaunt; the death toll was sobering. Their years with Mary Lyon had only confirmed in both girls their old-fashioned inheritance—the obligation to serve without heroics.

Abby had planned to visit Susan in Ware during the latter's spring vacation, and now the visit had to be foregone.

My dear Abby:

> . . . I looked for you yesterday & the day before, & yet I hardly dared hope to see you, and now I must not even hope more . . . I cannot but think you will be better when you are once out at sea & the last parting trial is over. You have had too much of fatigue & excitement for your

delicate frame the last two months . . . My Father's family feel quite acquainted with you & were much interested when I told them there was a possibility that you would visit us. Jane my youngest sister asked yesterday many times do you think Abby will come today? . . . I spent last evening at Mr. Gale's . . . [They] are going to attend the anniversaries in Boston next week. I told them I thought perhaps you would be there . . . Mrs. Gale said "I would go a good way to see that sweet face once more. She has what I call a beautiful countenance." Mr. G. always inquires about your health & says she looks very delicate. I cannot bear to hear anyone say so although I know it to be true . . . I go back to Hadley next week Thursday. Shall I hear from you before I go back? . . . I want to know when you sail . . .

They never met again. Their mission posts lay on opposite sides of a wide country. Abby Fairbank died at Ahmednugger in 1853. Long after, a younger woman wrote of her: "I realize more and more that it is what we are rather than what we do that influences the world."

four

"GO YE INTO ALL THE WORLD . . ."

HER STUDENTS USED TO SEE MARY LYON EARLY ON SUNDAY afternoons with Jonathan Edwards' *History of Redemption* in hand, eager to fill usefully the hour before afternoon church services by reading to a voluntary audience. The voluminous notes which Susan Tolman and many other students made upon their principal's chapel talks— sermons, had she been a man—reveal a theology sterner in many of its aspects than our generation knows. Her discourses were weighty with the sense of an imminent Last Judgment, the self-surrender of positive conversion, the confession of sin. She held that the whole aim of creation, to the farthest star, was the redemption of man on this little earth and that there was but one means of redemption. Her God was equally of the Old and the New Testaments; indeed, rather more the towering shadow of Jehovah than the luminous presence whom John knew. One misses in those notes the untensioned happiness of that story which ends the first chapter of the Gospel of John. But the authentic stories about her outside the chapel reassure us that her religion was kinder than her theology. Devout Bible reader though she was, she often showed a want of discrimination between the noble and the mediocre in her citations. Daniel was to her as lofty as the herdsman of Tekoa, Proverbs or the Pentateuch as spiritual as Isaiah; the Song of Songs was literal Messianic prophecy, and a detail of early Jewish ritual as valid as if Isaiah and Jesus had never denounced it. In these records of her chapel talks there is no evidence that she ever faced the growing question of her time: if scientific truth run counter to the letter of Genesis, what shall one believe? How shall man learn to trace through the fable of experience and all the racial childhood's fumbling with the alphabet, the heart of the matter: "To the truths we keep coming back and back to"?*

The sense of mortality lay somber across her world; she felt it a blessed privilege to prepare souls for death. With their own hands she and her young women washed and clothed their dead for burial. Intelligent inquiry was strangely benumbed; they regarded the prevalent tuberculosis as willed of God. The heaven of Revelations was factual to them, yet the sense of mortality gave all their songs a minor key. Yet here was a paradox: so intense that faith, the stories of the several deaths in the Seminary sound of an experience not bewildered and lonely. Her implicit faith in prayer for others made it hard for the independent to evade her, yet she seems not to have set herself in the accuser's seat over against them. Her code forbade a whole category of innocent amusements, but after all hers was not a negative morality; and it was very unlikely that her young women, geared to her own hearty propensity for work, would ever seek an escape in the immolation which makes mystic experience a main object. For on the practical side her religion worked. Those disciplinary section meetings wherein each student, made to toe the mark both by her own conscience and by the listening social group, owned up in public to her shortcomings—what were these Puritan confessionals but a prompt and regular psychological house cleaning, a habit of keeping one's accounts square with the community?

The more one reads those pages of eager concern that every girl find a living, working faith, the clearer one truth emerges: Mary Lyon and her students were trying to accomplish by religion the same things that our generation undertakes through psychology and the preaching of social obligation. In that school, so free from cultural and social snobbery, they found in the Bible the cure for the oldest psychological ills and a working basis for democracy. Modern scholars know more about the Book—its slow growth as an anthology of racial experience—than Mary Lyon did; but her

* "The Black Cottage." From *Collected Poems* by Robert Frost. Copyright 1930, 1939, by Henry Holt and Company, Inc. Copyright 1936 by Robert Frost.

students, with their old-fashioned habit of reading and memorizing, knew the Book itself. Religion gave them motive for living and doing. Even with their evident lack of discrimination they could not but find in that uneven wealth of word a brave condemnation of arrogant power, a pleading compassion for the wronged and helpless. Though literalists, they must have felt more than they realized in their reading the passionate effort of man to free religion from ossified formalism. Stumbling over a thousand contradictions and indirections, man had somehow found his way again and again to a belief that this quintessence of dust holds a spark of divine fire. By some strange economy in the universe, the humblest, the least gifted person, had a significance. Even the most timorous among them felt herself moved and strengthened by a power beyond human contriving. Altruism (a word they had never heard of) would have seemed more abstract than love; and good taste, as an end in life, lacked the virtue as of some wild herb to save one from despair. "He restoreth my soul." Here were poets who had had all the prettiness and falseness winnowed out of them, men whose anger was a sharp sword; men who saw, past bigotry and racial prejudice, a light that would reach all nations. Self-sacrifice, a respect for the essential dignity of man, a fear of violating the soul of another—these became second nature to many a girl in that fervent little school. In those chapel meetings, in the daily Quiet Hour, one might acquire, without analyzing the how and why of it, the reader's gift of taking a high excitement from words written long ago. "We likewise dare all things if we hear a horn blown from some far height of being and remember that some who lived before us reported that they too heard that horn."* In her early twenties Susan Tolman echoed many of the stock phrases of theological dialectic, as students of a later era repeat the clichés of their time; but with more than an average instinct for the beauty of the King James English, she had, and could communicate to others, that best reader's gift. That reading had done strange things to men, turning them into reformers or saints or martyrs or madmen, making them overthrow the stubbornest wrong foundations and build better. A hundred years ago it kindled a few hundreds of American students to one of the strangest of all undertakings—to try to convert the world in their generation.

That part of the missionary movement which concerns our story began in 1806 when five students at Williams College met in what later became famous as the Haystack Prayermeeting. Out of that beginning the American Board of Commissioners for Foreign Missions was founded in 1812, to act jointly for the Congregational and Presbyterian churches of the United

* From *The Interpreters*, by Æ, with permission of The Macmillan Company.

States. Other denominations soon organized their own missions, the Baptists and Methodists being especially zealous. (Churches in England and Scotland had been active long before the movement became general in America.) By 1848 the American Board had missions in India, Ceylon, Siam, Persia, Syria, Turkey, Greece, South Africa, West Africa, the Sandwich Islands, China, and Borneo. The movement had become a campaign on many beachheads, more enthusiastic than systematic in the management. The men and women at these outposts wrote regular formal reports to the Board in Boston, and the busy *Missionary Herald* posted these accounts of progress and of setbacks as on a bulletin board, for the folks at home. Other letters, personal and more revealing, came to families and friends; and as in wartime, the folks at home were prayerful and anxious, devoted and critical too, responsive to the heroic incident and curious for realistic details. Almost every church had heard a recruit, tense with consecration and excited with high dreams, or the more sobering story from some veteran, home on sick leave, winnowed of illusions but still unwavering and terribly earnest. And somebody in almost every church knew the kinsmen of a missionary, and could pass along the informal and more confidential stories that came in family letters, and share the family's sorrow when word came of a son or daughter who would never return.

Eighteen Mount Holyoke women went as foreign missionaries before 1848. Five of these had left the Seminary before Susan Tolman entered, but she was bound to know of them by report. Six more had been her teachers, and the seven others either her classmates or her students. From 1843 on, throughout her time in the Seminary, at least one teacher each year resigned to enter the service—three in 1846, including Abigail Moore and Lucy Lyon, nieces of Mary Lyon. Both young women were loved at Mount Holyoke; Miss Moore, as one of the vice-principals, had been a mainstay, and Miss Lyon felt she had given two daughters to the cause. Besides these eighteen, fourteen others whom Susan Tolman knew as students or fellow teachers were preparing to go, and most of them did go by 1850. Feeling was high; a cause that had earlier seemed an abstract good, a romantic dream, was now actual, pressing upon thought and emotion daily. The many letters which these women wrote back from their outposts to the Seminary were lost in the fire which destroyed the main building in 1896, but we know that those letters possessed the minds of the school; and Susan Tolman, as author of the answering letters through two years, was in the full force of that current. Missionaries were no longer persons whom you prayed for in a general way; they were now Persis Thurston Taylor of your own class, and

Nancy Foote Webb of the class just before your own, and Miss Fiske and Miss Reed (Mrs. Howland) for whom you had felt a freshman's ardor, and—dearest of all—Abby Allen Fairbank herself—"my sister Abby," as Susan called her. No wonder that Ooroomiah and Kailua and Ahmednugger and Batticotta became as Scriptural as the names of early churches in Paul's letters.

I now turn to Susan's private notebook as distinct from her missionary journal. It is a plain little pocket memorandum book in marbled paper cover. About one-third of the entries are in ink, the rest in faded pencil—and her hand was never easy to read. The book was begun on April 12, 1846; the last entry is dated April 6, 1848, shortly before she was released from teaching, to make ready to go as a missionary. It is not a diary; a few fast days (prayer days) are dated, with phrases from Miss Lyon's remarks and citations of Bible readings, but there is no sequent record of events. Names of persons appear but with no comment; her interest in them has to be learned from other sources. The book is an agenda of personal discipline, as private as her room in Quiet Hour, and certainly not to be invaded out of mere curiosity. The very artlessness of it furnishes the best unplanned, unselfconscious portrait of this terribly earnest girl of twenty-one. The book begins:

Objects *for which I wish stately to pray*
Monday *The Missionary work*
Tuesday *My country in all its interests & bearings*
Wednesday *This family*
Thursday *My little praying circle*
            The Middle Class
            The circle of impenitents with which I meet
Friday *The Sailor The Slave & His Master*
Saturday *My friends & my own church*
Sabbath *The Church*
        "   "   at home
            General subjects
The class with which I graduated
The school for Armenians in Persia
The missions at Bombay, Ceylon, to [the] Nestorians,
            Ahmednugger
Individuals for whom I wish to pray
            My Father—Mother—My Sisters, especially
                Julia & Jane who are not pious.
                My Brothers in law. My aged Grandmother.

As has been noted, her brother John and her sister Elizabeth De Witt died in 1845. Her sister Emily was married to John Condron; whether they were then living in Ware or had moved to Rochester, New York, is not known. Her sister Sarah, married to Freeman Foster, was living in Palmer, a few miles south of Ware. And sisters Julia and Jane were "not pious." The words *piety* and *pious*, which occur often in certain letters, have lost tune like a neglected piano. To us they suggest a self-conscious righteousness, doing good by rote, a tithing of mint and cumin; but Mark Hopkins and Mary Lyon surely meant something much more positive, more fluent and lively.

"My aged Grandmother" was of course Eleanor Boutelle Nichols, then aged eighty-one and living in far-off Enosburg—she whose stored memory of good verses had started all this passionate earnestness. A little way down the page come two cousins, indicated only by initials. "T. B." was Thomas Brainerd Nichols, who had been a valorous flanking party against Barnum's bull in the stony pastures of Enosburg. He and Susan favored each other among those large families of cousins. He became a physician at Plattsburg, New York, and at least once in the 1870's Susan and her husband visited him there. The other cousin, "J-a S." remains unidentified. The initials do not fit any first cousin; the child of a Leominster cousin may have been in mind.

Then come the names of twenty-four other persons, most of them associated with Mount Holyoke. First, of course, was Abby Allen Fairbank. Next was Nancy Foote ('44), who with her sisters Sarah ('45) and Mary ('47) came from Cayuga, New York, and were close friends of Susan and Abby. At the time of the notebook entry Nancy had married Edward Webb, an Englishman who graduated from Andover Seminary in 1845, and the two were on their way to India, where they were stationed successively at Madras and Madura. The third name was that of Susan Reed Howland ('39)— "dear Mrs. Howland, my first section teacher"—who, with her husband, was already stationed at Batticotta. Throughout Susan's life in Ceylon they would be next-door neighbors.

Four others in the list were, or soon became, missionaries. Foremost of these was Fidelia Fiske ('42), the first Mount Holyoke teacher to go into the mission service. Her call had moved the entire Seminary deeply; coming as it did in Susan's impressionable first year, its effect upon her was great. Indeed, in all that growing company of enlistees Miss Fiske continued to be, by common consent, pre-eminent. They started the missionary journal mainly for her sake; and Mount Holyoke and the churches continued to think of her and her school for girls at Ooroomiah as the best proof that missions were worth while. One feels that if she had failed, morale at home would have collapsed; but Fidelia Fiske, with more than a little of Mary Lyon's own qualities, was not given to defeat. After fifteen years in Persia she returned to South Hadley and taught for five years, besides writing the biography of Mary Lyon. Another name is bracketed with hers—that of "John the Nestorian." It has been suggested that he was Mar Johannan, a Nestorian bishop who visited America in the 1840's and made quite a stir among the college recruiting centers; but I am now confident that this John was not a bishop. Susan informed her alumnae readers that she had received letters from Miss Fiske and from John the Nestorian; and again, when letters had arrived from Persia: "One was from Miss Fiske, & one from John, a pious Nestorian, to myself." Here was an early experiment in pacific relations between Persia and Massachusetts. Not precisely romance—a dangerous force, connotative of novel reading, but mayn't a young lady decorously encourage a pious young Nestorian to attain even deeper piety and help him with his tenses?

Then comes the name of Persis Thurston ('45), and near it that of her brother Asa. Born in the Islands, he too had been sent around the Horn, to be educated at Williams College. Susan had probably met him; and it would seem that Persis had confided a private worry about this sophomore brother, who was in danger of running somewhat wild. Remoteness from home and the excitement of the States were proving a little heady for the boy from the Islands. It is a satisfaction to record that Asa became pious.

The list includes still another classmate and one of Susan's students who became missionaries. Then "my minister and his family," Mr. Nahum Gale; and two De Witts, also of Ware. "E. De Witt" (Eliza), related to Susan's brother-in-law, married Susan's cousin, Joel Hyde, of Winchendon, and became the mother of William De Witt Hyde of Bowdoin. Another woman of Ware, Miss Harriet Goulding, had been a missionary among the Choctaw Indians; she visited Mount Holyoke at commencement in 1848. She was related to Cynthia Goulding (x'56) who, many years later, was Mrs. Mills' right hand in managing the preparatory department in Mills Seminary. Also on the list was Miss Susan Lincoln, the maiden lady in Leominster for whom Susan was named. Besides, there are nine others who were either classmates or students of Susan, among them Mary P. Thompson, "the New England nun," and Harriet Niles, whose sparkle was to delight the alumnae in 1912. Five of the six others are identified; the sixth, "M. Bingham," may be one of three Mount Holyoke women whom the name and initial fit.

The notebook contains resolutions for Bible reading—two chapters a day—and for still more memorizing of good verses and the daily practice of two quiet half hours. She promises to set down in the book any failures to keep this schedule, with the reasons thereof. "It was during vacation and I was not careful enough to record the time." "I did not make plans aright." "No good excuse." She arrays her worst faults for correction: too great haste in doing things, passing hasty judgment, thinking ill of others, want of perseverance, and she warns herself to speak nothing but the truth. And page by page the appeal for missionary recruits becomes more urgent.

The pieces fit together perfectly; and the kingpiece was the Reverend Rufus Anderson (1796–1880), Corresponding Secretary of the American Board. A Bowdoin and Andover man, he had served as undersecretary in Mission House in Boston, and had then been advanced to the higher office in 1832, where he became really the brains and voice of the Board. A born executive, he was personnel manager, diplomat, comforter, unraveler of snarls, and was altogether even busier than he seemed. He had been an early champion of Miss Lyon's school; when invited to give the anniversary (commencement) address in 1839 he did so despite the warnings of Boston clergymen that he would lose caste by lending his prestige to so brash an educational venture. Rufus Anderson was a great mixer, and though not nominally the recruiting agent for the Board, he knew everybody and recruited out of hours. His oldest daughter, Sarah Jane ('48), was one of Susan Tolman's students, and evidently she carried back to Boston glowing stories about the young teacher, for Rufus Anderson had Susan Tolman in mind as a likely candidate long before she became an active one. He had visited her home in Ware, and when she applied formally as a candidate the friendship between them was accepted as being stronger than most testimonials.

And so on April 6, 1848, the final entry in the small notebook runs:

Fast Day   *Apr 6, 1848*   South Hadley
In my little room at Holyoke—All is beautiful without, within all is quiet. All have gone to tea & I am alone. Thoughts of the past, of the precious seasons I have had in this dear home are with me—The future too rises before me. Oh where will a year from this day find me? It may be in eternity. Solemn thoughts . . . If my life is spared doubtless I shall be in Ceylon far far away from these hallowed scenes—The Ch[urch] spire I

have so often looked upon from this window will not meet my gaze then, no church going bell will sound upon my ears. Instead——I shall be in a land of strangers a land of darkness & heathenism—My heart shrinks at the thought & yet—I wish only to go Forward.

Friendliness had been wonderful at South Hadley; but even in that warmth (she confessed to her alumnae readers) she dreaded her assignment to meet with a group of students who were unbelievers. Somehow Miss Lyon could face unbelievers without a quaver; Susan was not sure that she could do that. And yet, here was the call.

Mr. Nahum Gale did not share Susan's mistrust of herself; he wrote a nice letter to the Board in her behalf. And Miss Lyon's altogetherness was like a ninth wave. She wrote to Dr. Anderson:

SOUTH HADLEY, April 3, 1848

DEAR SIR:

By request, I write a few lines relative to Miss Susan L. Tolman. She has been connected with Mount Holyoke Female Seminary 6 years— three as scholar, & three as a teacher. With us she has been highly valued & greatly beloved. I regard her as possessing a rare combination of requisites for the work which she is now contemplating. Her general characteristics, her health and personal habits, her intellectual powers & mental culture, her industry, faithfulness & perseverance in the performance of duty, her activity & versatility of adaptation, her social character & disposition, her piety & disinterested benevolence, all combine to fit her to be an excellent missionary. Her loss from our band of teachers will be great, but we are reconciled to this by the hope that our loss will be gain to the cause of missions,—a cause so worthy of our confidence and support, & of all the sacrifices which we can make.

Yours with much respect,

MARY LYON.

five

THE YOUNG MAN FROM LENOX

WHEN CYRUS MILLS OFFERED HIMSELF FOR APPOINTMENT AS a missionary in 1846, two of his professors in Union Theological Seminary wrote of him to the Mission Board, saying the same thing but with a difference. Dr. Edward Robinson said:

> *The personal appearance of Mr. Mills is at first not prepossessing,—perhaps diminutive. But on acquaintance and in conversation, this impression vanishes, & his address, though at first somewhat awkward, is easier & even agreeable . . . He is a person of good judgment, discretion & common sense, of good literary and theological attainments, diligent in the improvement of time and opportunity of usefulness . . .*

Dr. Robinson spoke as umpire, not as morale-building coach. Himself a Connecticut man, trained first for the law, then for divinity at Andover, then deep-rooted in sacred literature at Berlin and Halle, he viewed awkward young men with complete objectivity, a Presbyterian discipline of judgment, a Scottish economy of enthusiasm. But the Reverend Asa D. Smith, who was also Cyrus' pastor in New York, put the same point with a manner:

> *His talents, though not of the highest order, seem to me respectable . . .*

76

His bodily presence is not, indeed, greatly superior to St. Paul's, but that, I presume, will be no objection to him,—and I have observed no other natural infelicity. His piety is of a high order, & he is much devoted to doing good . . . His views of the work he aspires to, are not, I think, romantic, but simple and scriptural . . .

In Cyrus Mills' own letters through many years, two expressions sound a familiar note: "my clear and full conviction of duty," and "if there be any reasonable prospect." Cyrus' mind and grammar were judicious: "If there be." No racing emotional excitement, no color of audacity; a sober mind, arriving slowly at a set plan and sticking to that plan. With no conceit of superior talents, one might still do something. Besides St. Paul, there was another diminutive man who climbed a sycamore tree when taller men got in his way, and won thereby a favor denied to loftier Hebrews.

Little is known of his early years or his forebears. "As to my early history I can say but little which has either interest or importance." His parents, who died before he was grown, seem to have left no store of family or tradition in his memory, or his diffidence caused him to judge such matters not worth recording. His parents were poor; and not being pious, they left no trace in church records. Vital records for Hillsborough County, New Hampshire, where they grew up, have many disappointing gaps for the period shortly following the Revolutionary War, and there are only scraps of record for the frontier counties of central New York where they died.

This much is known. Cyrus' parents, William and Mary Mills, were living in Hillsborough County when David, first of their three sons, was born on December 21, 1814. Nothing is known of William's ancestry except that his father was Henry Mills. There is one plausible clue to the ancestry of Cyrus' mother. Irish place names are abundant in the northern part of Hillsborough County, and the county swarmed with Taggarts, one widely branched family of that name being descended from Archibald Taggart, who came with his wife from Ireland around 1738 and begat a scriptural family. In 1819 when Mary Mills named her second son Cyrus Taggart she may have been weaving her own or her mother's maiden surname and the full name of a cousin into the record. For there was a Cyrus Taggart, grandson of Archibald, born in 1790; and Mary Mills may have been his cousin.

William and Mary Mills moved to the neighborhood of Paris, Oneida County, New York, at some time before May 4, 1819, when Cyrus was born. They had a third son, Giles, whose birth date is unknown. In 1823 they moved to Lenox, in Madison County. Family tradition has it that the boys were orphaned early and were brought up by an Aunt Rebecca, whose surname has been forgotten. In his modest autobiography, furnished to the Mission Board, Cyrus wrote: "As my parents were poor and lived in a back place my advantages were limited." Of Aunt Rebecca and the boys' debt to her we know only that at some time in the late 1860's Cyrus, hearing that she was a helpless invalid, had her brought to the home of a kinswoman in Iowa and paid for her care. Parents and aunt—the unknown poor; but there was some leaven of character, of hope, for the two older brothers graduated from college, and Giles is said to have attended.

In Cyrus' boyhood the village of Lenox was already losing its small importance. Settled around 1800, it had been for twenty years a trading station and part-time county seat on the road by which settlers from New England and the Mohawk Valley moved to the Genesee country—the road that became the Seneca Turnpike. From not too lofty Quality Hill in Lenox township one could see trains of wagons, as many as forty together, crawling westward. Land-hungry families were transplanting into western New York and northern Ohio some of the qualities they had inherited from Puritan or German or Dutch ancestors. Religion and education, industry and community life, would become a blend of these various inheritances, all considerably changed by a new frontier. Then soon the opening of the Erie Canal, a few miles north of Lenox, left the village far enough off the line to lose what importance it had.

What impressions the people and the country, the fluctuating and the stable, made upon Cyrus, we do not know. We only know that down to the time he left America (1848) he continued to think of Lenox and Chittenango (a few miles to the west) as home. Unromantic though he was, the home county meant a great deal to him. For that reason, or by mere coincidence, some of his most trusted friends in later years, especially in California, were men born in either Oneida or Madison County.

In the little that he told about his youth, in his first letter to the Mission Board, he dwelt mostly upon his religious experiences. He had never attended church or Sunday school until after he was ten; at fourteen he was "somewhat awakened" for several weeks during a revival meeting, then lapsed into what he considered a rather wild life, until in February 1838 he found himself converted, though without any mystical experience. The Reverend Alvah Day was minister of the Presbyterian church in Lenox at that time, but record and memory of minister and church have disappeared with the village itself. The personal clue that would mean most in this connection is lost: the man or men who first turned the minds of David and Cyrus Mills toward Williams College. Alvah Day was not a Williams man.

In the decorous, newsy pages of Calvin Durfee's *Biographical Annals of Williams** one finds a score of alumni who were near enough to have known the Mills brothers. Williams drew many youths from the lake district of central New York in the 1820's and 1830's, and many Williams graduates settled as ministers, doctors, lawyers, and teachers in Utica, Rome, Syracuse, and the villages between; but I can find no clue as to the person who encouraged David and Cyrus to hope for a college education. David prepared for college "at a school on the Hudson River, under the care of the Rev. David Smith," but here again is no clue leading to Williams. David entered college in the fall of 1837; the inference is that Cyrus turned the same way because his older brother was already a student there. Cyrus wrote that, after being converted, he began the next winter (1838–39) to study Latin. "I fitted for college at Williamstown and at Manlius, N. Y." One might at first suppose that he meant Williamstown, Massachusetts, but doubtless he meant Williamstown, New York, a village in Oswego County, north of Oneida Lake. Evidently he found there and at Manlius, nearer home, some kindly professional men who could coach him through the preparatory subjects.

A saying attributed to President James A. Garfield, though it may be apocryphal, has fixed Mark Hopkins upon one end of a log and a student upon the other: the image of a university. This aphorism has been quoted impressively and for various ends, upon academic great occasions, and still there is a core of truth in it. Mark Hopkins was a great teacher; and the sound Williams tradition had gathered a good faculty before he became president in 1836. When Cyrus Mills entered Williams there were six teachers besides the young president; and it is no disparagement of the early Mount Holyoke to say that these Williams professors were, in scholarship and teaching experience, superior to the women at South Hadley. Only one besides Mark Hopkins was a minister. Tenure was steady; there were no changes in the faculty in Cyrus Mills' time. Mainly they were young men.

* Williams was lucky in having a Calvin Durfee to antedate the modern alumni files with these curious winnowings. A prosy old gentleman, clerical and proper, he recited men's honors with not too much monotony, and their failures with a gentle sigh. One alumnus "opened a bookstore in Hartford . . . but he was too convivial in his habits." Alumni who failed at everything else did not farm; they "engaged in agricultural occupation." "He published a work of fiction . . . which was quite readable." "He taught for a time with acceptance." Even shocking carnage was given a verbal decorum: "He fell upon a circular saw which was in rapid motion." There may have been the italics of a chuckle in his voice when he summarized a certain teacher: "The French language was his vernacular tongue, and, though said to be wanting in dignity of deportment, he was a successful teacher of that language."

Mark Hopkins was thirty-eight; his brilliant and able brother, Albert, was thirty-three; Lasell, Alden, and Tatlock were a year or so younger. Emmons, equal of Albert Hopkins in science and more widely known at the time, was forty-one. The Nestor of the group was Ebenezer Kellogg, a Yale and Andover man, almost fifty-one, who grounded youths in their ablatives and second-aorists, and seems to have been the caricature figure of the conscientious proctor. "It was his practice," wrote Calvin Durfee, "to call at all rooms [in his dormitory] as often as once a day, to see that the students were in their rooms, and attending to their studies . . . He was a man of great particularity."

Joseph Alden, a Brown and Union College man, had the bulging portfolio of political science, history, language, and literature. Edward Lasell (Williams '28) was professor of chemistry; and John Tatlock, born in northern Wales but educated at Williams ('32), was professor of mathematics. The times required a man to know more than one subject. Tatlock was a relief teacher in languages for a year, and Albert Hopkins, physicist and astronomer, also taught French for a time. Ebenezer Emmons, though he had become professor of chemistry in the Albany Medical College, continued as lecturer in geology and mineralogy at Williams. Himself a Williams man ('18), trained for college by Moses Hallock (still a man to remember), Emmons had early published a *Manual of Mineralogy and Geology*, and was one of four men who made the first geological survey of New York. He also wrote a four-volume work on agriculture, showing its dependence upon soil chemistry, geology, and entomology.

In fine, Mark Hopkins, great teacher of moral philosophy, was not alone upon the teacher's end of the log. Students idolized his brother Albert, who, once he knew that teaching was to be his work, went to Europe chiefly at his own expense and visited university laboratories to observe better methods and to select improved apparatus. The astronomical observatory on the top of Graylock was his undertaking—the plan, the execution; he was foreman of the student laborers who did most of the building. To a degree unusual in his time, he created his courses without slavish dependence upon textbooks. Not even Thoreau was a truer lover of nature. Intensely religious, finding the Bible still a living word, he was eager to free religion from theology, and as willing as the men of Concord to trust the God of nature. He was impatient with "lily-fingered clergymen who never went into the Heart of Graylock or the heart of anything." Had he been in control of missions he would have sent out not exhorters, but "colonies of young Christian craftsmen and tradesmen with their families, who by their example would show . . . the Christian life in its entirety." His religion was a welling overflow of goodness with energy. In the spring of 1848, shortly before Cyrus Mills went as a missionary, he hoped to spend six weeks or so in study of advanced astronomy with Albert Hopkins, though it is not clear whether he carried out that plan.

That observatory on Graylock had at least one visitor who, though fairly soaked in classics and preclassics, was anything but academic. In a leisurely digression in the Tuesday chapter of *A Week on the Concord and Merrimac Rivers*, Thoreau tells how he climbed Graylock on a gusty, showery afternoon—taking an unorthodox way, of course—ate his frugal supper with a wooden spoon whittled out on the spot, and half-slept the chilly night through in the lee of the observatory, and—of course—saw an original sunrise. During the night woodmice came, hunting crumbs: "They nibbled what was for them; I nibbled what was for me." An epigram which might serve as a relief to that one about the log.

Henry, eager as any preacher to have a thought for the occasion, left an advice about the topography of learning:

> *It would really be no small advantage if every college were thus located at the base of a mountain, as good at least as one well-endowed professorship. It were as well to be educated in the shadow of a mountain as in more classic shades. Some will remember, no doubt, not only that they went to college, but that they went to the mountain. Every visit to its summit would, as it were, generalize the particular information gained below, and subject it to more catholic tastes.*

That same observatory drew incidental attention from another writer whose world was more populous than Thoreau's. Hawthorne, spending a week at North Adams in 1838, was bound to note that the driver of the Bennington stage was the very man who had hauled the materials for that building—"the only man that had ever driven an ox-team up Graylock." Nathaniel's week was packed with seemingly desultory observations: the glint of marble along the creek below Hudson's Falls, the far-off sound of a bugle from a stagecoach in a mountain pass, "the remnants of a thunderstorm" in a sunset sky, and common people who became strangely memorable in his notebook.

> *To commencement at Williams College . . . At the tavern, students, with ribbons, pink or blue, fluttering from their buttonholes—these being the badges of rival societies . . . Country graduates—rough, brown-featured, schoolmaster looking, half-bumpkin, half-scholar figures, in*

black ill-cut broadcloth,—their manners quite spoilt by what little of gentleman was in them.

The next day his eyes were kindlier; he may have remembered himself a freshman at Bowdoin only sixteen years before.

The next day after commencement was bleak and rainy . . . and a good many guests were added to our table in consequence. Among them some of the Williamstown students—gentlemanly young fellows, with a brotherly feeling for each other, a freedom about money concerns—a half boyish, half manly character; and my heart warmed to them.

But the nub of the notebook was that he attended the commencement exercises and yet blissfully was not there. He seined a page of live impressions of the crowd outside the church: a wrestling match, a drunken man, a few Negroes, a crippled boy, and was immensely taken with a York State peddler who auctioned his wares with magnificent patter. Moreover, the Bowdoin man was among the audience that filled the church; he sat watching the well-dressed ladies "in silks and cambrics—their sunburnt necks, in contiguity with the delicate fabrics of the dress, showing the yeoman's daughter." All this. But of the dignitaries on the platform—the trustees, the valedictorian, and the orator, and what they said—nay more, of the great Mark Hopkins himself—not a word. And if the masterful young president, himself tall as Graylock, noted the mild-faced other giant somewhere far back in the audience, he in turn left no record of the fact. And so, the log again, now worn smooth and sittable by decades of polishing; the log with Mark Hopkins on one end and Nathaniel Hawthorne on the other, sitting forever with oblivious backs to each other. There's Honor for you.

By 1840 the college had acquired a quota of mildly distinguished alumni, approximately one-third of whom were ministers, with law and medicine next in favor. It was something to be a Williams man, and already the bent twigs were making it what it has been ever since, a family college. The enrollment was around one hundred fifty, everybody knew everybody, and there was a fair diversity in backgrounds. Approximately forty percent of the students came from Massachusetts, about one-third from New York (mostly upstate), and the rest from New England and the Middle States, with a few from as far west as Michigan and Indiana, and four from the South—three young gentlemen from Virginia and one from Georgia. There were not many college itinerants among them; of the fifty-eight men who entered in the fall of 1840, thirty-three graduated. In only five classes during the first half-century of the college had the staying power fallen below fifty percent.

The curriculum was rigid. In but one term during his four years was the student allowed the not very seductive option between French, Hebrew, and Fluxions. Three years of Latin, Greek, mathematics, and science and, in the senior year, a more varied spread of Butler and Paley, President Hopkins' pet philosophy courses, a segment of Civil Polity, and one course which smacks of frosty tartness: "Leslie's Short Method with Deists." As if prayers in an unheated chapel at six of February mornings were not enough to discourage potential young deists, one had also to be short with them. The sophomores were marched through conic sections, with fluxions in the offing; through Sophocles and Euripides, with Demosthenes waiting in the junior year. The course was more severe than at Mount Holyoke, and the science teachers were not limited to what the textbook said. The curriculum was weak in history and void in English literature, though the regimen of weekly (and in some terms daily) themes must have impelled the student to read a little on his one allotted day in the library, which was open to upperclassmen on Wednesdays and to the others on Saturdays.

Four of the buildings Cyrus knew are still in use, but in his day the campus was but a wide street, a quarter of a mile long, with college buildings and faculty homes scattered along, and a nucleus of village at either end. In 1910 Horace Davis, grand old man, regent of the University of California and trustee of Stanford, told California students about his sophomore year at Williams, the year after Cyrus Mills graduated. His pithy account shows the universal tendency to remember the Big Cold Spell: morning prayers when the whale-oil lamp sputtered out, frozen, and the professor had to leave off reading and resort to prayer by candlelight. (Mary Lyon would have gone on reading from memory.) After prayers, a race of a quarter of a mile back to West College, where the sophs and freshmen roomed—an eager race, for the recitation room would be warmed and a fellow could partly thaw out during spherical trigonometry or Cicero and be ready for the combustion of breakfast. Later would come the daily visit from Professor Ebenezer Kellogg, that man of great particularity, and calls from other professors. President Hopkins himself would come at least once a term.

There was a vacation of six weeks from mid-December, when students with ambition and little money taught village schools; by borrowing (with permission) two or three weeks from the last of the autumn and the first of the spring terms a young man could get in the usual winter term in a village or country school and earn a good half of the expense of a year in college—estimated at from $101.50 (which must have been shaving it close) to $134.00. And in spite of the Spartan details—split your own wood, carry your own water, build your own fire, trim and fill your own whale-oil lamp, and all this without a co-ordinator of recreational activities—they had their share of fun: Chip Day when they tidied up the buildings and grounds; Gravel Day when they repaired paths and roads; and, of course, Mountain Day, when Albert Hopkins would be in his element. On Chip Day and Gravel Day a fellow might, by a fine of ninepence, buy release from broom and shovel and go fishing along the torrent brooks that feed the Hoosic. Fishing—but strictly no hunting.

In his freshman year Cyrus roomed with his senior brother David in the Southworth home in the village; but in his sophomore year he moved to West College, and as an upperclassman to East College. And though never a professional mixer, he was very much a classman and a Williams man. The men of '44 liked him, elected him permanent class president, and later in Ceylon and Hawaii and California the warmth between him and them was very real. Cyrus was twenty-one when he entered; three of his class were a little older, and the average intrant was about eighteen. Eleven of his class became ministers, eleven lawyers, and the remaining eleven went into medicine, teaching, and business. Three of the class were to attain some distinction in California—of which, more later. Five of the class "made" Phi Beta Kappa. Cyrus tied with Henry P. Coon (later mayor of San Francisco) for the seventh rank in the class—one step behind the Phi Beta Kappa men. Mark Hopkins wrote: "His improvement was more marked as he proceeded." But the most significant point is that four of the class became foreign missionaries, and a fifth was training for that work when cut down by early death.

When Cyrus entered college eighteen graduates and five nongraduates had already gone as missionaries. Several had gone in the first wave before 1820, most of them to die soon. There had been a second wave in the late 1820's, and the class of 1844 came at the crest of a third wave, as strong at Williams as at Mount Holyoke. Although Mark Hopkins was a power on the Mission Board, it does not appear that he preached missions to his young men with a fiery ardor comparable to Mary Lyon's; rather, a zeal was in the air, and the students themselves created it. Cyrus later said that a missionary society of but three members in his freshman year grew into a large organization before he graduated. Of the seven classes whom Cyrus knew, one man from '41, two each from '42 and '43, five from his own class, and three each from '45 and '46 were training for missionary work—sixteen in all and quite the largest group for any equal period in the history of the college. His classmate Jacob Best was designated to the Gaboon Mission in West

Africa; Joshua E. Ford, best scholar in the group, to Syria, where he became a notable linguist; David Rood, a Plainfield boy, to the Zulu Mission; and William L. Silcox, who died untimely, was training for China. One Williams veteran who was to affect Cyrus considerably was Henry Richard Hoisington ('28); a hard-working scholar, he had charge of Batticotta Seminary in Ceylon, retiring—worn almost to death—when Cyrus took over that post. Practically all of these Williams missionaries spent three years in theological seminary before ordination. Andover, Yale, and Auburn had been favorite seminaries, but Union Theological Seminary, opening in New York City in 1836, was drawing strongly from Williams men. Seven men of '44 went there, including Best, Ford, Mills, and Silcox.

Whatever personal comment reticent Cyrus made upon his teachers in New York City has been lost—or at least I have found none. He had Systematic Theology from Dr. Henry White, Biblical and Ecclesiastical History from Dr. Samuel H. Cox, Sacred Literature from Dr. Edward Robinson (the one who allowed that Cyrus was diminutive and awkward), and Pastoral Theology from Dr. Asa Dodge Smith (who said Cyrus was no smaller than St. Paul). Besides, he probably had a jot and tittle of Hebrew from a young teacher, and may have been urged to carry a hymn tune with sharper attack by the very young Edward Howe, who was then creating a course in Sacred Music. The first three professors were somewhat older than most of the teachers at Williams. Doctors aplenty, but from Cyrus' point of view, no Mark Hopkins among them. In graduate school and to the end of his days, Cyrus remained a Williams man. This was not a case of the small-college man's being overawed by a great university; the seminary was little bigger than the college. The difference lay, I think, in the power of the Hopkins brothers to establish self-confidence in rustic youth; and it is quite possible that the Williams men were, all round, the better teachers, less objective but more creative.

The seminary gave Cyrus his first experience with city life. The ministers of the two churches there to which he successively belonged wrote of his helping in parish and home mission work; but mainly we have to judge of his life during those three years by the aftermath of the friendships he developed among his fellow students. Of the fifty-five who entered the Seminary in the class of 1847, thirty-five graduated; and here, as at Williams, the striking thing was that this class came at the crest of missionary enthusiasm. From the seven classes that had graduated before Cyrus entered, only three men had become missionaries, and from the men whom he knew as upperclassmen, only three more. But from his own class eight graduates and two nongraduates went into the service, and the tide ran high for the next five years. Cyrus and J. E. Ford, writing back to the boys at Williams, commented upon the fact that missionary zeal did not originate in the theological seminaries but in the colleges; and clearly, in this instance, the Williams men brought their full share of that zeal with them. As a freshman in the seminary Cyrus knew William W. Howland ('45), who soon married Susan Reed of Mount Holyoke ("my dear Mrs. Howland"), and through his first two years, Eurotas P. Hastings ('46), who was to be tragically connected with the Mills' arrival in Ceylon. Townsend E. Taylor, of his own class, married Persis Thurston— "the beloved Persis"—of Mount Holyoke. Four other men whom he knew in seminary were to touch his life importantly in California, and at least ten other graduates of Union Theological Seminary during the early 1850's, though they did not know him in New York, were drawn to him in California. But the best friend of all, and finally the best interpreter of Cyrus, was Israel Edson Dwinell ('48). He became an abler scholar and preacher than Cyrus Mills; his respect and affection for Cyrus deepened with the years, and there was not a grain of condescension in that feeling.

Beginning in his junior year at Williams, Cyrus taught a winter term of school in Plainfield, Massachusetts, and returned for three more winters. His call there came through two of his classmates at Williams—David Rood and Martin S. Pixley, both of whom were Plainfield boys, and Rood was Cyrus' roommate in their senior year. The call may also have been helped by William Agur Hawley, Jr. ('42), whose father ('15) was settled as minister in Plainfield in 1841. And so, from Williamstown and from New York Cyrus rode the stage back to Plainfield each winter, and developed there some of the most lasting friendships of his life. In October 1846 he felt brave enough to offer himself by letter to the Mission Board; he had set his heart on this as early as 1842:

> As to the field of labor I have only to say that ever since I desired to be a missionary, which was 4 years ago, my attention has been directed to the Tamil mission. I have paid some attention to the language and have tried to gain what knowledge I could of the people. I prefer to go there unless there is some more difficult and dangerous place where no one else dares go.

The letter reveals—still with reticence—another matter.

> As to the matter of a companion I have none in prospect. In the early part of my course I formed an attachment for one whom I regarded as eminently qualified for the missionary work. But during the summer of

'45 an all-wise Providence saw fit to remove her to a better world. *This will explain to you why this important matter is yet to be arranged. My feelings have been such as to preclude my turning my attention to it. This has been a severe trial . . .*

The girl's death had hit him very hard. In '47 when word went out that he was assigned to Ceylon, Henry R. Hoisington wrote from Batticotta a sharp letter to the Board. The Ceylon Mission had wanted Joshua E. Ford, whose promise as a linguist was widely spoken of—and now Ford was assigned to Syria. In another note, the nerve-wracked Hoisington voiced an astonishing rumor: the brethren in Ceylon had heard that Mills "has been sick and insane." Rufus Anderson answered soothingly; he had heard (he wrote) that Cyrus Mills had, at his own request, spent a few weeks in The Retreat, a hospital in East Hartford, but that he was quite well again. What truth is in the story? Hoisington gave it as rumor; Rufus Anderson, usually explicit enough, "had heard." The records of that excellent hospital, well preserved and said to be complete, contain no record of Cyrus Mills as a patient. He may have been a voluntary guest for a short time. If further reassurance were needed it would appear to be plentiful in the growing respect which Cyrus continued to receive from his college and seminary friends. If a brief breakdown did occur, I think it was between the time of his sweetheart's death and his application as a candidate—at some time before October 1846. His affections ran deeper than in a more voluble man.

six

THE COURTIN'

FOR A PAGE OR TWO THE STORY WILL BE CONFUSING AS AN OLD photograph album when a great-aunt is initiating her grand-nephew's bride into family history. Great-aunt and album belong in a staunch old house in Plainfield, which was one of the most intellectual villages in Massachusetts, and mainly because of one man—Moses Hallock (1760–1837). Graduating from Yale in 1788, he settled as minister in Plainfield, found it hard to raise a family on his salary, and started a one-man academy to train boys for college. It was no cramming school; he was a real teacher, and his recommendation was a good bond at Yale and Amherst and Dartmouth, and especially at Williams. Time and again Calvin Durfee gives a kind of preliminary *cum laude* to a Williams man by saying, "He was trained by Moses Hallock." During forty years that village minister prepared more than three hundred youths for college, among them William Cullen Bryant, and Marcus Whitman, later of Walla Walla; and John Brown, whose soul goes marching on, is said to have been for a little while one of Moses Hallock's boys. There ought to be a book about that Leonidas and his Three Hundred. And be it heredity or environment or both, there is something in a family. Two of

88

Hallock's sons, both of '19 at Williams, became notable, one as an executive of the American Tract Society, one as editor in Boston and New York. One grandson reached distinction as editor and author; and, though the biographical dictionaries do not name her, one great-granddaughter, Fanny Rouse Carpenter, wrote a college hymn that some of us think is better than any song of Yale or Harvard.

Moses Hallock died a few years before Cyrus Mills first came to teach in Plainfield, but his son Leavitt was living in the old homestead and he too was a man of character. Cyrus boarded in Leavitt Hallock's home and became adoptively one of the family. Leavitt was a great friend of Mary Lyon; his twin daughters, Eliza and Fanny, graduated from Mount Holyoke in 1850. (It would be a nice touch to say they were pupils of Susan Tolman, but, being Hallocks and brought up on Euclid and Latin, they entered the seminary as middlers, the year after Susan quit teaching there.) And the Hallocks were all tied up with missions. Leavitt Hallock's older brother, William Allen, had married Fanny Lathrop, of Norwich, Connecticut, and her four sisters had all gone as missionaries, three of them to Ceylon and the fourth to the Madura field on the mainland. A sister of Mrs. Hallock had married the Reverend John C. Smith and was with her husband at one of the Ceylon stations. Indeed, Plainfield had been militant ever since the time of the Haystack Prayer-meeting, for James Richards (Williams 1809), a Plainfield boy and one of the Haystack group, became one of the first American Board missionaries in Ceylon. His brother William, classmate of Moses Hallock's sons at Williams (1819), became the foremost translator in the Sandwich Islands mission and later minister of education in the royal government.

While the great-aunt is confusing us with the before's and after-that's of the album, we may as well hear that Eliza, one of Leavitt's twin daughters, married Thomas Henderson Rouse (Williams '47 and U.T.S. '50). Rouse later taught in Mills Seminary at Benicia, and it was his daughter who put into the college hymn the sunset hills and the light blue smoke ascending. Further, Leavitt's little son, named after his father, was greatly taken with the shy young teacher boarder. More than forty years afterward, when young Leavitt Hallock had become minister of the Mills College church, he recalled his small-boy idolization of Cyrus. He hadn't thought him awkward at all, but very nice. For Cyrus those were happy winters in Plainfield. The Reverend Mr. Hawley liked him, found him helpful in parish work, scanned his doctrine and found it "truly evangelical and sound, as impressed with such men as Edwards, Bellamy and Dwight." He added that Cyrus was "habitually listened to."

I have not the exact date of the next episode, but it happened in the summer of 1847. In April Cyrus was licensed to preach and was looking forward to graduation from the seminary in June. He had been studying Tamil for a year or more, and was tentatively assigned to Ceylon. Ready for the field—all but one thing. It is not true that the Board never sent out an unmarried man, but they advised and practically required marriage. If ever a man needed a good wife a missionary did. And now began a three-cornered benevolent game of matchmaking between the Hallocks, Mary Lyon, and Rufus Anderson. The Hallocks still have a family tradition that Leavitt helped Cyrus clear up his seminary debts in order to enlist with a clean slate; and Leavitt's oldest brother, William Allen—he of the four missionary sisters-in-law—already knew Miss Susan Tolman. He had had her audit the really huge accounts of his Tract Society; he considered her "keen as a razor." Miss Lyon believed in Marriage and Missions and Miss Tolman and everything good. And Dr. Rufus Anderson was avid to pair off his recruits and get them to the harvest field. The mission archives would furnish a chapter on Rufus Anderson as matrimonial go-between and cheerful suggester, and he saw no reason why two decent young people should not fall in love, and less reason why they should procrastinate.

For a fair sample of dutiful expeditiousness, take the courtship of Asa Thurston and Lucy Goodale, who became parents of Persis. This happened way back in 1819, long before Rufus Anderson became a power on the Board, but the case is not untypical of his time. This is Lucy Goodale's own account of her romance. She was teaching in a country school, boarding away from home, and had to face her grave problem alone.

> *Sept. 18, 1819. Yesterday, during my noontide intermission I received at my boarding house, an unexpected call from my cousin William Goodell. He gave me information that a Mission to the Sandwich Islands was to sail in four or six weeks . . . At length, having prepared my mind, the proposition was made. "Will Lucy, by becoming connected with a missionary now an entire stranger, attach herself to this little band of pilgrims, and visit the far distant land of Obookiah?"*

(Obookiah was a Kanaka boy who had come to New England on a whaler and, being converted, had become a magnetic object lesson in mission recruiting.)

> *The Gentleman proposed as the companion of my life is Mr. Thurston, member of the Senior Class, in Andover Theological Institution . . . he has no personal knowledge of one who is both willing and qualified to go*

with him to a foreign land. Some of his classmates were admitted to his private confidence. One of them, in passing back and forth, had been entertained at Dea. Goodale's. He spoke of his daughter Lucy being fitted for such a position. Next week on Thursday is the anticipated, dreadful interview of decision.

Meantime her sisters came from home to comfort and sustain her. She took a leave of absence and went home; and on Thursday came cousin William morally supporting the young and Reverend Mr. Thurston to the dreadful interview.

The early hours of the evening were devoted to refreshments, to free family sociality, to singing, and to evening worship. Then one by one the family dispersed, leaving two of similar aspirations, introduced at sunset as strangers, to separate at midnight as interested friends.

But only as interested friends. One should not rush headlong into a more serious relationship. They did not become engaged until the next forenoon; and then they waited three full weeks for the proper crying of the bans in church. Married in October, they sailed with the Whitneys and the Binghams and four other couples on the brig *Thaddeus*. A cold marriage? You should see the photograph of the two in 1864 when they were beloved patriarchs in Hawaii. Asa, white-bearded, with steady eyes and strong nose and mouth; Lucy, bright-eyed, in a best dress that looks like silk—very handsome —with the Puritan equivalent of a black lace mantilla over her head. Good faces, both; comfortable in the Old Testament sense of that word; good but not gullible—a peddler of wooden nutmegs would never try his salesmanship upon these two. Judged by their faces, and even more by the way they were loved in the Islands, they seem to have got on fairly well together—even to have become, one might say, fond of one another.

But that was the Courtin' of the Thurstons, and even with the pushing help of their well-wishers, Cyrus and Susan were positively not to be rushed —not too fast. One of the two women yet living who knew Susan best has given me what she remembers of Susan's own version of their Courtin'. Many details have been forgotten in the forty-odd years since Susan last told the story. If I touch it up to bring out small details, as in copying a faded daguerreotype, I do so with circumspection; and the Question itself is still as she told it.

Miss Tolman is summoned into the big white parlor of the Mount Holyoke Female Seminary: there is a visitor whom Miss Lyon wishes to introduce. Whether there had been any preliminary sounding-out of Susan's feelings by that masterful lady, no one knows; but even if there had been, Miss Tolman enters the parlor with ladylike poise as if to meet the parent of a student, or some elderly minister who knew her grandmother. "Miss Tolman, allow me to present Mr. Cyrus Mills, a senior in Union Theological Seminary. Mr. Mills, as you may have heard, is a Williams College man, well spoken of by President Hopkins. Mr. Mills is, as it were, a member of the Hallock family of Plainfield. We trust that the Hallocks are all well, and that Miss Eliza and Miss Fanny make good progress in their studies. I should say, Mr. Mills, that Miss Tolman is our mainstay in botany. Our valley is very attractive at this season—or so we think."

Cyrus guardedly agrees that the valley is indeed very attractive—at this season. And now Miss Lyon hopes that he will excuse her, as certain pressing household problems demand her attention. With Miss Lyon out of it, the parlor becomes immense, frightfully spatial. Across the distance between one horsehair chair and the other (one has been too well-bred to sit upon the invitational sofa) conversation is impeded. Pause. Polite question. Polite answer. More pause. Comment upon one's favorite teachers. Comment upon the telescope at Williams College. Miss Tolman has studied astronomy only in the book and with a few well-conducted star-gazing excursions; she has never had the great privilege of observing the heavenly bodies through a telescope. Pause. Does Mr. Mills know young Asa Thurston? Not directly, but his friends at Williams have spoken of that young man. But Mr. Mills does know Mr. Townsend Taylor, who is—er—the—er—interested friend of Miss Thurston. Mr. Taylor is well regarded by his classmates. And slowly the ice in the Connecticut goes out. Comment upon Dr. Rufus Anderson, who is indeed a powerful servant of the Lord. Comment upon the difficulties of the Tamil language. Yes, Mr. Mills hopes that his lifework will be among the Tamil heathen. Warming comment upon the Howlands, now at Batticotta, for Mr. Mills has great admiration for Mr. Howland, and Miss Tolman's voice runs like a bird's song when Mrs. Howland is the subject. Yes, indeed—Batticotta. The field is white unto the harvest. And—the laborers are—few.

(Mental comment from the one chair: Her mind is quick, much quicker than mine. Mine will always have to plod. And she is—well, I mustn't be too emotional—but she fairly takes my breath away. I wonder if there be any rational prospect . . .)

(Mental comment from the other chair: He's terribly shy. And he needs some advice about his clothes. His voice is upstate New York. He will never pronounce *Israel* as Mr. Condit does, and he will never be at ease in the pulpit. No, nor wave his cane and speak commandingly. He will need lots of encouragement in life. But he *is* kind, and he doesn't show off. I wonder how much persistence he has.)

And now Mr. Mills finds he must go. Is he returning to his studies in New York City? No, only over to Plainfield for a few days' visit. And so the call is over.

And to nobody's great surprise he comes again after a decorous interim. Meantime he has thought of other subjects. Miss Fiske in Ooroomiah. The great opportunities in teaching those children in a land of darkness. The climate on the Bombay side of India; the climate on the Madras side; the climate in Ceylon. (This time the young lady risks the invitational sofa, but the young gentleman keeps the safe chair.) The—er—we were speaking of Ceylon. Mr. Howland writes very hopefully of the work there. It is regrettable that Mr. Hoisington's health is so low. The work at Batticotta is very pressing.

(Here I quote verbatim.) "I—am designated to the Batticotta mission, and I hope to be sent soon. And I have been wondering whether you—er—might like to—go to Ceylon with me."

(Go to Ceylon! I'm eager to go to Ceylon. Eager! But—why, he hasn't said he loves me! He hasn't said any of the things a man ought to say when he's courting.) The answer perts off her tongue: "I am not at all sure that I would." (There, that ought to wake him up.)

And presently he is on his way back to New York City and the baffling difficulties of the Tamil tongue, which are ever so much harder—or are they?—than *amo, amas, amat*. And we go up to Room 32 and have a good cry, for we did really want to go to Ceylon.

How long he waited, what letters passed—these details have been forgotten. But the faithful rememberer recalls that Susan used to say, "When he asked me again, I said: 'Yes, I would like to go to Ceylon.'"

When Rufus Anderson heard that they were engaged he was all for immediate marriage. That good man's executive habit of settling his missionaries' personal problems for them with cheerful readiness might in time become irritating—a point difficult for him to comprehend. The inference is that Cyrus went to Mission House in Boston to talk over his plans and was somewhat overcome by the Secretary's large certainty. On August 28, 1847, he wrote to Dr. Anderson:

I returned to Ware as you requested me, and presented the subject to Miss Tolman . . . We both came to the same conclusion that unless there were reasons of a weightier kind than we now see, we could not go without violating our sense of propriety in such matters.

He cited their minor objections: Miss Tolman needed more time to prepare for the special work they would be doing in Ceylon, and she felt an obligation not to leave Miss Lyon shorthanded by such a late withdrawal. But there was a nicer reason: they were engaged but not long enough engaged.

> *The two main objections were the shortness of time we must have to become well acquainted with each other, and the unfavorable influence it must have upon the minds of others. We cannot do it with our present sense of the importance and sacredness of the relation.*
>
> *I presume you are aware how many in the field have made these arrangements. I know of half a dozen or more who have done it in a week. This is improper and the sentiments of both of us are strong against it. We have both held our sense of propriety strongly violated and have spoken strongly and decidedly against it . . . We would not add to the reproach or set an example unsafe for others to follow though it might be safe for us.*

Recruits, complaisant as nice freshmen, did not ordinarily take exception to the Secretary's ideas. A perfectly respectful tone, and yet dissent, based upon personal scruples. Rather preposterous scruples which scores of other young ministers dutifully waived—or didn't even feel. Pshaw. And Mills looks to be the meekest little man. Have we enrolled a potential rebel? Hardly that, but—well, he has some spunk. We'll let him wait a year.

What made Cyrus's position the harder during his year of waiting was his almost total dependence upon the Board for the barest means of subsistence. As a pledged recruit he was honorbound to give most of his time to further preparation, but he would draw no salary until he reached the field. Used as he was to poverty, still his occasional appeals for expense money sound embarrassing; money for a trip to Rome, New York, on missionary society business; money to enable him to attend the annual meeting of the Mission Board in Rochester. He was making ready to spend the fall and winter at South Brookfield, Massachusetts, studying Tamil under Samuel Hutchings (Williams '28), who had spent ten years in Ceylon and Madras and had helped compile a Tamil-English dictionary. He estimated his living expenses at $2.50 a week, and $20 for winter clothing. He touched upon these needs without abjectness, nor did he ever lard his requests with piety; Cyrus could not take on the tone of the clerical mendicant. And this situation was to last for nine years. I am confident it deepened in him a determination to become financially independent, to recognize his own knack of making money.

And so from September until April he studied with Samuel Hutchings at

South Brookfield. Meantime, in February, he was ordained at the Brainerd Street Presbyterian Church in New York City—the church of his friendly former teacher, Asa D. Smith. With early summer he was growing restless for definite word as to when he would sail. Sailings from Boston to Madras were vague; the Board could only pester the several merchant firms whose cargo vessels could make room for a few missionaries, and then put the recruits upon an indefinite alert.

Late in June Cyrus wrote from Ware. He had been supplying Mr. Gale's pulpit for a few weeks—an arrangement in which Deacon John Tolman probably had a hand. There would be kindness as well as family pride in giving Susan's intended a chance to prove, and improve, himself. In July he supplied the pulpit in South Deerfield. Early in August he attended the anniversary (commencement) at Mount Holyoke; young ladies (he learned) have a way of displaying their men on such occasions. He spent most of August in a farewell visit to friends and kinsfolk around Lenox and Chittenango, and returned to Ware about the first of September. It was settled by then that they and their company should sail from Boston "at some time" in October or early November.

He and Susan were married on Sepember 11. Many years later, when bringing his report to his Williams classmates up to date, Cyrus wrote of this: "Here the *I*'s end and the *we's* begin." And that was the simple truth.

The letters of these and of the scores of other recruits in the Mission archives are hard to read coldly, they overflow with such humility, confidence, and pitiful unawareness. Sabbaticals were as yet unknown; there was the level probability that they were bidding farewell forever to America. But this was their call—no sudden impulse but the fixed hope of years. In his last letter from Ware (September 28) Cyrus wrote to Rufus Anderson:

Our packing is nearly done. We are both in good health and spirits. We shall leave here on Thursday morning by the first train of cars.

seven

AND THIS IS CEYLON

THE SHIP *Bowditch* SAILED ON OCTOBER 10, 1848. MISSIONARY records are replete with stories of farewell gatherings on the wharves in Boston or New Bedford or New Haven, when families and friends came to see their loved ones off with prayers and hymns and many tears. I have found no record of such a meeting when the *Bowditch* sailed, though there may have been one. In any case, clerks from Mission House would be at the wharf to attend to last minute matters, and good Dr. Anderson would be doing his cheerful best to carry everybody through the ordeal with assurances and habitual blessings. As was usually the case when Mission House persuaded owners and captains of cargo vessels to make room for a small quota of passengers, the comfort and even the decency of the improvised quarters were something of a gamble. The *Bowditch* may have been one of Tudor's ice ships—at least, ice was her main cargo.* Generally the Board furnished provisions for its missionary personnel; and in 1847 another party bound for Madras reported back that the drinking water was brackish and

---

* In 1844 Dr. Henry M. Scudder and his bride sailed to Madras on a Tudor ice ship; their cabin was four by six feet and without a porthole.

96

insufficient, there was not enough rice and potatoes, the ducks were stringy, and the salt meat was nauseous. That complaint had not brought much improvement, for Mrs. Mills recorded:

The ship was not intended for passengers, so temporary quarters were built between decks for a party of twelve. The cabins were dark and small, and the furniture of unpainted pine boards was made for the occasion. It was all about as primitive as a mining camp. Our fare was very poor and our service most imperfect. It was before the days of canned fruits and meats; no cold storage supplied us with delicacies. Our fare was very much like that of the sailors before the mast . . .

The cargo was ice, but the missionaries had a short allowance of water. And though time might blur other details, no missionary ever forgot two items of his first journey to the field: the length of the voyage in days, and the disposition of the captain. The *Bowditch* took one hundred thirty-two days, and Captain Pike was very unfriendly—at first.

There were really fifteen missionaries on board. John Dulles and his wife were assigned to Madras; he was a Yale man ('44) and U.T.S. ('48). Mrs. Dulles was a daughter of Miron Winslow, a veteran in the Madras field; her mother, who had died in India, was one of the four missionary sisters-in-law of William Allen Hallock. Her stepmother, returning from sick leave, was also in the party, with her small son. Charles Smith Shelton, M.D., and his wife were going to the Madura Mission; Joseph T. Noyes and Thomas Burnell and their wives, to Ceylon. Noyes was an Amherst and Andover man; his wife, Elizabeth A. Smith (Mount Holyoke x'49), had been a student of Mrs. Mills. Burnell, a printer, was to have charge of the mission press, relieving the overworked missionary who had doubled in that work. Mrs. Burnell was Martha Sawyer (Mount Holyoke x'39). Besides these twelve appointees of the American Board, a Dr. Day and Mr. and Mrs. Jewett were in the service of another mission board—a connection that I have not traced.

One hundred thirty-two days: the long slant around Good Hope, then up through the Indian Ocean. "We tasted the sublimity and awfulness of gales at sea, and felt the power of calms under a torrid sun, and headwinds within a few days' sail of port." After their first spell of seasickness they gave their forenoons to the study of Tamil grammar under Cyrus Mills; and ever so eager to be at their chosen work, they were taken aback when Captain Pike forbade them to start a Bible class in the forecastle and indeed to have any word with the sailors. Whether from experience or hearsay, the captain wanted no revivalist technique on the *Bowditch*; his wife had taunted him about that. But after fourteen weeks, something touched his heart; he began to listen to their daily prayer service between decks and gave them permission to talk with his sailors. "Do all you can to make me and my crew better men." Although the tradition that they converted the entire crew is something of an overshot, they did win the captain and at least two of the sailors, and had respectful hearing from the others. The burial at sea of a Greek sailor was solemnly impressive. Our first voyage into the rough world; we have prayed so long, so earnestly; the ocean is wider and men are more indifferent than we supposed. But we are nearing our field. Captain Pike says that purple blur, dim in the west, is Ceylon. We can almost catch a breath of spice in the wind. A few more days, then Madras. And here come our first catamarans with their lateen sails, the fishermen standing in water half the time.

There was no harbor at Madras, only open roadstead, and the *Bowditch* anchored four miles offshore. Fatherly Miron Winslow and Brother Phineas Hunt came out to bring the missionaries off in massulah boats, which "were sewed, not nailed, thus making them very flexible." Twelve shouting oarsmen to each boat drove them in through three lines of heavy surf—"a frightful passage," wrote Susan. Then natives waded out, waist-deep, and carried them to the beach.

I can see now the crowd of naked children and half-clad men and women who surrounded us. From their mouths was running what seemed to be blood, but it was the saliva simply colored by the betel-nut which they always chewed. Specimens of humanity I have never forgotten.

And this was India's coral strand.

The Dulles were of course at home with the Winslows; the other three couples spent a week resting from the voyage, the Mills being guests in the home of Dr. John Scudder. From the flat roof they saw "heathen temples without number," and one place where self-torturers practised hook-swinging. And when the newcomers ventured from the door, jugglers and beggars squatted on the verandah—not without guile.

Then the Ceylon party chartered a dhoni, and on February 27 sailed for Ceylon—a voyage of from three days to two weeks, depending on the weather and the poor skill of the dhoni-man; this trip took eight days. There should be in Mission House a model of a dhoni to commemorate those weary voyages between Madras and Ceylon. The cramped quarters made the cabins on the *Bowditch* seem palatial, and the food was from hand to mouth. The pioneer missionaries in 1816 had landed at Colombo and made their way over tortuous roads to Jaffna, but for three decades every missionary had gone by dhoni, and those who lived had returned that way.

They landed at Point Pedro on March 7, and went a few miles to the nearest mission station, Oodoopitty, where they stayed overnight as guests of Mrs. Apthorp, whose husband had died in the service. She herself was in very frail health, but chose to stay at her post—and did stay until death. On the second day they had to wait until the sickening midday heat had passed, then they went on by oxcarts along the borders of rice fields to a half-way station—presumably Tillipally; and that evening most of the mission families from the scattered villages rode over to welcome them, hungry for new faces and for talk about the homeland, hopeful and perhaps a little anxious to size up these recruits upon whom so much would depend. And Cyrus and Susan were eager to meet the men and women they had heard about for years. Excerpts from letters printed in the *Missionary Herald* presented one side of the picture; faces marked with exhaustion were more eloquent. Adin Fletcher, who had been in the field only three years and who had written with boyish enthusiasm at first, was so ill he could hardly ride a few miles; the man was in the shadow of death. But there were Benjamin Meigs and Levi Spaulding, who had come to Ceylon before Cyrus Mills was born; they were tired, yes, but hearty and humorous, taking their work in easy stride. Spaulding, saltiest and shrewdest of the veterans, wrote privately of Cyrus and Susan: "Our new brother and sister are very good people, and if they were greater they might not be so good." There was prophecy in that sentence, Brother Spaulding.

On the third day Cyrus and Susan left their shipmates and went on to Batticotta, the station nearest Jaffna. At first they were guests of the Howlands, who had rooms in one end of an old stone church built long before by the Dutch. The walls were of coral, the ceilings of cloth, the unglazed windows shaded by Venetian blinds. After five months of ship and dhoni, it was good to be with home folks—with "dear Mrs. Howland, my first section teacher." One could not help noticing, though, that Mr. Howland, only two years in the field, was showing the strain. And Mr. Hoisington, whose bungalow was only a few yards away, was so very feeble, one caught the anxiety that all the Mission felt lest he would never live to reach America.

This new land was strange and more than a little awesome. One had to conclude that the author of the favorite missionary hymn had colored his dream of far-off things, for they had seen no coral strands, and the breezes that came across rice fields and crowded villages were, even by poetic license, not spicy. Nature was more lavish than one realized. Almost too lavish. One missed the clean-washed coolness of New England valleys, the lift of mountains on the sky line. The tamarind and mimosa trees in the

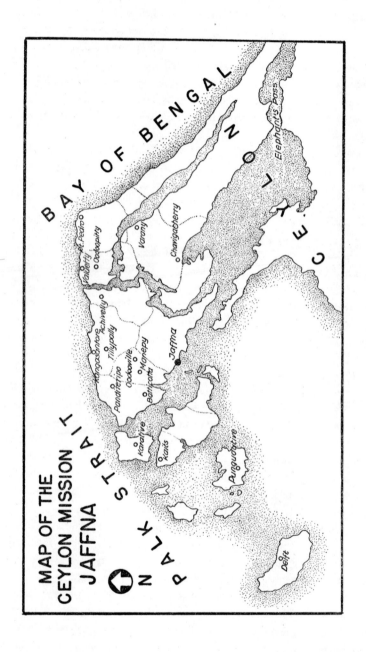

dusty mission compound had a dubious novelty; the palms, though, were Scriptural—palms in the village gardens and lining the narrow crooked lanes that passed for roads, and dense beyond the rice fields. The Howlands were weary of palms, and wished there were a hill or even an observatory to climb—anything to give a view above the dead level of the lowland. One had been schooled not to expect too much of the heathen, but now there was a disquieting irony in that "too much." One had not guessed how prolific the heathen could be. Around the school and the church were mud-walled compounds crowded with huts of the native teachers and servants and with kitchens and stables and baths and godowns—all swarming and babbling. And beyond these the town, crowded with incomprehensible ways of life. The language must be Tamil, but it races ever so much faster than it reads in the grammar text. And we—we are strangers. Aliens. Mr. Howland tells us how the priests in the largest temple display malicious ingenuity. On heathen feast days they halt their procession in front of *our* church as if to convert *us* with their abominations, which include certain dances by the temple prostitutes—a type of unrestrained self-expression that differs somewhat from calisthenics at Mount Holyoke. One heathen temple were surely enough; but in this town of three thousand lost souls there are fifty-four temples and shrines. Yes, there is surely a great work to be done, and we are eager to be at it. But the voyage seems to have tired us more than we realized, and this tropic climate has strange ways: the night chill reaches the very marrow of the bones—and then the hot lassitude of the day. Friendly Dr. Green cautioned us, when we passed through Manepy, not to overdo. The Howlands keep reminding us. Clearly, there are unfriendly forces to be reckoned with. Susan never forgot how they were awakened on the first Sabbath morning by a wailing in the streets: a native woman, going through a thatched gate, had been bitten by a poison serpent and died within three hours; and already the funeral procession was passing, the son of the dead woman leading with a torch to light the funeral pile.

Within ten days Cyrus and Susan came face to face with stark reality, in an episode touching the Scudder family. Dr. John Scudder, first medical missionary in this field, had come out with Levi Spaulding in 1819 and had long been a tower of strength in Ceylon and later in Madras. In the 1840's his two older sons returned from college in America and took up the work, Dr. Henry on the mainland, William in Ceylon. Born in the field, they were acclimatized in body and mind, and naturally acquired a mastery of the vernacular, an ability which, with other sterling qualities, made the family a power in the service. Early in March 1849, William Scudder and his wife and baby girl were returning to Ceylon from Madura, where they had gone to recuperate. With them in the dhoni on the voyage down the coast was Eurotas P. Hastings, a kinsman (I believe) of Mrs. Scudder. All seemed well; the young wife had been exhausted, but now felt able to take up her work again. Then one morning she felt a slight illness; by evening, they knew she had cholera. Though not a doctor, her husband always carried the stock remedy that his father and other medical missionaries prescribed for the dread disease. He and Hastings did their best, but the young mother died at three the next morning. Her last wish—that her child be spared and that her husband continue to be a good missionary—lifts the story above all cavil of sentiment.

The dhoni put in at some wretched village. With great difficulty Eurotas Hastings made a coffin of rough boards, and they buried her in a thorn grove overlooking the ocean. Meantime William Scudder had dangerous symptoms of cholera and the baby was stricken. When they reached Jaffna they were quarantined for a week, still on board the dhoni. By some mercy the child lived; and when they finally landed it was Susan Mills who took charge of the baby and through many weeks nursed her back to health. The grateful aftermath of that story came more than forty years later on the Mills campus; Susan's part in it, though not recorded in the Mission archives, is cherished by William Scudder's descendants.

A few months later word reached the mission posts that the natives were bringing flowers to the young woman's grave and lighting candles there. Some of the missionaries on the mainland were greatly disturbed; such homage might betray the heathen into building one more temple. So they forbade the tribute, and later they removed the body to a mission cemetery. Poor dusky benighted children, we hope God was not too angry with you about the flowers.

From the beginning the Mills set themselves a disciplined program for learning the language. Susan wrote:

> *I found that I had a great advantage because of my study with Mr. Mills on the voyage. I knew my two hundred and thirty-six letters with their variants, and could read a little, but oh, the pronunciation! One day I asked my Pundit why he was not as patient with me as with Mr. Mills when I did not pronounce correctly. He said, "You are only a woman, and he is a man and a teacher."*

Mrs. Apthorp had given her a motto: "By erring you learn, so talk, talk." There was opportunity. Daily she went with Mrs. Howland to the near-by villages, trying to do something for the women and children. Girls from the native schools gathered on the mission verandah, and the two Mount Holyoke women patiently spelled with them the first syllables of better living—sewing, singing, the beginnings of health and cleanliness, a gleam of hope. Then the household affairs of the school needed management; and because there were no hotels, the Mission was open house to travelers; in all of which, the native servants showed a sad lack of upbringing, a reluctance to scrub and to scour. We came to bring them the Bible; but sanitation, like salvation, is suspect to the Oriental mind. One boy, indeed, took the Bible too literally: he stole the copy Susan's father had given her, tramped six miles to Jaffna, and sold it for a few coppers. (She redeemed it, minus the fly leaf, for a shilling.) After a few weeks, she and Cyrus moved in with the Hoisingtons, who were too feeble to complete without help their packing for the long journey home.

The American Board had eight mission stations and four outstations in the northern tip of Ceylon, and these were its only missions on that island. These, as a group, were generally called the Ceylon Mission, or sometimes the Jaffna Mission, though Jaffna was a misnomer, as the Board had no station in that city. During the Mills' time there were usually about ten men, with their wives, assigned to these stations, with one doctor and a printer for the entire group. Though the Board advised and controlled general policy and most details, these ten or twelve men in the field practically controlled reassignment to posts, short-term sick leave, and such emergency matters. They were, in effect, an ex officio presbytery in which the native churches had no share; the fifty or sixty native teachers, catechists, and licentiates were only servants.

The area was compact; stations at opposite points of the district were hardly more than twenty miles apart, yet travel was exhausting. New England walkers soon found that a seven-mile walk to visit a colleague depleted them strangely, and the wives, unless they dared ride horseback, had to travel by oxcart or bandy or rickshaw. There was no official capital of the Mission; monthly meetings were rotated among the stations; but Batticotta, seat of the main school, and Manepy, where the press was established, were rather more important than the other stations. Banking was through London exchange. Salaries were uniform regardless of tenure and ability: £150 a year for a married couple, with graded allowances for children; £100 for a single man (the doctor and one other missionary being single at this time); and £75 for the faithful Miss Agnew, who taught in the girls' school at Oodooville, and for Mrs. Apthorp.

Each station had in its area from one to ten free primary schools, with native teachers, not all of whom were Christians. Above these were two seminaries: the girls' school at Oodooville under the capable management of Levi Spaulding, and the more important seminary for boys and young men at Batticotta. The Board had designated Cyrus Mills to teach at the latter school; the Mission could have reassigned him to another post but, for various reasons, kept him there. In reassigning their colleagues the members of the Mission appear to have been unselfish and to have had a consideration for the varying needs of the different stations and the strength and ability of the man. But plainly the work at Batticotta Seminary had become a man-killing job, and few veterans relished a second assignment to that post. They doubted their own qualifications and felt incapable of doing what the Board expected of them there. Instruction was given through the medium of English; and men who were zealous to save souls by preaching in Tamil begrudged the Seminary assignment, which ate up time and strength and curtailed that free mingling with the people whereby a man could master the vernacular. This issue between teaching and preaching was already a touchy point and soon became crucial—more so in Boston than in Ceylon. The entire Mission was understaffed, yet the tiredest preacher in the field could fever himself counting the villages that were not yet evangelized, and planning to extend the work farther inland south of Elephant's Pass or among the low-caste fishermen on the little islands northwest of Jaffna. And Batticotta was sadly undermanned. With from a hundred to a hundred twenty-five students, the Mission could spare it only two, often only one, capable American teacher, to supervise the five or six native teachers and carry the executive duties, together with a full teaching load of his own. William W. Howland's time was fully taken with preaching and parish work. Soon after the Mills arrived, Henry R. Hoisington, long in charge of the Seminary, left for America. And so Cyrus Mills began, first as teacher of science, and soon as principal.

In the twenty-five years of its existence Batticotta had grown into certain functions hardly foreseen at its founding. At the outset the pioneers had gathered boys of the poorest families, orphans, whosoever would; and eager to attract possible converts, the school had given free board and tuition with a small bonus of cash or books. The founders expected the school to furnish native preachers for the Tamil missions—Ceylon, Madura, Madras. Slowly the school had won a certain esteem among the small minority of native families who were reached by the Mission, and by 1849 many of its students were bent twigs. Batticotta graduates were in considerable demand as teachers, interpreters, court and government clerks; and most of the Mission helpers—catechists and lay preachers—were former Batticotta men. Boys who were courteously passive to the new religion had a secular eye upon the technical and social advantages of the training: better pay, a step up in society, a more lucrative marriage. Or so at least the critics of the Seminary believed; and New England investors in missions misdoubted whether that sort of education was worth what it cost. From their remote point of view education was not saving souls; and indeed only one in seven of the students was a church member. For that matter, all the churches in the Mission comprised only 325 native members—and this after thirty years of hard effort by fifty men and women, one-third of whom had died in the service; and in the entire Mission there was not yet one ordained native preacher. Many a good man, at the breaking point, agonized in prayer, wondering what was wrong. From the Sandwich Islands came word of conversions by the thousands. Titus Coan had baptized more converts in one day on Hilo than the Ceylon Mission had won in thirty years.

Repeatedly the enthusiasts in America cited analogies from *The Acts of the Apostles*: the early Church, consecrating missionaries by the laying on of hands, had sent them out pretty much on their own to all quarters of the Roman world, and had they not converted that world in no longer time than it takes to read The Acts? And if consecration and faith and martyrdom worked in the first century, why not now? Why could not modern missionaries lay consecrating hands upon ready converts and set them at once to establishing all over India and Persia and Turkey and Zululand and China new churches that would carry on like orderly congregations in New England? Few mission supporters, few indeed among the Board members, had begun to surmise that the word *heathen*, with its other demerits, was altogether too broad and vague a term; that it were well to know the ethnical and cultural backgrounds of these various peoples. Slowly the best missionaries were coming to realize this; their successors, best of all some of their own sons and daughters, learned the virtue of adaptability.

But if you are on a remote beachhead in 1849, you do the best you can. In spite of the heavy going Cyrus felt encouraged. He wrote about the boys who crowded his office at the opening of the new year—three times as many applicants as the school could admit—pleading earnestly, tearfully, for a chance; and of their fathers, some of whom were doing their bewildered best to live up to this new religion in spite of caste and the dead weight of tradition, and who wanted their sons not to lapse back into despair. With his natural humility and the memory of his own struggle, it was hard for Cyrus to deny any boy. The school with its inherited conditions was on his shoulders. Even had it been within his nature to make radical changes he was not free to do so; the Mission controlled the school and the Board controlled the Mission. But he had the courage of common sense; he put the school on a more businesslike basis. The school was charging some students the actual cost of board, a little more than a dollar a month. Cyrus cut out the gifts and arranged that half the students should pay full cost of board, one-fourth should pay half-rates, and one-fourth should be admitted free. He made some sensible changes in the curriculum. The eight-year course gave much training in English and the Bible, some science and considerable mathematics, a little history, and fair attention to Tamil literature. There is no way of knowing how efficient the five or six native teachers were; they were Batticotta alumni and poorly paid, one or another of them being tempted over to the Wesleyans in Jaffna. The curriculum was weighted with theology—Paley and Butler—and other carry-overs from New England tradition. Mr. Hoisington had even introduced Bacon's *Novum Organum*—a use of that profound work which must have awakened in its ghostly author that feeling which the Elizabethans called "admiration." Hoisington had defended his use of the book on the ground that Oriental students were much given to dialectic. Cyrus felt that they were too much given that way—without Bacon. There was too much abstract teaching, not enough personal counsel, and he established "divisions" like those at Mount Holyoke, and impelled his teachers to have heart-to-heart talks with the boys. Susan had a hand in that move.

I have seen but one catalogue of the school, a printing job which does credit to Mr. Burnell and the mission press. The names of the boys appear in both Tamil and English, the former being as pretty as a page of Greek. Something to display with solemn, and perhaps timid, pride in one's home village. In his reports to Rufus Anderson and the Board, Cyrus was painfully conscientious about curricular changes, daily regimen, and the conduct of his boys. In these reports, which were copiously quoted in the *Missionary Herald*, he continued his predecessors' usage of classifying the students as "impenitent," "well-disposed," "serious," and "church-member," and of listing their fathers as Christian, heathen, or Catholic.

But what is this we read? Heathen fathers—the roster plainly says so; but the sons are Edward Beecher and John Orr Fiske and Joseph Lafayette Leeds and David McGregor and—save us!—Mark Hopkins himself. Each of them is either impenitent or well disposed or serious. Can Mark Hopkins be anything less than serious? It sorts with dignity that Moses Hallock should graduate from Batticotta: how could any Hallock fail? But it's a world of mares' nests when we find Cotton Mather also among the Batticotta alumni. And from collateral reports we learn that Margaret Purviance and Phoebe McLean and Catherine Ann Devereux and Jane L. Wadsworth were faithful to their Bible verses and plain sewing in Oodooville.

Early in the life of the Mission some bustling mind in America conceived this promotional idea of stirring each church, each Sunday school, to sponsor a boy or girl in Ceylon. Surely it would hearten the waif to be told he was the protégé of Wachusetts Center. To spur him to high endeavor, to Americanize him, why not rechristen him with an uplifting name—a name which, incidentally, we in America can pronounce? And so it was done, by paying a certain amount. There is no record of what the dark-eyed Tamil boys thought about the matter, or what names their home villages and hostile relatives called them by. In time a practical difficulty arose: the bent-twig son of, say, Israel W. Putnam was placed in a cloudy position by being tagged Edward Dwight Payson. The Mission had to rule that the son should keep the father's surname and wear the gift name as a prefix, which usage must in time bring a handsome string of initials into the catalogue. All of which imposed upon tired teachers a smother of bookkeeping and correspondence, with no infrequent embarrassment when lads whose names sounded of bank presidents and college trustees—names with gold-headed canes—were expelled for sins that had no redeeming touch of gentility.

The bother of it all. An undersecretary in Boston writes an undersecretarial letter, tartly citric: the Juvenile Missionary Society in Evansville, Indiana, had bestowed the name Eliza Tappan Drew upon a little heathen girl. Two years have passed. *The donors have had no word* from or about little Eliza Tappan Drew, "her age, disposition, appearance, progress in her education, & c." The undersecretary is pained. "Let me hear by the earliest opportunity." We suppose that Levi Spaulding answered, for he was a kindly man. Famine and cholera were bad that year, and pestilence walked by noonday. Besides his work in the school at Oodooville, where his wife Mary and faithful Miss Agnew helped him, Levi was a real preacher. He liked to go into the crowd, to reach them in their own idiom, and he knew the native mind and heart as few men did. After an arduous day he could still summon strength to translate one more page of the Bible into Tamil. A tough-fibered resilient man, kindly but fiery too. He doubtless answered the undersecretary with decent patience, and managed to throw across the crowded and shadowy world of his work some pin point of particularity upon little Eliza Tappan Drew; but as the nature of the man is revealed in the salty tang of his known letters, his side comment to Mary—if we had it— would pain the ears of piety.

And so Cyrus and Susan carried on at Batticotta Seminary, sometimes with the help of one other missionary, but often with none. The morale of the native teachers needed strengthening; school discipline was not a matter of controlling energy but of inducing it. The native servants—cooks and steward and sweepers and all—were given to abstract meditation; and somehow the servants' compounds became crowded with the huts of their cousins and in-laws, all plausibly receptive to Christian charity. Nature herself seemed strange: death lurked in every crevice, in the air itself. Termites had no sense of religion: they devoured a dedicated chapel and a beggar's hut with the same gusto. In cool New England Paley's orderly pattern of a moral universe seemed complete. Could it be that Nature, east of the Holy Land, did not subscribe to Paley? But fortitude, when made a disciplined habit, still carries on. The Mount Holyoke habit: Mary Lyon would be depending on Susan and Cyrus. In the first midsummer came letters from South Hadley: Mary Lyon was dead. She had died in the very week the Mills had arrived in Ceylon. So strong and confident, so Scriptural and right. And that ideal of hers *was* right—right and exciting as Isaiah's "Ho, every one that thirsteth, come ye to the waters." A share in whatever good there was belonged to every man. But nobody in America could begin to understand the inertia, the indirections, the rooted fears and prejudices of the Orient. Still there was hope. With apostolic simplicity, a few of the boys and one or two of the native teachers made week-end trips among the outcast fishermen on the small islands. Then too there was a stir of the dramatic to rouse courage. A boy whose family was one of the wealthiest in the village offered himself for church membership. The Mission had learned to scan such professions, but he was a good boy. Threatened with being disowned by his parents, threatened with a beating by his uncles and brothers, he still wanted to be a Christian. His male kinsfolk tried to browbeat Mills and Howland, but they stood firm, and Cyrus put the decision squarely up to the boy. On Sabbath morning the relatives came to church, sat through the sermon, and when the lad stepped forward to be received they became abusive and laid violent hands on him. The missionaries called upon the native policeman whom the English deputy had posted, and he, though also a cousin and strongly opposed to the new religion, was, above all other gods, a dutiful policeman. An order was an order. He stopped the row and the boy joined the church. By the last accounts the lad's parents had relented, but the uncles remained stiff-necked.

The stir of this occasion, together with word of a great revival in the Persian Mission, started the deepest religious feeling anybody could remember at Batticotta. For a few weeks apathetic boys and teachers felt something of the self-abnegation, of warmth and hope, that seemed to be second nature in Hawaii. Cyrus was wakened at dawn by the murmur of their volunteer prayer meetings, and he had to use kindly admonition to get them to break up at night. The feeling reminded Cyrus and Susan of their own college days, seasons when youth made its own greatest discoveries and trusted the inner flame. This, they felt, was the way missions should go. Both were wise enough to know that this feeling could not be constant; if they could only learn how to waken it again. . . . And if their own strength were not so steadily depleted. . . . Word of their progress had sifted back to America through letters from their colleagues. Even Mr. Hoisington, not easy to please, had to admit that Batticotta appeared to be in good hands.

At the end of his first year Cyrus summed up his impressions in a long letter to the missionary society at Williams. (The Mills Society it was called, after that earlier Mills of the Haystack Prayermeeting.)

A person of an excessive go-ahead spirit will be sorely tried here, because he cannot make things go to his mind always, and he will be very liable to discouragement. So a person who is very full of new ideas and plans, now for schools, now for touring and now for something else, will not do well here . . . Again one who is very set in his own opinions and wants everything in his own way, will be sure to have trouble with his fellow labourers . . . Again one needs a large stock of patience, next to piety and good judgment nothing is more important. You cannot now realize how much there is here to try and even torture poor human patience. The climate seems to affect the nerves more than anything else. One cannot be here long without having his nervous excitability greatly increased, so that things which did not affect him, become very trying. There is a strong tendency to morbid sensibility, which inclines one to be fretful and peevish . . .

For one may have piety and a heart to do good, and yet fail for want of common sense, from a want of knowledge of men and things, and an acquaintance with business . . . I would say with emphasis that a mere book educated man though the valedictorian of his class, is not the man for a missionary . . . A missionary to a people so crafty and full of metaphysical subtlety should be a good scholar . . . But this is not enough . . . You cannot give yourself to simple preaching, but you must manage all sorts of business. If you do not understand business matters the natives will soon find it out and take every possible advantage of you. They are very shrewd in playing their games . . .

You cannot witness from day to day the misery and degradation of the people, without pain. And when you find that all you can do is only like dipping the ocean dry with a bucket, your heart will ache and sicken within you.

He usually reported to the Board three times a year; and whatever the varying tone of hope, one trouble was pressing upon him steadily: he felt he was not learning to speak Tamil as readily as the Board expected. Then in October 1850 a greater trouble appeared: Mrs. Mills' health was none too good; they hoped she would soon be well again. That was the last letter which was not weighed down with anxiety.

eight

"THE PESTILENCE THAT WALKETH
IN DARKNESS"

*T*HE STORIES OF THE MEN AND WOMEN WHO FORMED THE THIN
and overextended lines in the campaign are preserved mostly
in their official correspondence with the Board.* All but a few of their more
revealing private letters have been lost or hidden away too well to be re-
assembled. But Mission House kept the official correspondence: the out-
going letters copied in a writing-school hand; the incoming letters from the
hundreds of men and women who formed the lonely patrols through decade
after decade; and these incoming letters, in spite of their formality of style
and cliché, have the germs of story. Thousands of letters—the bound volumes, shelf upon shelf, stack after stack—enough to keep the most avid
prospector burrowing forever. Enlistment letters, telling all we shall ever
know of a man's background; letters from the field, losing tune through
illness and defeat or keyed to a kind of grandeur when a man stayed on the
front line for forty years; and when a man was invalided home, a series of

* I have read only the letters pertaining to Ceylon from the middle 1840's through
1857, a few scores from the Madras and Madura and Arcot men, and a smaller number
from Hawaii.

declining hopes and evasions, and a helpless casting about for other employment. Some of the incoming letters are in the hands of native copyists, but most are holographic, and the writing reveals the fatigue, the nervous and spiritual states of the man.

Tired and lonely men—very lonely, even when blessed with a good wife and staunch colleagues and a few sheaves of harvest. Taciturn men would have spells of needing to open heart and mind in sixteen to twenty pages of shop talk or in gatherings from their diaries, crowded with the human scene and its pathos. Now and then one would find healthy release in a travelogue, though such instances are rarer than we could wish, for some of the men had little eye for the innocent-exotic. As the Ceylon Mission had a grooved rule that no member might write to the Board about any matter touching the Mission's interest without submitting his letter to the entire group, the cramped and guarded style may be imagined. (The Hawaiian men could be themselves.) But now and then some man, usually a veteran, unbuttoned his collar, or by some blessed inadvertence a private note got bound into the volume —and then there is lively reading.

Home was far away, and the mails were slow and expensive. The overland mail was quicker—across the mainland to Bombay and thence by what routes I know not, to England and America—but it cost more, and the poor dears had to count their shillings. They used thin paper, crowding both sides and filling margins with overrun, until Rufus Anderson had to cry to some of the microscopic writers for mercy and send them a supply of thicker paper. If the good Secretary could have confined himself to the higher strategy of the Lord's work—but no, he had to be all things to all men. The wife of a missionary had inherited from her Virginian mother a one-ninth share in a parcel of twenty or thirty slaves: would Dr. Anderson set in motion the legal machinery to free her one-ninth share? Another wife who had gone to the States to place their children in school had her own grim-dry thoughts about giving all to the heathen, and downrightly refused to return to her husband. She would continue nominally to love, honor and obey him —but not in the Jaffna climate. Time and again the husband, good man, who hoped to convert Asia, pleaded with Dr. Anderson to soften a little the passive resistance of his helpmeet. There were more overt feuds to be umpired: one in which a missionary on the mainland, obviously a wild ass, snarled the nerves of half the Ceylon brethren and brought down an avalanche of long documents, attested with prayerful forbearance; and another in which the Madura Mission censured the Ceylon group for receiving a native whom they had dismissed for his unwillingness to waive caste and eat with his fellow Christians. Feeling became so strained that one testy veteran on the mainland refused to speak to his Ceylon brethren, and Anderson had to labor with him through many folio pages. Once the ladies of the Mission requested the busy Secretary to see to it that if a certain invalided couple returned to the field they should leave their problem child in the States. And one good man felt impelled to justify his criticism of a brother for using native bearers and a palankeen when an oxcart would have been more economical. So very human, all this. But mostly the letters were tender with considerateness, and many carried a heartache—anxiety of parents who had sent their children home for schooling and were disturbed by slow-sifting news: would Dr. Anderson please see that the boy was shifted to a better school or the girl to a kinder home? Yes, Rufus Anderson should have had his fill of letters, but he cried for more: more moving stories of conversions, more dying beds of missionaries and converts, which, when printed in the *Missionary Herald*, were potent to keep contributions flowing and stir imaginative youths to enlist. He was inordinately enthusiastic, prodigious and voluble with executive cares, and his zeal so filled his mind that he could not well brook any seeming hindrance. The ingrate meagerness of the harvest, the worst hardships of climate, should not (he suggested) be played up too strongly lest recruiting drop off.

Some of the Ceylon men escaped to a degree the stultifying decorum of censorship. Benjamin Meigs had come to the work in 1816; he stayed in harness until 1857. Cheerful, sturdy, fluent in Tamil, he had an inexhaustible affability. His letters are equaled by those of only one other man for the light they throw upon mission problems in general and the Mills in particular. His analyses were logical, practical, and honest. Then, too, his boyish interest in small things. His spirited Burmese saddle pony died mysteriously, and then a second pony. He had Dr. Green and Cyrus Mills make an analysis; they proved arsenic poisoning, which nefarious sabotage, he discovered, was the work of his bearers, who did not propose to have the rice taken out of their mouths by ponies. His letters contain almost the only references to food which I have found: he cheerfully told how his digestion was upset by "eating too freely of the sweet and very delicious grapes" of the land. His station at Tillipally being nearest to one of the small north-shore dhoni ports, he often rode five miles to the shore when missionaries were about due, that he might welcome them. He saw the morning light on the ocean, clear as glass, and a dhoni slowly drawing in. "I sleep very soundly and sweetly, and rise very early to my labors, and take my coffee at five o'clock." A younger colleague wrote: "Brother Meigs looks at everything in an easy sort of way." Essentially kind, magnanimous to his colleagues, he knew the actualities of the work better than any member of the Board. He had the courage to dissent, but shrank from controversy—a point which will have a bearing upon our story.

Daniel Poor had come to Ceylon with Meigs in 1816. Deeply serious, greatly loved, he was inclined toward mystical abstraction, a devoted preacher living in an intense world of his own. His letters (for the period noted) have only a moderate by-play of comment upon his colleagues, and as he was on rest leave during much of the Mills' period, there is little occasion to quote him. Hardy veteran though he was, and used to taking care of himself, he died of cholera in 1855, just before the visit of the Deputation.

The third gray veteran, and spiciest of the three, was Levi Spaulding. His humor was not the habitual cheerfulness of his old friend Meigs, nor was it a turn of exhibitionism. His dry acidity had no malice, it was rather a litmus honesty in the man; he had patience with many things but not with sanctimoniousness. Can a man fill his belly with the east wind? Brother Meigs could call a spade a spade, but would be troubled lest the Board's feelings might be hurt. Brother Spaulding would say, in effect: "For the Lord's sake, dig one acre and you'll know your tools." His bluntness, his freedom from the flattened decorum of clerical style, give his letters pungency. Whatever effect the fresh wind of his honesty had upon his own times, it clears the issues now. Once he wrote to Rufus Anderson:

> *In your communication you have several times referred to the 'excellent committee of 13.' You will pardon me if I say most frankly that I hope you and I shall never see the time when you will think me capable of entertaining the least respect for the opinions of any committee, or of any man, who can stoop to such measures as you and I know that committee has done.*

The gift these older men had of working hard brought sighs from some of their juniors. W. W. Howland wrote:

> *In such a climate and with such exciting work as ours there is danger of the nervous system becoming deranged; sleepless nights and dreadful headaches follow days of preaching and mental labor. It is a noticeable fact that our oldest brethren, Poor, Meigs and Spaulding, can sleep anywhere.*

Spaulding himself summed up the labor he loved:

> *They [the missionaries] must be book makers from a—b—c to dictionaries and astronomies. . . . They must be managers and editors in the printing*

*and binding office. They must be pastors of churches, catechists and Bibli-
cal agents . . . treasurers, secretaries, colporters . . . evangelists to
preach the Gospel on the Sabbath from village to village, & hewers of wood
and drawers of water at home . . .*

In an atmosphere where there was too much conscious and wistful goodness,
his irony was curative. He could penetrate through the wrappings to the core
of a man, yet he was no cynic. When someone in Mission House wrote
pityingly about having a severe headache, Levi snorted. And when at last
the Board announced it was sending out the Deputation to inspect the harvest
field, Levi candidly suggested these brethren should stay at least a year,
through hot season and rainy season and chills and plague. His very fatigue
is more stimulating than another man's good cheer, and his approval would
be dearer than any other praise.

Eastman S. Minor had been in the service for sixteen years when the Mills
came, and had been mainly responsible for the mission press before Thomas
Burnell. Considerate and forbearing, he stated problems with great clarity;
and though he had not Spaulding's tart humor nor quite the tenderness of
Benjamin Meigs, he was close to Spaulding for plain speech. W. W. Howland
made almost no comment upon his colleagues; to compensate, no other man
in that period told more about his native helpers or gave more complete pictures of the country. Though not robust, and compelled to work hard for what
he achieved, he remained forty-six years in the service, and his daughter,
Susan Reed Howland (Mount Holyoke '70), enlarged the good work after
him. The Scudder family—Dr. John and his sons, Dr. Henry, William, and
Joseph—were gathered as a family mission in Arcot on the mainland early in
the 1850's. They were the sole exception to the Congregational-Presbyterian
scope of the Board; they were of the Dutch Reformed Church. The father and
the older sons had much to do with the Mills.

But from the bulky old volumes the personality of still another man
emerges with refreshing difference—the Mission doctor, Samuel F. Green,
who came out in 1847. Most of the ordained ministers simply couldn't help
sounding like one another, but Dr. Green wrote about things. Even before
sailing, he spoke little of his feelings, rather about assembling instruments
and medicines, trying to persuade the Prudential Committee to underwrite a
daguerreotype outfit (and we wish they had), pricing saddles, and having a
shay made to order by Messrs. Tolman and Company of Worcester. At
Madras he grew impatient of waiting for a dhoni, and struck off down the
coast on horseback with three coolies and a horse-tender. He was stationed
first at Manepy, and then at Batticotta, where his crowded clinic added to the

busyness of the Topsy-growing compounds. After one look at diseased India en masse and concluding there were more ulcers than one man could cure, he started a medical school, choosing four or five of the likeliest Batticotta graduates for students. If the undertaking appear preposterous—what with his meager equipment and his own professional limitations—still he made better progress toward turning his youths into practical doctors than his colleagues did toward making effective preachers of theirs. Hard put to it for texts his students could understand, he wrote his own text, which was printed on the mission press—a duodecimo of 148 pages with "three rather sad cuts." (A copy of this should be a collector's item.) Naturally he taught in English—a point which will be pertinent in the next chapter. He thought the Mission coddled its graduates too much; he was for turning his young men loose to find their own places. In that crowded and distressing scene he noted many curious things: the technique of chewing betel, and the endemic mouth cancers; the ways of climate and weather and diet; vivid symptoms of malnutrition, and wealthy characters whose "fat is so crammed under the skin that the abdomen really shines, & the navel becomes a bottomless dimple."

At some point the letters of every man spoke of the difficulty in mastering the Tamil language. Except the three oldest veterans, hardly a man but confessed his shortcomings. True, the Scudder brothers minimized the problem somewhat; they did not realize their own advantage in having heard the language from infancy. One of them pointed out the similarity between Biblical rhythms and imagery and the poetic quality of Tamil, but few indeed of their colleagues got beyond prosaic needs. Nathan Lord voiced the average experience when he said that it would take five years in the field to become "so familiar with the language of temples, bazars and fields as to catch readily and accurately the idioms and imperfections." All agreed that preaching through interpreters saved few souls. Benjamin Meigs reviewed the cases of twenty of his former and present colleagues: two men were too old when they began; one man had no ear for music; another had "some defect in his ear and voice which prevented his acquiring a very good pronunciation"; another man, an exceptional scholar, had lacked the health and perhaps the temperament for mingling freely with the people. Spaulding wrote:

> [The new missionary] must be quiet at his studies while he sees his seniors overworked, and important interests suffering. Of course he falls a sacrifice to over-exertion, or fails to get the language, without which he can never sympathize very much with the people, nor feed them with Bible truths, nor legislate for them excepting on foreign principles and by foreign weights and measures.

One man suggested that the recruiting agents pay more attention to the linguistic aptitude of candidates; another, that a qualifying course in Tamil be taught in America. The fact that Dulles, Noyes, Burnell, and their wives studied grammar under Cyrus Mills during the voyage on the *Bowditch* would indicate that he had gone farther in preliminary study than the average. Veterans and all agreed that new men required more time after reaching the field than the conditions allowed, and that Batticotta was, in that respect, the hardest post. When that post was offered to Levi Spaulding before the Mills' arrival, that doughty man threw up his hands; he could speak Tamil with the best of them, but he could not do what was demanded in that position. Benjamin Meigs ended his summary by saying: "Mr. Mills will obtain the language if he can have such help in the Seminary as to relieve him of a part of his labors and cares."

But Mr. Mills had a deeper anxiety: Susan had become seriously ill. When he first mentioned this in October 1850 he was hopeful of an early recovery. A statement made later by Dr. Green indicates that her sickness began within six months of their arrival.

Sickness, too, was a steady subject in the Ceylon letters, deeper than Tamil. The older men felt that one point should be clearer in Boston: that Ceylon, though tropical, was not a health resort. Again, Benjamin Meigs' summary (though not applicable to Mrs. Mills) is worth noting. Many of the breakdowns were due to overwork; but too many were the result of physical unfitness which should have been apparent when the candidates were accepted. He checked off man after man who was tubercular or otherwise unfit before he left America. Levi Spaulding was even more revealing: Mr. X "was a dead man before they sent him out, an invalid dyspeptic minister & came out for his health, & looked as careworn & near death when he struck off the first sheet in the press at Manepy as he did before he left." (He was not speaking of Eastman S. Minor.) Another man was "consumptive when he left home— had a fever & a deep cough when he arrived in Jaffna." The stoutest constitution was none too good against the depleting heat and malarial mists, and the heat itself was less harmful than an earth and air contaminated with filth and disease. By 1849 the Mission had built a health bungalow at Valverty, on the north shore a little west of Point Pedro; the change and the sea air, even at that short distance, gave relief to exhausted families. The Madras and Madura missions on the mainland had built their health bungalow some fifty miles west of Madura, where the Pulney Hills rose to an altitude of seven thousand feet. They passed the word along to their Ceylon brethren, who at first shared that bungalow and then built one of their own near it. To worn men and women the Pulneys were an exciting joy, not unmixed with nostalgia; to have to close doors and windows and gather round a stove reminded them of home; and the exciting lift of forested mountains and cataracts and a feeling of snow in the wind moved more than one letter writer to extend himself. Dr. Henry Scudder, stationed in Madura, told how he had sent his wife and little girl to the Pulneys, the child so frail he had not expected to see her again; and then of his own jolting crawl by oxcart across the hot plain when he went to join them, and the slow climb up the steep pass, and the joy of seeing the child ruddy and racing. His account of the return trip—three married couples and the children—has more physical exhilaration than anything else I have found in the dusty volumes. So steep and narrow the road, the women and children had to ride in improvised blanket litters borne by carriers, and the men on shaggy hill ponies. Rested nerves and an almost secular laughter confirm Brother Meigs' opinion that the missionaries would do well to devote a briefer part of the early morning hours to prayers and Tamil, and more to a canter on a pony.

But Mrs. Mills' sickness was no laughing matter. She became a victim of amoebic dysentery which, when chronic, passed into dangerous ulcerations. In December 1850 she went with the Howlands to the Pulney Hills and seemed at first to improve, but soon found the cold altitude too hard for her weakened condition. In March Cyrus joined her; he himself was near a breakdown. They returned to Madura, consulted Dr. Shelton (their fellow passenger on the *Bowditch*), and by his advice went to Coimbatoor, a hundred fifty miles northwest of Madura—a two weeks' journey by oxcart. (The patience needed for those journeys!) There, at a gentler altitude but well above the air of the plains, she was under the care of Dr. Porteous, an Englishman, reputed the best physician in all that country. In June Cyrus' letter betrayed for the first time the heartsick fear that they might have to return to America; but by early September Susan felt improved enough to undertake the long journey by cart and dhoni back to Ceylon. They were touched by Dr. Porteous' refusal of a fee.

And so they took up their work again at Batticotta. Cyrus wrote:

We did not know before how much our feelings here have become enlisted in the welfare of this people or how sore would be the trial of separation from them. But a merciful Father has averted what we feared so much . . .

But early in December Mrs. Mills' increasing weakness so alarmed her colleagues that they requested the Prudential Committee to permit the Mills to return to America. Benjamin Meigs, as secretary of the Mission, enclosed a statement from Dr. Green: she was so weakened that there was no hope for her recovery in a tropical climate. On another occasion Meigs had intimated that another couple "did not wish to remain"; now he was explicit regarding Cyrus and Susan Mills: "Their whole desire is to remain and spend their strength in this place." Levi Spaulding, too, wrote in fatherly concern; unless their Christmas vacation at Valverty helped the invalid, he urged the Committee to permit a return to the States.

Again in March 1852 the Mission urged action, but Cyrus and Susan felt obligated to see the term through, and were reluctant to leave Ceylon without the Committee's permission. Some sort of permission reached them before the end of June. No copy of that document is in the files, but it seems to have been a dubious consent, and Secretary Anderson spoke disparagingly of the matter to some of the brethren who were on leave in America. (Hastings was on leave for matrimonial purposes, and Minor and Hoisington and their wives, though not expecting to return to the field, were in friendly correspondence with their former colleagues. Minor was the most likely to resent any official criticism of the Mills' position.) From other letters it appears that the Prudential Committee suggested a voyage to the Cape and a recuperative side trip—a sort of postman's holiday—to the mission in Zululand, where at that very time Cyrus' classmate, Samuel Dexter Marsh, was near death.

In any case, Cyrus Mills' patience was near the limit. Their own deep disappointment over having to leave their chosen work, he wrote,

> *is now made far more trying to us both, particularly to Mrs. Mills, by . . . the qualified language of the permission, and the remarks made to three or four of our Mission in the U.S. about the undesirableness of our returning. I am sure if you fully understood the case you would not have made the remarks that have come to us . . . After so many changes of air and medicine with no permanent benefit, we do not feel called on to make any more uncertain experiments . . . Still we cannot help feeling tried and grieved to feel obliged to take a course not fully and certainly approved by the Committee.*

The brethren of the Prudential Committee were directing global strategy on terrain none of them had ever seen. Shortly after he issued this "qualified permission," Rufus Anderson had written to the Ceylon brethren:

> *We are exceedingly perplexed in accounting for the failure in health of so many in your fine climate of Jaffna . . . You will need to write a good deal and ably, for a time at least, to induce our most promising young men*

to devote themselves to India Missions . . . Your climate must be one of the best in India. Your children have lived beyond what is common in missions, excepting the Sandwich Islands . . . Has your climate deteriorated? Are your employments less active? less in the open air? less favorable to the flow of animal spirits? less exercising to the lungs?

And in 1853, after Cyrus and Susan Mills were disabled, the Secretary could still write:

I have long supposed your climate to be one of the most salubrious in the world—almost an oceanic climate. It [now] seems you are subject to fever & ague east of you, & that cold night dews abound everywhere in the winter months.

His overflowing good will made it hard for him to perceive that his cheerful raillery was hardly the best manner; nor is it easy to harmonize his suppositions with the staring fact that one-third of the Mission had died at their posts—none of old age—and that another third had been retired because of physical and nervous breakdown.

Late in August 1852 the Mills went to Madras, planning to sail to the Cape in October and wait there for a ship to Boston. Again, weeks of uncertainty; the impact of their own seeming defeat was sharpened by the fact that John Dulles and his wife, who had come out with them on the *Bowditch*, were already compelled to leave the field. But Mrs. Mills improved a little, and Dr. John Scudder advised them to tarry in Madras. Their stay was prolonged to nearly seven months, during which time they were guests in the home of Isaac Hurd; and again, the grateful aftermath of that visit was to be repaid twenty-five years later in California. Cyrus studied Tamil, and noted the practical sense of the Scottish missionaries, who had ordained three native preachers. "I do not see that they are superior to *ten* men in our mission except that they are ordained." One small episode during their stay accents a problem. The Madras Mission held its annual fellowship dinner, when missionaries and converts ate together of rice and curry with an afterdish of fruits and sweetmeats—really a test dinner (as Miron Winslow confessed) to see whether all professing Christians had abandoned prejudices of caste. "There was a little question about two of the members actually eating any of the boiled rice, but when it was noticed and spoken of, they ate, and all seemed happy." The touchiness of the problem came out on another occasion when a convert timidly requested his missionary pastor, who had come to call, not to enter his house lest it involve him in loss of caste.

In March 1853 Cyrus and Susan dhonied back to Ceylon, riding out a bad storm, with twelve thousand rupees in their care. In this, their last term at Batticotta, what did they think of missions? They did not know it was their last term. They fully expected to return to the field, once Mrs. Mills' health was restored. They were disabled, not defeated. Early illusions were giving way to level-eyed perception. They knew that much of their good work with the boys was destroyed during school vacations. They began to see that the natives must be impelled to help themselves. Cyrus' remark about the Scottish missionaries indicates that he was well ahead of most of his colleagues on that point. Their own theology had had a shock; a good many Batticotta men avowed a belief in one God but not in the orthodox doctrine of salvation through blood sacrifice, and Cyrus was not ready to meet them on that ground. Would he have become an effective preaching missionary? It is now too late to grade him in Tamil Conversation, whatever that test be worth. He never became a notable preacher in any tongue, but he had the steady patience of the teacher. On still another point their eyes were clearer: good will alone was not enough. Much of the misapplied energy, the over-extension of the lines, the wastage of missionary power was due to impractical theorists in America. I think their perception of this fact became the deciding principle in their lives during the next ten years. Missions were still the Lord's work, but remote foremen could make mistakes: a conclusion which conservative Cyrus and Susan did not quickly reach, but which affected them profoundly. The word "expendable," in our current sense of it, was not in their vocabulary, but many a worn and bereaved man and woman must have had some grim intimation of its meaning. Were the many deaths as necessary, after all, as the home folks and the missionaries themselves had believed? Mary Lyon's brightest and dearest had enlisted; in this one year, 1853, Lucy Lyon Lord died in China, Abigail Moore Burgess and rare Abby Allen Fairbank in India. (If the fourth had died in Ceylon there would be no Mills College.) Missions were hardest on the women and children. I have been competently warned against sentimentality; still, a scrap of story in a folder at Mount Holyoke moves me more than reports drawn up by conclaves of the great. The Burnells, who had sailed in the *Bowditch*, stayed in the service all their lives. Their little girl fell suddenly ill; the mother started with her in an oxcart to reach the doctor—a slow journey through dust and heat. They halted under a banyan tree, and there the little one died. Long years after, a younger daughter recalled how her mother, grown gray and wise in the service, never passed that banyan tree without speaking a little, as old-fashioned mothers would do, of that child.

It takes many defeats to prove what truth is in the old poets. A few Mills

nine

APPARENT FAILURE

THEIR SALARY STOPPED WHEN THEY LEFT CEYLON, BUT THEY were still at the command of the Prudential Committee; while Mrs. Mills was recovering health, Cyrus was on call as a field agent for missions, for which twofold purpose they were allowed $400 a year. Eastman S. Minor, likewise under command until he resigned, was allowed $500 for himself, his wife, and nine children. When advised by the Prudential Committee to be frugal he tartly suggested that some one of the Committee feed, clothe, and house the Minor family on that sum and learn the meaning of frugality: "The policy that would place a missionary and his family, on their first return from a foreign land, in circumstances of so much want, is impolitic and un-Christian." While the Mills remained under pledge to the Board their allowance was never enough. There were many doctors' bills; three times Cyrus had to ask for small additional amounts, and he said that but for the generosity of friends they would be in still greater need. They considered Ware their home for the first year and a half, but Mrs. Mills was in New York a great deal, and then for five months in Rochester, for medical treatment, and Cyrus was on the road much of the time.

Her family circle was smaller. Her sister, Sarah Foster, had died at Palmer in 1852. Her other married sister, Emily Condron, was living in Rochester, and Susan may have stayed at the Condron home while taking treatment in that city. Coming and going, Cyrus attended the tenth reunion of his class at Williams, and together they visited Mount Holyoke at anniversary time in 1854 and 1855. His field work took him well over New England, and he mentions towns in upstate New York, from the northern tip to Rochester, where he had spoken or planned to speak. Once he went into the "far West"—inferentially as far as Ohio. Mission House praised him and wanted more. The churches were eager to hear at first hand about the working conditions in Ceylon, and Cyrus, less emotional than most speakers, evidently gave them food for thought. In May 1855 he spoke at Broadway Tabernacle in New York and at Tremont Temple in Boston. Charles Demond, a Williams classmate and then a rising attorney and man of affairs in Boston, wrote to the men of '44 regarding Cyrus and missions: "I heard him deliver the best speech upon this subject which I remember ever to have heard, in Tremont Temple at the Anniversaries." All was going well. Even with his "want of address" he was moving his audiences with a simple, rational force. In another year Susan would be well again. "We hope ere long to return to our chosen field." On August 9, 1855, he wrote to Undersecretary Pomroy, who had praised his work as an agent: "I know people listen to my statements everywhere with interest, but I have regarded it as their interest in Missions, and not in my mode of presenting the cause. But of that, others must judge. The cause, I am sure, is dearer to me than any other cause in the world." The next day the blow fell. Word came from his colleagues in Ceylon that the Deputation had made cataclysmic changes affecting Batticotta.

Of the heated and vociferous war that grew out of the Deputation's visit, a very little may suffice here to show how the future of Cyrus and Susan Mills was changed by that affair. In 1854 the Prudential Committee, deciding at last that it were well for some of the general staff to view the coral strands and sunny fountains of the remote terrains, appointed Augustus C. Thompson and Secretary Anderson to that duty. They were to visit India and Ceylon, and then the more accessible of the missions in the eastern Mediterranean countries. They went by steamer, via England, and began their inspection on the Bombay side. The purpose was well meant, and the final results of that visit were salutary. The Board needed to have its abundant good intentions shocked and alkalized by reality. The weary men in the field needed to shed their decorum and find a cure for lost effort. And mission supporters at home needed to stiffen sentiment with common sense, and study how to do good to alien peoples. The final results were wholesome; the immediate as upsetting as a row at a love feast.

The Deputation met each mission group in turn for a conference lasting usually three weeks. They began at Ahmednugger in December 1854 and reached Ceylon the next April. They brought with them an agenda which was practically uniform for all the Indian missions: teaching versus preaching, English versus the local tongue, health and health vacations, finance and accounting and budgets, physical properties and architecture (including termites), caste and polygamy and intermarriage between converts and heathen, printing, censorship, further extension of the lines, the acceptance or rejection of British government aid—these and many others; twenty-one points in all. (The nice question whether wine for the mission infirmary was a legitimate budget charge, and whether it could be considered medicinal unless made unpalatable, was not one of the points, but was gravely considered as a footnote in the Ceylon agendum.) Each point was assigned to a committee, and in a back-bending effort toward disinterestedness, committees on touchy subjects were "chaired" by whatever brothers knew least about the matter—or so it seems. Then for three sultry weeks there were two general sessions daily, each lasting from three to four hours; and between whiles, committees labored timidly or bravely, and each brother had much ado to keep up with his committee assignments. (One poor man at Ahmednugger was on eleven committees.) And the wives looked on and listened, and carried the tune in the hymns, but no woman spoke—not in public. At best, some committee reports could only be innocuous; many of them clarified an issue and pointed to better practices—for example, the conclusion that it were better to take a vacation before breaking down. But at least two committees dealt with explosive subjects. It would be sheer prejudice to attribute all the good sense to either the Deputation or the missionaries, and indeed the latter were not unanimous on many subjects. But clearly, the Deputation had brought its conclusions from Boston, and those prejudged conclusions were apparent in Secretary Anderson's presentation of the agenda. For better or for worse, the ultimate findings of almost every committee were forecast in the very wording of the subject.

The touchiest subjects were: teaching versus preaching, and the type and methods of education in the mission schools; and the two were so interknit as to be well nigh inseparable. The Deputation, backed (or so it believed) by a considerable opinion at home, held that education beyond the training of native preachers was not proper missionary work. Batticotta and the seminary in the Bombay Mission should be turned into preacher-training schools and should give instruction only by medium of the local vernacular tongues. Education for any other purpose was a luxury, and the use of English in teaching was a handicap upon evangelization. Though Dr. Green's little medical school was not slated as a topic, the Deputation was not ready to admit that the training of native doctors, either, was any part of the Lord's work; in any case, if such training were continued, it too should be only through the Tamil tongue. (In earlier correspondence, the Prudential Committee had implied some blame to Dr. Green's predecessor because, though busy healing the sick, he had not learned Tamil well enough to preach directly.)

There is no record of what the missionaries said in these conferences. But in all the letters, from the middle 1840's down to the Deputation's visit, I have found no instance where any missionary spoke out against education as a legitimate part of missionary effort. One man on the mainland did not like Batticotta—but on grounds so personal as to have no bearing upon the principle; and one man in Ceylon doubted the use of teaching science: it saved no souls. The Ceylon men agreed that the Batticotta post was a hard one. If for themselves they preferred preaching, still no man had previously expressed any sympathy with revolutionary changes. Meigs, Poor, and Spaulding, who could outpreach all the rest, had been whole and positive in their defense of a liberal education. Meigs had written that the charge that the mission schools had failed to produce converts would lie with equal force against preaching the gospel directly. Spaulding had pleaded—not for two men at Batticotta, but four, and even more than four—make it a real college, as good in its field as Amherst or Bowdoin or Dartmouth, and it would transform Ceylon.

> *Two-thirds of our whole number might be engaged with Batticotta Seminary alone . . . In reference to Preaching versus Teaching, no man can tell where the one begins nor where the other ends . . . The warp & woof must go together. It is God's web . . . If schools and education in Jaffna . . . have been a failure, simple preaching of the gospel among the people has been a much more marked failure.*

Several men had urged the practical argument that the native youths were so insistent upon getting English that they would turn to other schools if denied at Batticotta; and to the objection that the Seminary was now appealing to well-to-do families, the Ceylon men had remarked that converts from such a group were more likely to be genuine, not rice Christians.

(The Deputation, for all its disesteem of education, could not well do much about the girls' school at Oodooville, which was really a house of refuge to save little Tamil girls from child marriages. The Mission had bravely tried—not always successfully—to prevent parent-bargained matches

with heathen husbands. But many of the young ones were poor, and even
Christian husbands were reluctant to take them without dowry. India being
no field for career women, they were saved but wholly dependent, and the
Prudential Committee had to consider the budget. One missionary [not Levi
Spaulding] blurted out that admission to the school would have to be limited
to the demands of the marriage market—a good-Gobbo logic: "We were
Christians enow before, e'en as many as could well live one by another.")

This had been the cumulative opinion of the missionaries before the Deputation came. But the Ceylon conference voted to close Batticotta Seminary,
with an indefinite intention to reopen it at some future date as a Bible school.

The report of the conference was drawn up by the deputies as they moved
on to the next scene, and was hurried to print. It contained the usual minutes,
the agenda as presented by Dr. Anderson, the committee's findings, and a
brief summary of the discussions as remembered by the deputies. Like the reports of the four other Indian conferences, it bore the printed injunction: "For
private use only." It presented a happy picture of brotherly accord; one
incident that especially touched the hearts of the deputies was the ordaining
of one native preacher—the first in the Mission. In their report the deputies
spoke of their good fortune in having so timed their visit as to escape the worst
heat, and were thankful that a kind Providence had caused the cholera and
smallpox to subside around Jaffna just before their arrival, noting with regret
that, only a week earlier, Brother Daniel Poor had been removed by cholera
from his earthly labors.

The Ceylon report had not reached America by August 10, but letters
from at least nine persons in that Mission did arrive by that date or very
shortly after. Besides, the printed reports of the earlier conferences at Ahmednugger and Madura had reached the States. It is not clear what persons were
supposed to receive them, nor why they were marked "For private use only."
They did not remain private very long; and by the time the printed report on
the Ceylon conference came in, the kettle was boiling over. Clearly, the Prudential Committee had sadly miscalculated public opinion; the volume of
outspoken opposition was greater than the gentlemen had foreseen. With
canny understanding the critics picked out the vulnerable points. Why were
the printed reports for private use only? Had not all supporters of missions
an interest in the case? Had not some degree of coercion been used? Else,
why this sudden and all but total reversal of opinion by the missions? And
why all these letters of protest and disclaimer from the men and women in
the field? What had really happened at the Ceylon conference?

The Deputation itself was not to be reached. Brother Thompson was on his way home; six months of dhonis and oxcarts and weather and conferences had been too much for him. And Dr. Anderson was riding saddle horses over unimagined mountain trails in Syria; two weeks in the saddle, on his visit to Aintab, gave him a fundamental basis for sensitive reflection. Upon the undersecretaries in Mission House the storm broke. The *New York Observer*, the *Independent*, the *Traveller*, the *Puritan Recorder*, all asked searching questions. Returned missionaries were besought for facts and opinions. Ebenezer Burgess, Henry R. Hoisington, Samuel Hutchings (who ranked with the ablest in his mastery of Tamil), all were outspoken against the methods of the deputation and especially against abolishing the seminaries; and incoming letters soon made it clear that many able men in the field—Miron Winslow, Benjamin Meigs, Levi Spaulding—were not satisfied. Edwin Poor, son of Daniel, led the laymen's attack. Reared in Ceylon and sent to college in the States, he had few illusions about the problem, and many persons felt that through him a hitherto silent group—the families of missionaries—found articulate voice. At the annual meeting of the Board in October 1855 controversy became so strenuous that a special meeting was set for the following March, at Albany. At that meeting the deputies presented a lengthy printed summary of all the conferences—not, this time, for private use—justifying their actions. When the clamor grew that this summary still lacked complete frankness, what was called a second edition (though really a new summary) was issued; it quoted considerably, but still guardedly, from hitherto repressed objections by missionaries in the field. Rufus Anderson was greatly hurt. He took the defection of Edwin Poor especially to heart. He had advised that young man through college, and now felt that his dissent amounted to personal ingratitude.

How did all this affect Cyrus and Susan Mills? Humanly enough, they felt crushed. All the work they had done at Batticotta was now officially voted to be "not proper missionary work." They had been assigned to do that very work; Susan's sickness had been a handicap, and their colleagues had agreed that the burden was excessive; but now it appeared that the Prudential Committee did not really believe in the very thing it had assigned them to do. Both of them were conservative by nature, and authority was authority; but six years of hard experience had made them impatient of pleasant varnish: what were the facts about the Ceylon conference? Upon receiving the first word from his colleagues, Cyrus wrote to Mission House, suggesting that his speaking dates be cancelled. (Most of his letters for this period were addressed to S. L. Pomroy, an undersecretary who lacked Rufus Anderson's persuasive finesse.)

With our present views and convictions of duty J cannot refrain from speaking out freely and boldly to pastors and others whom J may meet, in regard to these things. J regard many of the proposed changes as unwise and injurious. Why they should be forced on the Mission J do not understand. J am sure there is no public sentiment in the churches or among the pastors requiring it. When questioned hitherto about these doings, as J often am, J could say J do not know. Now J do know . . . and J am compelled to speak. The cause of Christ and my position as a missionary demand it. J wish J could look more favorably upon the matter, for it is very painful to be placed in antagonism to the Board or any of its officers . . .

But with my present feelings it seems to me you would not wish to send me about among the churches. If you do, J wish it to be with this distinct understanding, that J am under no restrictions. J shall speak freely on all proper occasions of the course pursued by the Deputation. J shall do it on the ground that the Board, the officers of the Society and the missionaries are all agents of the Christian public and as such responsible to them primarily.

Pomroy's answer is not in the files; it may be inferred from Cyrus' next letter.

J have no intention of "making war on the Board or Deputation," or of trying to nullify their doings. But J do not approve of the course pursued by the Deputation, and J cannot pledge myself to silence . . . J could not act conscientiously on your suggestion and say to the questioner, "J can judge better when J see the reports of the Deputation." J have read reports from nine members of the Mission, some of them very full. J have seen the whole docket of subjects discussed and presume J am informed as to every change of any importance and generally the main reasons for making it . . . Those who sustain missions have a right to know what has been done . . . My conviction of duty is just this: when asked for information, to give it frankly and candidly, neither to seek nor avoid occasions of expressing my convictions.

Those private reports from nine members of the Mission being lost or past recovery, we can only infer their tenor from other letters in the files, most of them written in 1856. Levi Spaulding took decided exception to the Secretary's claim that Daniel Poor ever opposed teaching. "Mr. Poor never dreamed of reducing Batticotta, but was always for sustaining it." "I would advise the entire ignoring of the 21 reports." Upon the sore question, what degree of pressure the Deputation had used, he held that it had "exerted tremendous influence—if not dictatorial authority—upon the minds of the younger missionaries." Upon this same point, Benjamin Meigs wrote:

> *I feel bound to say distinctly that I have seen nothing in this report or letter which indicates the amount of influence which they [the Deputation] had in the formation of these reports. They are said to be the reports of the Mission, & so in a certain sense they are. For they were passed, some unanimously & the rest by a majority of the Mission. But they were certainly shaped and altered and molded so as to meet in almost every respect the views and wishes of the Deputation.*

> *They [the Deputation] were clothed with almost unlimited authority. This I felt to the ends of my fingers . . . They also stated in what measures we should be sustained and in what measures not. These statements had great influence on my mind at the time . . . The diversity of views with respect to missions is much greater than I had been led to suppose, judging from the statements of the Deputation.*

It was being said in America that Secretary Anderson had even threatened the missionaries with stoppage of their salaries. At the Albany meeting, in March 1856, he was sure that he had made no such remark. But Benjamin Meigs reminded him:

> *The expression which you used was in substance as follows: "One means that we have of controlling missionaries is to stop their salaries." Had the remark been made only once, the impression would not have been so deep in my mind. But according to the best of my recollection, you stated this on three different occasions . . . What you said upon this subject was conversed upon by two of the Brethren and two of the Sisters soon after they were made.*

A spade is a spade; but charitable Brother Meigs could not bear to hurt the Secretary's feelings, and he promptly unspaded himself:

> *After reading a report of your remarks at Albany on this subject, two things are very clear to my mind. 1)That you had forgotten what you did say upon this subject while with us. 2) That you did not intend to make any application of them to us.*

But his unspading left a blame upon Mrs. Mills. He had written to her an unsparing criticism of the Deputation. She had sent his letter to the *Independent*, which had printed a part of it; and in the heated debate at Albany, Edwin Poor had used that letter with telling effect. Brother Meigs could not disavow the letter, and he still avowed its sentiments; but he protested that it was private. He had swept the room; but Mary Lyon would have held that it is not good housekeeping to hide the sweepings under the rug. It was the old battle between decorum and plain speech. But many persons on both sides were beginning to deplore the injury to the cause of the missions. Cyrus Mills wrote to Pomroy: "It is sad that we all have so much of the alloy and that it mars so much that is good, and divides the councils and paralyzes the efforts of those who should act together." The younger Ceylon men began to recede from their own boldness. The Deputation had persuaded them to repeal their own self-imposed rule of censorship; now paradoxically that was the one change that some of them regretted. None of them, it would appear, was capable of writing such an unsparing analysis as the Scudder brothers, in Arcot, had jointly addressed to the Prudential Committee on another occasion. And so, in the set-to between decorum and plain speech, decorum won. In after years both the Board and the missions managed things better. But the officers of the Prudential Committee could not forget that certain men had challenged them upon two sensitive points: a use of magisterial methods and a certain want of honesty. An undersecretary put into the files the memorandum that Burgess, Hutchings, and Mills had made trouble. "Mills has said and done more than anybody else."

From September 1855 through the following March Cyrus lived at Williamstown, and Mrs. Mills joined him there early in the winter. He supplied a few near-by pulpits. It was good to be back where everything had once been so clear; good to be near the Hopkins brothers. This was Susan's first opportunity to know Mark Hopkins well. Characteristically, she adopted him. And Mark Hopkins still believed in Cyrus. This was not wishful thinking on Cyrus' part: Mark Hopkins still believed in him—more than ever.

On March 8, 1856, he resigned as a missionary. The doctors agreed that Mrs. Mills could never safely return to Ceylon. His resignation was not forced by Mission House, nor does it appear that the Prudential Committee would have refused to send him back to the field. Some one in Mission House suggested that he return alone, but he would not hear to that. In his resignation Cyrus opened his heart a little to Assistant-Secretary Treat, for Mr. Treat had been good to them; and Susan added a page. She was brokenhearted; they had so loved their work in Ceylon—all the hopes and dreams—"and then to keep my husband from a work he so long ago consecrated himself to." She was still very frail and deeply shadowed. This looked like utter defeat.

Cyrus had to ask the Prudential Committee to extend his pittance of thirty-odd dollars a month until May, until he could find something to do.

For three months later in the year he supplied the pulpit at Southbridge, Massachusetts. Through 1857 he was "stated supply" at Berkshire, New York, and the next year at Richford—villages between Binghamton and Ithaca. His own health was not good; the years in Ceylon were beginning to catch up with him. A seed was growing in his mind: a distrust of opinionated management, a desire for independence. Henceforth he would have a clearer understanding of what executives meant. In 1859 they returned to Ware, and Cyrus entered some kind of business, the nature of which I cannot learn. He was forty, and rated something of a failure. "If there be any rational prospect . . . My clear and full conviction of duty . . ." It would be terribly sentimental, no doubt, but true to add that he also believed, "The heart of her husband doth safely trust in her."

Batticotta remained closed for a few years, during which time the Tamil boys learned English from a Tamil teacher, formerly a Batticotta man, who opened a private school in Jaffna—an enterprise which the Mission appeared to regard as unorthodox. Later the seminary was reopened as a Bible school; in time it was fully restored and become a liberal college. Its degree is now accepted by Calcutta University.

A by-play of the correspondence during 1856 reveals the odd fact that the guiding minds in Mission House were opposed, if not to abolition, at least to Abolitionists, and held William Lloyd Garrison anathema. Negroes in Africa were souls to be saved; in America . . .

The Mills were not forgotten in Ceylon. A Batticotta boy who chose or was assigned the name of Cyrus T. Mills graduated in Dr. Green's medical school. Long after the Mills were established in California he continued to write to them and sent photographs, one of his class, and later one of his family. There was a decent pride in the man, and a sense of gratitude.

ten

PUNAHOU

IN MARCH 1856 WHEN SUSAN MILLS ADDED HER SORROWFUL postscript to her husband's resignation as a missionary, she was deeply despondent; her illness had caused him to fail—or so she believed, and the ways of Providence were mysterious. Soon after she entered the scene at Honolulu in the autumn of 1860 she moved with confident energy, an air of assured leadership. Was this abrupt change due altogether to Hawaiian climate? Hardly—good as that may be. Or to the fortunate turn of finding herself a member of a company whose goodness was not too sorely strained by habitual defeat? Somehow a majority of the Hawaiian Mission had discovered that the will of the Lord may express itself in a variety of lively human activities, not geared to bewildered and tearful resignation. Or it may be that in those fallow years at Berkshire and Ware she had reached an understanding of religion. Eternity, the Last Judgment, could safely be left to God; the nearer human concern lay in feeding hungry students well, teaching them beyond the textbook, and learning a world of new things from them. The tempo of life was quickened. In India, an oxcart creaked toward the Pulneys; in the Islands, she rode a spirited horse, racing along the roads

133

and trails. No safe "missionary horse" for her; she plumb envied her school-boys who came tearing in from the gate to the school building with their horses on the dead run, and they in turn admired her daring. And though the Hawaiian period brought no such dramatic change to Cyrus Mills, it did help him to discover something he could do better than most men.

In the summer of 1859 William Patterson Alexander, one of the many strong men in the Sandwich Islands Mission, came to the States to raise endowment for the growing preparatory school and almost-college which the missionaries had established for their children, and to select a new president for it. Punahou School was founded in 1841. In 1857 its name was changed to Oahu College, but it continued to be Punahou by affectionate usage. The trustees usually called it by the more familiar name; and Mrs. Mills, in after years, preferred that name, Puna-hou—"the new, the never-failing spring." The school was controlled by a local board of trustees, most but not all of whom were missionaries; two were appointed by the Royal Government as a condition of certain land grants, and two or more were secular men. Because the American Board had given and still (in 1859) continued to give some money to the school, the Prudential Committee in Boston was allowed an advisory function. (The ambitious title, Oahu College, was fixed upon the little school by the Boston gentlemen; they thought it would make a more impressive appeal in the endowment campaign.) But control lay with the Island men, through an Island charter, and was legally and factually independent of the American Board.

William P. Alexander had been in the Islands for twenty-seven years. Eminent among the able men in that remarkable mission, he had resigned as a servant of the American Board in 1850, but had continued as teacher in a mission school not under the American Board's control, and as minister of an independent church. Characteristically he went about his business of selecting a new president for Punahou by going for advice directly to Mark Hopkins, though he himself was not a Williams man. But during the forty years of the Mission's existence several Williams men had been leaders in the work. Amherst and Yale had each sent more men into that field, but in the late '50's sons of the missionaries were showing a marked preference for Williams. Mark Hopkins first recommended a professor in New York University who, declining, nominated another professor, but Mr. Alexander decided that the substitute was *not* the man. (The italics are Mr. Alexander's —not belligerent nor emotional, merely independent.) However, Mark Hopkins also highly recommended Cyrus Mills, and Brother Alexander visited Ware, talked with Cyrus, and liked him. "A very *plain* man," he wrote, "one I think that will improve on acquaintance." He too noted that in bodily presence Cyrus was like St. Paul. After that visit he broached the subject with Dr. Rufus Anderson of the American Board.

The busy Secretary was once more on a touchy spot. He deprecated Alexander's going ahead in the matter without first consulting him, yet an inner prompting cautioned him against being too peremptory with the Island man. Some years earlier, Brother Alexander had joined a number of his colleagues in opposing certain policies of the Prudential Committee, especially the rule that forbade missionaries to own land or to piece out their wretched salaries by honest "secular" employment. A good preacher and teacher, Mr. Alexander was a land surveyor by avocation, and had used his vacation days to earn a little money toward schooling his children. Surveying was sorely needed, but Mission House ruled that it was "secular" and therefore improper. The Committee had to rescind that rule, for the Island men had the habit of standing by one another; once when the Prudential Committee cut off the salary of an honest dissenter, Jonathan Green, his colleagues had shared their pittance with him and he had continued to preach, independently of the Board. And so in the present instance Dr. Anderson could only remind Brother Alexander of the unhappy battle of the Deputation; he doubted Cyrus's health; he doubted his views on education. Mr. Alexander was courteous, even charitable, but not willowy. He had supposed—and still supposed—that Mark Hopkins was a capable judge. He himself was well impressed by Cyrus Mills and was taken by the extraordinary qualities of his wife. This was his apology.

The four-cornered correspondence that followed is revealing. Brother Alexander was diplomatic but not vague; he could be pleasant without blurring a plain Euclidian honesty. Even in the soft Hawaiian tongue the trigonometry which he had translated did not fudge. He now continued to sound out other men (including one of the Hallocks) for their opinions of plain Cyrus. From Honolulu his colleague, Richard Armstrong, kept him posted; the trustees needed to be considerate of "our friends in Pemberton Square" (Rufus Anderson and the Prudential Committee), but after all they had their own responsibility for Punahou School. They had no mind to sell a gilded nutmeg to any man; they wanted the candidate to understand that the school was little and poor, a college only in hopes, and needed a leader not too proud to turn his hand to spade work. From his corner, Cyrus Mills wanted no repetition of Batticotta. He took six months to make up his mind, and he requested that all the conditions be clearly stated in writing. Secretary Anderson had to balance deftly:

As it is now, if I make objection, it brings up a host of memories, & puts men in an unpleasant, & perhaps a false, position. Mr. M. would feel, if he should not receive the appointment, that it is all owing to me . . . His only way of regaining my confidence is, by the frankest possible statement of his position on the principles which are likely to come into controversy, as to the evangelical training & employment of natives in the work of the Lord in the Pacific.

Since Punahou was for Mission children and not for natives, and was intended for a liberal education and not for training missionaries, the good Secretary's point appears a fixed idea. He adverted once more to Cyrus' "not having sufficient address." Evidently Cyrus had no inkling of the hostile current in Mission House, for he kept Anderson informed of the proceedings as if valuing his judgment. Having acted fairly in the battle of the Deputation, why should he consider himself a marked man? It is equally clear that if William P. Alexander had wavered or been cunningly acquiescent, Mills would have been dropped. But Dr. Anderson conceded, "After all, Mr. M. *may be* the man." In February 1860 it was settled that Mr. Mills and his wife should take charge of Punahou as soon as he could satisfactorily dispose of his business in Ware.

They left Ware late in August or early in September, and sailed from New York to Aspinwall, their first ocean voyage by steamer. From Panama they took the steamer *Golden Age,* Captain Whiting; this lap of the journey brought excitement, for the *Golden Age* picked up the disabled *John L. Phillips* near Acapulco and towed her to San Francisco, arriving on October 6. There is a fairly well-authenticated tradition that the other passengers on the *Golden Age* noticed the brisk and perky-curled small lady who had so obviously set her cap to catch the shy little minister. Quite a comedy—until the audience was let down by discovering that the flirtatious couple had been married for twelve years. They may have been tipped off by Charles Judd and his bride, who had become acquainted with the Mills early on the voyage. He was the son of that Dr. Gerrit P. Judd who had left his work as medical missionary to become adviser and later foreign secretary in the government of Hawaii; and Charles Judd's wife was a Mount Holyoke girl, one year out of seminary. Cyrus and Susan were beginning to learn how warm and lasting those Island friendships could be. The Mills and Judds had three days in San Francisco. If they went to church on October 7 they had a choice of hearing the Reverend Edward G. Beckwith, late president of Punahou; he came down from Sacramento to supply the pulpits of the First Congregational Church in the morning and the First Baptist in the evening. If instead they visited the race track they saw the crown prince of Hawaii, who, in that very week end, was making a cultural survey of the city and taking a drive to San Jose by four-in-hand. The *Alta Californian* paid rather more attention to the prince than to Cyrus and Susan. On October 9 they and the Judds sailed on the clipper bark *Comet*, Captain Scott, and reached Honolulu on October 26. There for the first day or two they were guests of Eli Corwin (Williams '48 and U.T.S. '51), pastor of the Fort Street Church and acting president of Punahou.

At best, the Ceylon experience had depressed them with numb fatigue, meager returns, and baffling unresponsiveness. In the Islands the feeling was quite the other way. There had been some failures, but the dominant chord sounded the vitality and versatility of that Mission. Here more than in any other field under the American Board that dream which began in the Haystack Prayermeeting almost came true: virtually an entire people were converted in one generation. In the Islands the pioneers found a fertile seedbed for gospel simplicity—a people naïve and generous, primitive and emotional, sensual but more warmly receptive than tired India. Their very fears were near to nature, and they had a remarkable love of music and beauty. Parable and story seemed just made for them. And conversion was reciprocal; in a less friendly field the missionaries might have continued as spiritual aliens, but if they began with any such tendency the Islands surprised them out of themselves. It is not a trivial circumstance that the missionaries quickly adopted so many words and idioms from the musical native tongue, and felt the wild power and beauty of natural phenomena more than they would have done in America.

Those pioneers left a generous shelf of histories and biographies, diaries and letters, which their descendants have enriched with filial impartiality, each modern biographer writing as though his grandparents had been related by blood to all the company who called each other Brother and Sister; and indeed intermarriages between the mission families have interwoven a cousinly pattern almost like that of the fourth generation in Dorchester, and an outsider who would disparage Father Thurston or Father Bond would have all the Judds and Alexanders and Baldwins and Gulicks and Damons and Cookes and Emersons down on his shamed head. With a devotion happier than piety the Hawaiian Mission Children's Society has gathered an excellent source library, and has published, among other things, a biographical album of the hundred and eighty-odd men and women who were members of that Mission: ministers, doctors, teachers, printers and bookbinders, and business agents. Here you have the catalogue of the Twelve Companies that came out between 1820 and 1848, and of the ships that brought them around the Horn: the brig *Thaddeus*, the whaler *Averick*, the bark *Mary Frazier*, the *Sarah Abigail*, and eight more, with their tally of days (116 to 244) and their tonnage, and the kindness or meanness of the captain. With a sort of David-to-Goliath cockiness the *Thaddeus*, first and smallest of the twelve, got not only her tonnage into the record but her length and beam—to the half-inch. She was 85′5½″ long—and proud of it. That spunky last half-inch is important. For the pioneers and their children had to be sea-minded. If there had been dhonis on that ocean, boys of the second generation would have mastered and improved them.

Here you have also the twenty-one mission stations on the five islands, confusing to an outsider but musical and vivid to the Mission Children, each station needing a volume to tell its story. A book which tempts to other books. Best of all, it has pictures of most pioneers: daguerreotypes and photographs, some dim and rigid, some transparent with character; and early portraits, four couples having been painted by S. F. B. Morse, and a score of others by that uneven artist, Pictor Ignotus, whose work is sometimes hard to distinguish from the flat amateurism of his pupils. But the Pictor Ignotus who portrayed Henry Dimond, the bookbinder, deserves identifying, for he gave us a gentleman worthy of Stuart's brush. And Morse's portrait of Sybil Mosely Bingham sets the imagination toiling at the stone wall she built at Punahou— delicacy and stone. Reuben Tinker and Titus Coan might well be senatorial contemporaries of Andrew Jackson, and Sereno Bishop and Hiram Bingham II youthful understudies of Daniel Webster, supposing that Daniel ever caught the passionate fire of Isaiah. And the modernist who would raze the written troubles of the brain would do wisely to pass the psychiatrist by and take treatment instead from the pictures of Dwight and Charlotte Baldwin and compassionate Mary Alexander, and finally submit his real and fancied wrongs to Asa Thurston.

This cannot be a history of that Mission, but as the ripening work of that able company affected the lives of Cyrus and Susan Mills, some of the achievements of those men and women need to be noticed. As translators they were versatile and prolific. To name them by seniority of service: Hiram Bingham I and Asa Thurston, Artemas Bishop and William Richards (a Plainfield boy and Williams man), Lorrin Andrews, Ephraim W. Clark, Jonathan Green and Sheldon Dibble completed by 1839 a translation of the Bible, which was printed on the mission press and bound by Henry Dimond. They compiled and translated a grand shelf of lexicons and grammars and school texts; Lorrin Andrews wrote or translated eleven, Richards four, Dibble eight, and Artemas Bishop five (including *Pilgrim's Progress*). Samuel Whitney, Ephraim Clark, Jonathan Green, William P. Alexander, Richard Armstrong, and John Emerson added their quota of books upon science and history and mathematics. Moral didacticism was not the sole aim. This was a teaching mission, with faith in knowledge and technical skills. Many of these men developed that degree of observation where the amateur naturalist approaches and becomes the scientist—an intelligent interest, not content with merely accepting the first chapter of Genesis. Titus Coan, witnessing great volcanic eruptions, almost became a John Muir; and many boys of the second generation became youthful but respected authorities on ferns and crustaceans and vulcanology. Even before he went to college young John Gulick had collected fifty species of one genus of land shell animals, and had discovered a law of their distribution that modified the theory of evolution. The avocations of these mission folk were not drowsy; they wrote and drew and engraved, and at least one man painted good landscapes. Lorenzo Lyons, of the Fifth Company, by his sheer eloquence did almost as much as the translators to establish Hawaiian as a written language, and his joy overflowed in his lyric poetry. The children were avid for music. Boys schemed and bargained with ships' crews to buy or barter for flutes and accordions; and I like the story of how Mrs. David B. Lyman contrived homemade instruments for her school band of native boys, and did so well that a visiting sea captain presented them with an outfit of real horns and drums. That would not have happened in Ceylon.

Best of all, several of these men made themselves so useful to the native kings and princes that they became a power in government. The Mission early established a school for young chiefs. Dr. Gerrit P. Judd advanced through various advisory offices to become secretary of state and the real director of government relations during a period when France and England each had a mind toward taking the Islands. William Richards became an adviser to the government, went on one embassy to England, and was minister of public instruction. After his death he was succeeded by Richard Armstrong. Lorrin Andrews, one of the ablest scholars, became a justice of the Supreme Court. (It denotes the healthy independence of these men that Andrews, Jonathan Green, and Dr. Thomas Lafon all resigned from the Mission in protest against the American Board's failure to take a more pronounced stand against slavery.) These men and their colleagues codified the Islands laws, established courts, and made a constitution; and in so doing they refrained from imposing a purely American form, but rather made a wise combination of their own inherited ideas with native laws and customs and needs. Small though the kingdom was, these affairs were not a matter of comic opera; the power behind the throne was the intelligence and spirit of the Mission men, and theirs was the influence that eventually made the Islands eager to join with the United States.

It was men of this caliber whom Cyrus and Susan Mills came to know. Of those named, Richards and Dibble and Whitney had died some years before 1860, and Armstrong died a few weeks before the Mills arrived. Hiram Bingham I and Dr. Lafon had returned to the States. There had been some failures in health, and some cases of incompatability, though not so many as in India; but all in all the Mission was remarkable for the endurance of its members. In the final record, long after the Mills returned to California, we find men and women who served fifty years and upward and whose old age seems to have been only a prolonged Indian summer. David Lyman (a Williams man) served fifty-two years at Hilo, Lorenzo Lyons fifty-four years at Waimea, and lovable Elias Bond fifty-five years at Kohala—all on Hawaii; until, in the course of peaceful time, the mission and the man, the buildings he built, the fruitful landscape, the outlook on mountain and sea, and even the ways of the weather, all were spiritualized as one in the memory of the younger generation.

Amid all this activity Punahou School had grown out of a need common in most missions: parents absorbed in mission work found themselves unable to teach their own children well, yet could ill afford to send them to the States. The long voyage around the Horn, years of separation, anxiety of parents and heartache of children, fill many a remembered story. More than one mission family resigned rather than accept those conditions. Those who stayed believed they should meet the educational needs of their own children as well as they were providing, in many schools, for the natives. The American board was conservative on this point, the Island men more self-reliant.

The story of the Punahou land involves a native queen who was more like Queen Bess than like Queen Victoria, and a technicolor princess with her handsome but amoral husband; it involves also certain social reforms, many caprices, and a speculation in sandalwood—the telling of which had better be left to sober scholars. Briefly, in 1829 Queen Kaahumanu, who greatly liked the first Binghams, gave them some 224 acres of land two miles east of the village of Honolulu. There they built an adobe cottage; and, the land being pasturage commons for the mission livestock, they fenced their taro and cane patch with a stone wall. (It was a part of this wall that Sybil Mosely Bingham laid with her own hands, and it was by this wall that she planted the night-blooming cereus which has now become a hedge that excites awe

The President's rooms,
Mills College, about 1893.

142

Anna L. Sawyer

Fannie A. Madison

Rose porch in the 'nineties

Susan Mills
and "white angora"

Dr. Mariana Bertola

Giuseppe Cadenasso

Barney Barry

Michael Herlihy

146

Susan Tolman Mills and Luella Clay Carson, 1910.

Hettie Belle Ege

Persis Thurston Taylor

Eighthieth birthday letter, to
Mrs. Mills, 1905, from the
long-time cook, Yep Wo.

Mills College Nov. 17. 1905
My Dear Friend
Mrs S. L. Mills
I am Thankful that Yours So
Kindness and Treato Me Farithe
alway for I am Never forget
but Now I wish Yous
to joy Happiness Many More
as today and Hope God
Will Bless Yous Enjoy
and Comfortable for Ever
Yours Faritiful
Friend
Yep Wo

The Richardson portrait

and wonder, even in that land of flowers.) Later, because a rule of the American Board forbade missionaries to accept such gifts, the Binghams (with other colleagues who had received similar grants from Island chiefs) gave the land to the Mission. When the Binghams returned to the States in 1840 this Punahou land was chosen as a site for the school. In May 1841 the ship *Gloucester* arrived, bearing the Ninth Company—only four couples, but they assayed high: Elias Bond, Daniel Dole, John D. Paris, William H. Rice, and their wives. Bond and Dole had been fellow students at Bowdoin, and Paris had been with them through Bangor Theological Seminary. Rice was a teacher, never ordained as a minister. He and Paris had been designated for the Oregon Mission by way of Honolulu, but unrest among the Oregon Indians led the Board to keep them in the Islands. Daniel Dole, "tall and slender, with a dark complexion setting off his grave but kindly features, a good classical scholar, and fond of books," was made the first principal of the new school; and after three years at another station, William Rice became his assistant.

Except for the brave but limited work of the Binghams, the school had to be built and planted from the ground up, without architect and contractor and hired artisans. The Mission men drew plans and found materials; and they and the teachers and students turned a hand at stone and adobe, at rough-hewing timbers and thatching roofs and developing springs and digging ditches and a pool. As with their pioneer ancestors in the States, this was the only way. William H. Rice drove three yoke of oxen to break ground for more vegetable gardens; patrons and students set out vines and fruit trees. A school where no child had ever known other than these home-contrived ways of getting things; there was unconscious beauty in that simplicity. Before Punahou opened, Luther Halsey Gulick, first son of Peter, was sent on a whaler around the Horn to get his schooling in the States. Slight in body and very sensitive, he endured a deep humiliation on his first day at Sunday school. His homemade clothes and rough cobbled shoes and Island hat were so queer—especially the hat. The loquacious superintendent held the hat up for display, talked and talked about it, and called for a collection to buy "our little guest" a more becoming one. In time, Luther Gulick founded missions at Ponape and Ebon in Micronesia, and saw much of the world, from Italy to Japan; but it is recorded by one who knew him well that even in wise old age he still winced from that ineptitude. At Punahou no child could feel either snobbish or inferior. Daniel Dole had a way of spurring them by his stories of superior scholars in America; later, when his Punahou graduates carried off more than their share of honors at Yale and Williams, they perceived the method in his scrupulous avoidance of blarney. Home-cobbled shoes—but more Greek than most American colleges offer today.

At first, admission was limited to children of missionary families; later, some children of businessmen and planters were admitted. The boarding pupils came from Kauai and Molokai and Hawaii, or from distant stations on Oahu; the day students rode over from Honolulu in family wagons or carryall or on horseback. In spite of straitened budget and a supplement of student teachers, the school developed a rare spirit, a wealth of gay traditions and nostalgic memories—things which money can never provide. (Hoeing in the vegetable garden, the boys composed a song or a sort of chanted school yell, on the chopping rhythm of Pun-a-hoe-hoe-hoe.) Then in 1854 Daniel Dole retired to teach and preach at Koloa, and William Rice went into the employ of one of the earliest sugar plantations. They were succeeded by the Beckwith brothers—both Williams men. Edward G. Beckwith had been principal of a private school in Honolulu; his wife, daughter of Richard Armstrong (minister of public instruction), was a Mount Holyoke woman. Beckwith was not a member of the Mission, and was indeed only a layman, though he became ordained after his appointment because custom required the president to be a minister. He and his brother George were inspiring young teachers and did their best to make the school really a college, but ambitious older boys still preferred to go to the States, and the college course existed mostly on paper. The school was closed for ten months in 1857 while Edward Beckwith went to the States and tried to raise endowment—with only moderate success. George Beckwith gave up teaching to become a sugar planter, and in 1859 Edward resigned as president. His wife's health was a reason; besides, he may have despaired of the school's future. Trustees and patrons felt that the home life of the school had lost something of the quality it had enjoyed under the Doles and the Rices. In the interim following Beckwith's resignation, William De Witt Alexander was in charge of the school. Oldest son of William Patterson Alexander, he graduated from Yale in 1855, returned to teach Latin and Greek at Punahou, and married Abigail Baldwin, a Mount Holyoke graduate.

This was the situation when Cyrus and Susan Mills came; the pioneer days of the Mission were past and the leading figures in the drama had already achieved a modest greatness. Approximately half of the men and women who had belonged to the Mission were still in the Islands. How many of them did the Mills know well? Not all of them, certainly. Cyrus and Susan were fully occupied with Punahou, and they were not members of the Mission; at the annual May meetings in Honolulu, which they attended as guests, they could meet most of the families from remote stations, and it is known that they visited the homes of some of their students on other islands*

Of five Williams men who had been in the field before 1860, two were still in the service: David Lyman at Hilo, and Lowell Smith at Honolulu. Nine Mount Holyoke women were in the Islands; Maria Whitney Pogue and Melvina Chapin Rowell dated from Mary Lyon's time. Townsend and Persis Thurston Taylor had gone to California, and Father and Mother Thurston were venerable and friendly. The Mills made their closest friendships with certain families in Honolulu; next with remoter families whose children they taught. Punahou and the children attending it were the lively reality.

And what a connection! Away back in 1833 little Gerrit P. Judd, Jr., being then four and a half, dictated a letter to an aunt in the States:

Mr. and Mrs. Gulick are here in the house. Mr. Bingham has three children, Mr. Gulick three, and we three; three threes make nine. I have a wooden horse, it cannot walk, it has no head. I ride it sometimes. I have a wagon which father made. I have blocks with pictures on them. The carpenter made the blocks, Mr. Rogers printed the pictures and ma pasted them with poi.

Yes, son-man, three threes make nine, and in pioneer families nine nines make eighty-one. In time there were nine Judd children, nine Alexanders, eight Baldwins, ten Armstrongs, ten Bonds, eight Emersons, eight Wilcoxes, seven Rowells, eight Lymans, eight Clarks, ten Castles, seven Cookes; and "Mr. Gulick"—apostolic Peter J. Gulick—had seven sons and one daughter, all of whom became missionaries. The crop whom Cyrus and Susan Mills taught included younger children of the companies that reached the Islands in the 1830's, and from these on down to older children of latecomers; and they taught at least one child of the third generation.

Of the several accounts wherin Punahou boys and girls recalled that day when Brother Corwin drove over from Honolulu bringing President Mills and "his lady," Albert Lyons' story sounds most realistic. When he wrote it he himself was a veteran teacher, a doctor with a Phi Beta Kappa key, and knew the motes that trouble the mind's eye. While Eli Corwin and his carriage were exhibiting climate and scenery, young Albert Lyons and Justin Emer-

* The *Pacific Commercial Advertiser* for June 20, 1861, includes the Mills as passengers on the steamer *Kilauea* for the Windward Islands—Maui and Hawaii; and again in November that year, Mrs. Mills was a passenger with a group of Alexander, Baldwin, and Lyons children—the inference being that she spent a short vacation with some of those families. Again in 1862, while Cyrus was visiting in California, she visited the same islands; and she recorded at least one visit to the Wilcox home on Kauai.

son, being the entire sophomore class and therefore Punahou seniors, were having an adolescent binge of resentment against their Latin teacher. He, good and able man, was too young and sensitive to be inured to the irreverence of students. Distraught with duties, and with important company about to arrive, he was late in entering his classroom. Meanwhile these two youngsters had covered the blackboard with doggerel Latin, yapping indignities. Of course they wanted to enjoy their nervous-breathing wit to the last second. They would erase it when they heard him coming. They did not hear him. He popped in. And soon President Mills entered upon the vortex of a Problem. As Lyons tells it, Cyrus was calm; dry-drawling voice, enough balm for the hurt mind, a maxim or two for abject youth, and a suggestion of proper apologies. (They really had meant to erase the scurrility.) And then the entire student body—two sophomores, two freshmen, and thirty prep children—went to assembly and sang like brown thrushes, and Brother Corwin prayed for Punahou, and God let Harvard and Oxford and the Sorbonne and Padua go their proud ways like eagles in the air while He thought up some nice crumbs of blessing for all the fledgling schools in the world. And during the prayer more than one student stole glances at their new St. Paul–sized president, and noticed that Mrs. Mills looked ever so much like Mrs. Damon—their own Mrs. Damon over on Chaplain Lane—enough like her to be a younger sister. Which was a happy introduction for Susan Mills.

The Mills could have settled in the president's cottage—known officially as The Octagon, surreptitiously as Beckwith's Folly, and morally as a sore trial to ordained husbands who had to lay floor matting; but William De Witt Alexander and his bride were living there; and Cyrus and Susan, blending tact with policy, chose four rooms in the main school building, which was a capital E with the two courts opening upon a grand view of the ocean and Diamond Head. A sizable structure, two hundred feet long and with the three wings in right proportion, it housed dormitory, recitation rooms, dining hall and what not, with a cookhouse in the rear. One corner of the main stem of the E bore the honored name of Dole Hall; the other corner, Rice Hall. The orchard, mainly of figs and bananas, was bearing, some date trees were making up their minds that way, and a certain youthful tamarind tree was well started toward becoming a centenary landmark. Up the slope between the school and the famous Punahou spring was a mud-bottomed pool where the boys swam. Ordinary ablutions were managed by the fetch-and-carry system until Cyrus' Yankee mind devised a water pipe from the spring to the main building, with second-story outlets, and a tap in each court. He had a vision of fountains, but fountains cost money, and a plain tap served to fill the boys' pitchers and an outdoor washbasin; the girls could fill their pitchers without going downstairs. This new refinement was very impressive.

During the Mills' first year, kitchen and dining room were managed by young Warren Chamberlain and his wife; she and two of his sisters were Mount Holyoke women. The Mills and the Chamberlains appear to have got on amiably, but in the second year Cyrus and Susan took over the steward-ship and household management as a matter of economy. He reduced the school's small financial draft upon the American Board; he modestly suggested to the gentlemen in Boston better investments in the Islands, where interest rates were twelve percent. His economies saved for the school an amount equal to half his salary of $1,500; and Susan had the right to feel that she earned her stipend of $450—and board. She taught as though Punahou were Mount Holyoke: Physical Geography ("What a bright class it was!"); Phys-iology, Geology, Chemistry, and Botany; Natural Theology (Paley was happier in the Islands than in Ceylon), and Butler; *Paradise Lost*, and Draw-ing; and—to round out the day—a recreation of Calisthenics. A new wonder, this last, for Punahou girls. The boys had adapted or invented hearty games; now the girls could glide and bend rhythmically, to the very brink of orthodox dancing—but no further. "Presbyterian dancing," someone called it. Two or three girls, day students, really danced at a party in town. Cyrus was shocked; he told them they had crucified Christ anew. Susan seems to have had her doubts about that, for within a few years they would allow and even encourage dancing in their own school. She had the more intuitive sympathy with youth; from the Punahou days henceforth she would lead him to a more kindly liberality. One Christmas at Mount Holyoke she had written approv-ingly in her journal, "I have heard scarcely one 'Merry Christmas' all day." Her severity was but the accustomed Puritan attitude. In 1860 she freed Punahou from that same severity by giving the students their first Christmas tree, with a present for each—not just a trinket; Mary Rice treasured her bracelet of wood from the Mount of Olives. Students and parents soon noticed her knack of attending to many things; decorum in the dining room, flowers on the table, a spell of singing after dinner, prayer meetings not too grimly shadowed by apocalypse, and—best of all—plenty of tasty food. After one of his frequent visits Father Alexander noted: "Mrs. Mills is overdoing herself . . . Yesterday they baked 22 pies, 20 loaves of bread, 4 loaves of cake, & 300 biscuits." And under Susan's direction the student helpers made the school's supply of butter. The author of the last chapter of Proverbs would have approved, as most of the Punahou students did—especially the boys.

The children of Dr. Gerrit P. Judd were grown up, but the Mills developed a neighborliness with the doctor, who, after many years as adviser and member of the government, had resumed medical practice. Though he was sixteen years older than Cyrus they had an opening for talk; both had been born at Paris, Oneida County, and Mrs. Judd's family lived in the vicinity of near-by Clinton. And though Mrs. Mills had less Greek than the Mission translators, she and Dr. Judd had one interest in common:

> *Good Dr. Judd helped me to a spirit lamp, a few test tubes, and flasks. I procured an old retort, made oxygen gas on the kitchen stove with a wash tub for a pneumatic cistern, fruit bottles for receivers, and these I carried on soup plates, with the help of the students, from the kitchen to the farther room in the College building. But we had experiments that illustrated all our subjects with but little expense, but a great deal of labor . . .*

Labor, and one explosion—with no casualties.

Another friendship that lasted through life was that with the Damon family. Samuel C. Damon (Amherst '38) had come to the Islands in 1842, not as a member of any company but as chaplain of the Seamen's Friend Society. He served forty-two years, known and liked by a host of sailors in the whaling and clipper ships; and he founded and edited *The Friend*, which is reputed to be the oldest existing newspaper in the Pacific. His wife, Julia Mills (not related to Cyrus), did indeed look enough like Mrs. Mills to be a sister. Her daguerreotype is elegant with silk dress and best bonnet and black lace mitts. Once Brother Damon came to consult Cyrus in the matter of vocational guidance for young Sam. The father had his heart set on the boy's becoming a minister, but Sam junior didn't like Greek and Latin, and did want very much to go into business. Brother Mills thought this over, then gave his candid judgment: "If you insist upon making Sam a minister I think you will make a poor minister and spoil a good businessman." Cyrus may have been more autobiographical than he realized; in any case, young Sam went into business. Long after Father Damon and his wife died, Susan Mills was still mothering their children; she built Kapiolani cottage on the Mills campus as a guest house for one of their sons.

Were the Mills good teachers? Did the young people like them? They left Punahou in 1864, and no student of theirs in that school is living. (Or so I suppose, though one student died as recently as 1943.) Who are the vanished witnesses, and how revealing is their testimony?

The frequent notices of school affairs in *The Friend* may be considered as mild home-town journalism. Editor Damon reported the public examinations, some of which were held in town: "The Natural Sciences passed in rapid & animated review." "The young ladies have learned not only the theory of breadmaking, but have also been taught a practical application of the chemical principles." Brother Damon was quite taken with the calisthenics: "The music, the grace of motion & the precision of evolution of the young ladies, excited much enthusiasm on the part of the spectators." After one of his frequent visits to the school he lifted his editorial we in praise of the apple-pie order about the premises and the thrifty management of household affairs.

In letters more or less confidential, three trustees— Ephraim W. Clark, Samuel N. Castle, and William P. Alexander—reported the state of the school to Rufus Anderson. All three had children in Punahou and older children in college in the States, and all three had been active friends of the school from its beginning. Clark was an able missionary; Castle, after a lengthy service as business agent for the Mission, had joined Amos Cooke (a former Mission teacher) in a mercantile and banking business. I have found no item of doubt or disparagement regarding Cyrus Mills in their letters, except their regret over his frail health. Father Alexander wrote most often and with more details. The enrollment had doubled in the Mills' second year; and he, who during his long life drew a host of young people to him, praised the friendliness and happiness in the school. Samuel Castle was disappointed because one of his sons could not get enough advanced Greek courses and would have to transfer the sooner to a college in the States, but he placed the blame rightly upon the limited finances of Punahou; the teachers were carrying a heavy load.

And the students? A few of the girls thought Mrs. Mills a prim disciplinarian, and that her habit of entering their rooms promptly after knocking allowed scant time to readjust the conscience. As late as 1922 one man sounded a discordant note: he thought Cyrus was "dull, tedious, stereotyped," and inclined to value a memorized textbook recitation above bold, original reasoning. He felt that the Mills were jealous of the departed Beckwiths' popularity; that Susan was really the president, and that she resented all dissent. Once (he said) when she mispronounced a word and he corrected her she took it with ill grace. He thought she showed favoritism toward certain boys, and named four—his own brother among them. (For what value the fact may have, all four became distinguished men.) On the credit side, he spoke of her great energy and her ability to popularize her subjects. He attributed to her the establishment of science on an equal basis with the classics, and gave her personal credit for having inspired Albert Lyons to become one of the most brilliant alumni. And he admitted that she was a fine horsewoman. Some of his criticisms have a degree of validity. But hearts differ. Long after her Island days, Mrs. Mills characterized this dissenter as "conservative, obliging——full of information and always seeking more, and as ready to impart."

Some years after Mrs. Mills' death, Albert Lyons and Oliver P. Emerson wrote privately about her. Their evidence may have been selective, though there was no occasion for flattery. Albert Lyons—he of the doggerel Latin and the apology—wrote:

> *No one during my years at Punahou School touched so intimately the lives of every one of us, or exerted so profound an influence in giving those lives direction and impetus. Her human limitations only made her more dear.*

Oliver Emerson, notable in a large family of distinguished brothers, told how she quickened his ambition and gave him confidence. He recalled how she helped those Island boys and girls acquire social ease.

> *Sunday evenings her parlors were opened to us all and we were made welcome to join in a social sing . . . She loved to see things go, and when she was around they did go.*

Moreover, at eighty he still remembered her habit of bringing him a big cracker to munch at bedtime when he was feeling hollow after hours of study —"just the thing to send me to bed with a comfortable feeling." One hopes the august court will not exclude those crackers as incompetent, irrelevant, and immaterial. Another bit of evidence, tenuous perhaps but more revealing than formal resolutions: in writing to me about Cyrus and Susan, a woman in the Islands habitually calls them "Uncle and Aunt Mills." They have no relatives in the Islands; her usage is but long-established tradition, instilled in many Island households by mission grandmothers.

But the liveliest evidence remains to be given. In 1891, twenty-seven years after she left the Islands, Mrs. Mills, unable to attend the fiftieth anniversary of the founding of Punahou, wrote a long reminiscence of the students she had taught there. In the intervening years she had many hundreds of students in her own school, but she could still name eighty-three Punahou students, from thirty-seven families. And more than their names: her impromptu roll call brings them to life—face and body and voice, mind and heart; and incidentally she knew what had become of most of them, whom they married, and—in some cases—how many children they had. The letter is too long to quote in full: she remembered such an encompassing variety of things. An old-fashioned heaven still bent very near the earth; death was less gloomy than in her Mount Holyoke and Ceylon days; earth and Punahou and one's lifework were not all lugubrious.

> *Will Gilett—who can forget him with his mischief? With face as sober as can be imagined, he could fill the lamps with water, hide the matches, help himself and others from the store room, and stir things up generally— occasionally getting stirred up himself—but he was a good scholar, and has proved his ability in his calling.*

It was Willie Gilett who was helping her with some of Dr. Judd's chemical apparatus that time the explosion occurred, stirring Willie up and giving him his share of fame.

Sanford Dole, younger son of Daniel, was by native right a Punahou boy, born in the school and nursed by kind Mrs. Rice when his mother died at his birth. In the Mills' time he was tall, one of the older boys, and he resented Mr. Mills' strictures against dancing. Not that he wanted to dance, but he thought the rule rather inconsistent. But by 1891 small resentments were forgotten. Mrs. Mills wrote, "I still keep a copy of the essay he read in Fort Street Church, on *Astronomy*, of which we were all so proud." In 1894 when he was president of the new Hawaiian Republic, he and Mrs. Mills were exchanging letters, gravely earnest over the fate of the Islands. He respected her judgment considerably more than the muffled diplomacy of the United States government, talked neither down nor up to her, but "the word between them was the word of equals." Also he remembered to thank her for the box of apples she had sent him. Not given to dramatics, he did not tell her (but other Island friends did) that the deposed Queen Liliuokalani had vowed that *when* she was restored she intended to have him beheaded. *"That head, my lord?"* Not while any son or daughter or mother of Punahou could help it.

She wrote of Albert Lyons:

> *How many delicate ferns and shells he brought me, and helped me in my ignorance of those so new. Modest as a girl, and especially shy of girls, but strong in intellect and most manly in character, everybody respected him. It was right that he should take the highest honor at Williams. Those faithful sisters of his—Fidelia, rightly named, and Lizzie just as faithful! How many hours we worked together in that old store room making toothsome dishes to satisfy the good appetites, and feeling that we could dignify the humblest work by the spirit we put into it.*

She remembered Henry Baldwin—"earnest, pushing, reliable, and a comfort everywhere." Though she does not tell this, Henry was once called upon by his brethren in the debating society to eject a rowdy intruder, in which assignment he tallied perfectly with all four points she named. And she wondered whether his sister Hattie

> *has ever shown to her children the beautiful maps she drew. I can see her now in her dainty way decorating the parlor, stopping perhaps to put a few flowers at my neck, and leaving behind her the aroma of a sweet nature.*

Of the children of good Elias Bond:

> *Shy, earnest, reliable Cornelius; Ellen, a little blunt, but so very sensible; and Willie—my boy. We who cared for him during that long typhoid fever will never forget how God heard and answered our prayers and gave back to us our youngest—dear Willie Bond. To this day, one variety of rose I never smell without thinking of the little black-eyed, refined and manly boy. For he it was who watched his one rose bush and left each opening bud at my breakfast plate.*

She called the names of four Alexanders—a few lines for each; but the youngest, Charlie Hodge, quite stole her heart away:

> *. . . dear blushing boy that he was! absorbing so much more than he reflected. How full of vigor he was; ready to train a bucking horse, to ride with the fastest, or to lasso with the strongest; and yet those who knew him best found him so gentle and appreciative. I never knew him to come home from the valleys without a wreath of ferns for me. In numberless ways, known only to us two, he ministered to my comfort. A large warm place he had in my heart. His life went out under a shadow, but thank God it was into the sunlight and glory of heaven.*

The young man met his death in an accident while he was managing a ranch, some ten years after his days at Punahou. As an example of the intermarriages of the mission families, his wife was a granddaughter of the Asa Thurstons and the Dwight Baldwins, and his brother, William De Witt Alexander, married a daughter of the Baldwins.

And so the roll call went on, and even the single line or phrase is more than perfunctory: "Albert Wilcox with sober face and self-contained manner"—"scholarly Justin, reticent to all those who did not come near him, but warm-hearted and true as steel to his friends"—"moderate James, old beyond his years"—"beautiful Annie, whose confidence I shared"—"Willie Rice, staunch and reliable like his father"—"Lottie, musical—overflowing like a glass of champagne." Surely that dissenting witness who thought her partial to a few never realized how dear the humble ones were to her heart; over and over again she recalled the "patient," the "painstaking," the ones who were "unobtrusive but with real worth of character." She wondered whether one boy remembered the drawings he had made for a certain composition. She couldn't help feeling sorry that Oliver Emerson had never married: "What a good husband he ought to have been!" (There was still time; he married after 1891, and he was one of the last of her boys left to honor her memory.) She spoke of the Armstrong sisters, whose minds were much upon their brother Samuel. He, with other former Punahou boys, was in the Northern army; later, as General Armstrong, he founded Hampton Institute for the education of Negroes; and he was the chief orator at this same fiftieth anniversary of Punahou. Rereading her letter many times, I noticed how often she remembered singing voices; she was not disconcerted by vivacity, and prized it above conformity; she remembered with intuitive sympathy both physical and spiritual pain in her students; and above all she valued being above achievement. To her there were no nonentities in that little school.

At the fortieth anniversary, in 1881, she had been piqued because the historical sketch of the school mentioned her only as Matron. Being house mother to that brood was something, but had she not taught ten or twelve subjects? In 1891 she recalled that story, but the ruffle of resentment had passed.

The moonlight rides, the picnics in Nuuanu Valley, the merry Christmas, and the commencement days with their following reception. Never was I happier in my teaching, never were students more responsive. Often I have heard Mr. Mills say the same.

In November 1863 King Kamehameha IV died, and the royal house, decaying toward its fall, gave him its modernized conception of a kingly funeral. As a youth he had traveled in Europe and been made much of in England, and the missionaries had tried to make a man of him; but if the tall ghosts of his ancestors attended the lying-in-state they averted their faces from the imitation of Victorian elegance. There were tailored ushers, the corpse wore a colonel's uniform under the traditional royal mantle of costly feathers, the Masonic brethren wore their aprons; and the people knew the king had died of drink. It cleansed the air a little when old John Ii, a prince and very much a man, interrupted the English bishop and his ritual by breaking into an old Hawaiian *me-le*—a ghostly saga-chant of former Island kings. And all this within two miles of Punahou—but if Cyrus and Susan were greatly awed, no record of the fact remains. Later in their homeland they might decide to give a campus tea honoring another king; in any case, they saw no point in losing their own dignity over such a matter.

An important change in the Mission in that same year, though it did not directly concern the Mills, did affect their business affairs and their understanding in after years. The American Board was in financial straits, largely because of the Civil War. Compelled to shorten its lines, it decided that the Hawaiian Mission, by far the most successful, should be put upon its own resources. There were forty churches manned by native pastors, the Hawaiian people had largely evangelized Micronesia, and now it seemed that religion in Hawaii should be self-sustaining. Naturally the Board wanted the able missionaries to continue in the field, and they wanted to continue, but it was unthinkable that their Islanders could support them. It was a real crisis to men who had been in the field from twenty to forty years, both the former regulations and their own literal acceptance of gospel poverty having forbidden them to make money. Now they must make money or starve. They planted sugar, and some of them had larger returns in two years than from a lifetime of missionary work. It is unsafe to generalize, but I have found no instance where discovering unsuspected ability turned any man's head. Father Alexander kept a level mind and heart. Elias Bond gave back to missionary work all of this easier wealth beyond his family's simple needs. There has been much satiric comment upon sugar and pineapple fortunes of the missionary families. First, let the story of their selfless giving through the hard years be read—and slowly. One point is clear: the discovery that an impoverished preacher need not be forever beholden to charity made a deep impression upon Cyrus Mills. He planted no sugar, but his mind was busy thinking.

In one particular Rufus Anderson's misgivings were justified: Cyrus Mills' health was not equal to his work. Those years in Ceylon were taking their toll. His friends in the Islands noticed how exhausted he was. In the summer of 1862 he went to San Francisco to recuperate, making the voyage "up" on the bark *Yankee*, Captain Claxton—a sixteen-day run. He was in or near San Francisco from July 4 until August 22. Either during that visit or in 1864—and most likely on both occasions—he foregathered with two of his Williams classmates, Dr. Henry P. Coon and Henry B. Livingston. Coon, after graduating in medicine from the University of Pennsylvania, went to San Francisco in 1852, and was well established in his profession. In the civic housecleaning that followed the work of the Vigilance Committee he was drafted to reform the police system, and was a judge in the city courts for five years. He led in putting down land frauds and other graft, demonstrating such ability that the reform party elected him mayor in 1863. He held that office for four years. Livingston, a forty-niner, was editor first of the *Sacramento Index*, then of the *Sacramento Union*. He too was a staunch man in those troubled times. He moved to San Francisco in 1858 and was for many years on the editorial staff of the *Alta Californian*. Cyrus may also have visited his seminary classmate, Townsend E. Taylor, who was preaching in Petaluma. In any case, the president of Oahu got around among men. On July 20 he preached in Calvary Presbyterian Church;* and during his seven weeks he was observant. "I have gathered a large amount of information respecting this young giant among the states." Returning to Honolulu on the bark *Speedwell*, he had time to think things over. His classmates were doing well under rough conditions, and California had its points.

In 1863 Dr. Rufus Anderson paid a long-deferred visit to the Islands. The difficult nature of his errand called for good cheer and finesse, for the American Board was putting the Mission on its own. One detail of his visit belongs here, a private appeal in which Mrs. Mills opened her heart to him:

> *I want to ask you to speak a word of encouragement to my husband. He is not very strong, and is often a very great sufferer, much as Mr. Hoisington was. Those ill turns often oblige him to neglect some duties, & he feels that most of his work is not done as well as it should be, & often says, "I am not fit to be here—it needs a well and strong man." But I know he does far more than he gives himself credit for, & far more than many strong men.*

She went on to praise young William Bailey, an assistant teacher—so very dependable, she said, and so kind to the smaller boys. He was like a son to her and Mr. Mills, but they feared they would not be able to keep him; the trustees, especially Mr. Castle, were sticklers for economy. (Twenty years later William Bailey, when he was a trustee of Mills College, helped her again through difficult times.) She continued:

> *I do hope you will convince our trustees that it is better economy to give Mr. Mills the help he needs, for I do think he has shown his ability to economize & make the most of little, & he is not strong enough to bear all the work it is in his heart to do . . . Once he was never depressed, & would not be now if he were well, the doctor says.*

One burden of dubious value was imposed upon the school by Rufus

---

* Calvary Church had recently installed as minister the Reverend Charles Wadsworth, mentor and inspirer of Emily Dickinson.

Anderson's pet theory—the teaching of the native tongue. Though the Board had withdrawn from the Mission, it continued to grant some aid to missionaries' children at Punahou, but insisted that they learn the Hawaiian language. The trustees could see little sense in that; the school was not a training school for missionaries. In the pioneer days many parents had tried to prevent their children from learning Hawaiian from natives whose anatomical frankness of speech was disconcerting. In time most of the children picked up a sociable margin of the vernacular, but why study what was in the air? William De Witt Alexander organized one class, but no one at Punahou appeared to regard this new enrichment of the curriculum as heaven-inspired. It only grated on the nerves of principal and teacher.

On February 20, 1864, Cyrus Mills turned in his resignation, to be effective at the end of the school year. Confronted by the resignation, the trustees offered him a leave of absence, but his decision was made. I believe that the Mills wanted to be free henceforth to manage their own work. They had learned to trust their own judgment and their ability to find resources. Samuel N. Castle, likely to have the coolest impersonal judgment of any of the trustees, wrote to Anderson, "We can hardly hope to fill Mrs. Mills' place in the institution, or get a president and his wife so efficient as they have been." Reviewing the history of the school, Castle felt that Beckwith had been the more popular president, but that Mills had been the superior business manager. Ephraim Clark wrote with warmer regret, and William Patterson Alexander with personal sorrow.

With Brother Clark and several young men and women from the mission families, the Mills sailed from Honolulu on July 8 on the bark *Yankee* and had a three weeks' run to San Francisco. Young Sam Damon wrote back to his family that Mrs. Mills kept organizing picnics and parties all the way over, and that they had a weekly newspaper. The Mills spent the next eight weeks in California. Conjecture is only conjecture, and I have no documentary proof that they visited their respective classmates, Townsend Elijah Taylor and his wife Persis (Thurston), but the Taylors had been in charge of a church in Petaluma since 1862, and not to visit them would have been unnatural. On August 17, 1864, William De Witt Alexander wrote: "It is whispered that Mrs. Taylor and Mrs. Mills think of setting up a second (or third) Mount Holyoke Sem. in California, at Petaluma perhaps." On September 18 Cyrus Mills preached at the Howard Street Presbyterian Church in San Francisco. On September 23 they sailed on the steamer *Golden City* for Panama. They reached Ware late in October, and had a talk with Rufus Anderson in Boston early in November. A note by Anderson indicates that at least a few of the

Punahou trustees still hoped that Cyrus Mills would reconsider his resignation.

In Ceylon, much disillusionment—necessary before they could really find themselves; in the Islands, discovery. Only once, and that very early at Punahou, did Cyrus in his letters to Anderson repeat the worn Ceylon formula of numbering the students who had "indulged hope." He and Susan—and especially Susan—had learned better ways of judging young people; "hope" had become a vibrant and responsive quality in youth. Those Island friendships were very personal; to the end of their lives the broad and general theory of doing good would resolve itself into an endless series of friendships, happy and natural as the story that closes the first chapter of the Gospel of John.

eleven

BENICIA

EARLY IN THE SUMMER OF 1865 THE MILLS RETURNED FROM Massachusetts to California, arriving at San Francisco by the steamer *Sacramento* on June 26. This time they came for good; they were ready to buy a school and develop it independently, but they had not decided what school they would buy. It is useful to know some of their friends who were then active in the Bay region. Neither pushing nor diffident, Cyrus had an exceptional predisposition toward men he had liked at Williams and at Union Theological Seminary, and even toward alumni whom he had not known in his own student days. In '62 and '64 he had foregathered with his Williams classmates, Livingston (of the *Alta Californian*) and Dr. Henry P. Coon; and Coon, who was mayor of San Francisco when the Mills settled, was a layman leader in church and school affairs. The Townsend Taylors were being transferred from Petaluma to the directorship of home missions on the Pacific Coast, with headquarters in San Francisco. But besides these men, Cyrus Mills had a broader circle of college and seminary friends who were outstanding as founders of schools; and most of these men had preached with distinction in interior towns. To rehearse a series of pastorates—Shasta

164

City, Marysville, Placerville, Grass Valley, Columbia—might sound disparaging to the modern ear; but these were the most populous towns in northern California, next after San Francisco, Sacramento, and Stockton. Those pioneer preachers went where the people were; and the hearty adaptability of the preachers was thereby developed.

Isaac H. Brayton, a Hamilton College man and two years after Mills in seminary, had come to California in 1850, and after pastorates in San Jose and San Francisco had established Oakland College School—the preparatory department of California College, which later became the University of California. Besides his management of the preparatory school, Brayton was associated with the college proper. Both the school and the college were in the center of the village of Oakland, and—as will soon appear—Cyrus and Susan Mills taught within three blocks of Brayton's school in the autumn of 1865. Edward G. Beckwith, their predecessor at Punahou, was associated with Brayton; later he became a staunch friend of the Mills, and in time one of their trustees.

Foremost among the pioneer Protestant ministers in northern California was Samuel H. Willey (U.T.S. '48), who had founded many churches in the mining towns and in the Bay region, and had led in establishing California College. Willey had known Cyrus Mills well in seminary; and in California Willey was everywhere, active, warmhearted, an encourager of men. Associated with him in California College was Martin Kellogg, another U.T.S. man; Willey has been rightly called the father of the University of California, and Kellogg became its president. Henry Durant, associated with Willey and Kellogg in that venture, was not a fellow alumnus, but he became close to Mills in friendship. Not until these four ministers—Brayton, Willey, Kellogg and Durant—proved their working faith in education did their college win full support from the State. Even the secondary schools were, until 1870, almost solely the creation of educated ministers who led the way before the state was ready to support public high schools. Edward B. Walsworth (U.T.S. '51) had founded the first church in Oakland; in 1865 he was conducting a school for girls in Oakland, and two years later he bought land from Cyrus Mills. Of the men named, all but Beckwith had worked in the rough-and-tumble conditions of the frontier, and all but Livingston and Coon were teachers. Capable and adaptive, they knew the needs of their time. In any case, the Mills did not come as strangers.*

* Joseph H. Budd (Williams '44) was a rising attorney in Stockton, later a judge of the superior court. John E. Benton (U.T.S. x'50) was preaching in the Mother Lode towns; later he edited the Oakland *Transcript*. Hannah J. Jayne (Mount Holyoke x'55) is said to have been the first public school teacher in Oakland.

But the Mills' closest friends from the alumni groups were George Mooar (Williams '51), minister of the First Congregational Church in Oakland, and Israel E. Dwinell (U.T.S. '48), Congregational minister in Sacramento, both being called later to the faculty of Pacific Theological Seminary. They were men of singularly fine sympathies, and they had the clearest insight into the quiet nature of Cyrus Mills.

> *And you must love him ere to you*
> *He will seem worthy of your love.*

Dwinell had been drawn to Mills ever since their student days. It is not known whether the Mills visited him during their eight-weeks stay in the summer of 1864; they did consult him about their plans in 1865.

For a time they considered buying a school for boys in Oakland. Mrs. Mills, telling of this in her old age, did not identify the school, but Brayton's appears to have been the only one available, and if they aimed at it they probably lacked enough capital. But they also had in mind the Young Ladies' Seminary of Benicia. Mary Atkins, owner and principal of that school, had taken a vacation voyage to Japan, China, and Siam in 1863–64. She sailed as a sort of adventurous supercargo and personnel manager on the brig *Advance*, she and a coltish boy, Charley Hare (son of the owner), being the only passengers. Stopping in Honolulu on the outward voyage, she had visited Punahou and met Cyrus and Susan Mills. Tradition, now deeply grooved, runs that she urged them to come to California if their health should require a change, and that their coming was, one might say, personally conducted by her; and it has been supposed that she even then negotiated with them to buy her school. This tradition, like many others touching Mary Atkins, ignores the facts. Cyrus Mills had spent seven weeks in California in 1862 and had observed the field with independent eyes. Further, Miss Atkins was not free to offer them her school at the time of her visit in Honolulu. She had already given an option to Miss Margaret Lammond and she confidently expected to sell to Miss Lammond. Indeed, the invitation ran the other way: the Punahou trustees, anxious for their overworked staff, invited Miss Atkins to stay on and teach. She accepted that offer, but when she returned to the *Advance* to break the news to Captain Barlow her heart failed her. She would have been glad to escape from Charley Hare, whose adolescent weather baffled her; but the voyage appealed to the strong romantic hunger in her nature, the captain's clothes wanted mending, and so she continued on the *Advance*.

As has been noted, the Mills had visited in central California for eight weeks in 1864. Did they see Miss Atkins then? Possibly, but not certainly. She returned from Siam on September 6, they sailed for the Isthmus on September 23; but until September 18 she still expected to sell her school to Miss Lammond. If they did see her, it is apparent that they came to no agreement then; had they done so, surely they would have taken charge of the school in August 1865.

Instead, they taught during the summer and autumn of 1865 in Mrs. Mary K. Blake's school for girls, which occcupied a building on the west side of Washington Street at Eleventh, in Oakland. Brayton's School and the struggling California College were within three or four blocks. It is not known where the Mills lived during that term. As to their recreation, one advertisement stirs the fancy: E. and A. Newland, whose livery stable was at Seventh and Broadway, offered carriages, buggies, and saddle horses for trips into the country. Did Cyrus and Susan explore country roads as far as Berkeley, and drive out the old county road toward San Leandro (then the county seat), and turn up some grassy lane among the farms that Robert Simson was selling—land that, only fifteen years earlier, had been the domain of Don Luis Peralta's sons? This road—that road; you crossed the hills into Redwood Canyon, and you might meet on the mountain grade a timber rig drawn by six yoke of oxen bringing a redwood log to the mill at Brooklyn. New orchards, too, and brooks that, even in the dry season, kept a low voice of waters. Did they drive, and begin to like one road better than others? I believe they did. From their friendship with Brayton and Willey they may have met Robert Simson; and within a little more than two years they were buying land in Simson's neighborhood. The record of their careful buying was in hand before we knew of their connection with Mrs. Blake's school. How had they learned the country so well? That brief sojourn at the Blake school gave the answer.*

They had very little money, in which respect they were on a par with every owner of a school in California. No school needed a comptroller to study investment trends in Poore's Manual. A score of little schools, small and hopeful as oak and madrone seedlings in competition of the forest. See: we have four leaves. If we can survive one more dry season we may have six, for in this growing empire of salubrity our spot is most salubrious. In San Francisco, the Reverend P. V. Veeder's City College (southeast corner of

---

* That connection came to light by accident. Being interviewed upon a quite different matter, a woman whose mother had been a student at Blake's in 1865 brought out keepsakes that Susan Mills had given that mother—photographs, and a topaz from Ceylon.

Stockton and Geary), with masculine courses in assaying and metallurgy; and the Reverend Townsend Huddart's Union College, at Second and Bryant; and Mrs. Swedenstierna's California Collegiate Institute at Silver and Third; and Grace Female Institute. In Oakland, besides the schools already named, was the Reverend E. B. Walsworth's Pacific Female College. In Sonoma, the Reverend W. N. Cunningham's Cumberland College, which had survived seven years of dry salubrity. In Napa, a Young Ladies' Seminary. And the Reverend D. Tuthill's Collegiate Institute in Santa Clara; and Miss Buckmaster's San Mateo Institute; and Sacramento Seminary for Young Ladies— "Herman Perry, Esq., and Lady, Principals."

Benicia had no less than four: an Episcopal school for boys, a Catholic school for girls, Miss Atkins' school, and C. J. Flatt's Benicia College, which had a branch—a law school, recommended by a long list of gentlemen who were prominent, and perhaps often, at the bar. Benicia was an educational forest. During a few months, back in 1851, there had been a Benicia University—on paper only. Three trustees were elected, but—so busy the times, so many directions in which men might throw their energies—it appears these gentlemen forgot to meet. Thus far no college or university has claimed to be descended from that squirrelish acorn.

With so many hopefuls wanting to live, a prophet could have foretold that the Episcopal and Catholic schools might survive, and that California College (with Willey, Brayton, Durant, and Kellogg at its head) might become a real college. For the other strugglers, what hope? And what hope for Cyrus and Susan Mills if they decided to risk all on one venture and buy Miss Atkins out? None, unless they could be wiser and more practical than a score of others. A school that depended upon a succession of transient teachers could never become permanent. Together they had learned—with Susan the best learner—what youth will do with enthusiasm, what as a duty, and what it cannot be driven to do. They wanted independence and permanence, too. Here at last they had the chance to prove their faith in the ideals of Mark Hopkins and Mary Lyon.

Israel Dwinell came down from Sacramento and talked the matter over with them, and this is the way he remembered it:

The purpose, in general outline, was as distinct and solid in Dr. Mills' mind as a temple of granite.

The plan seemed to contemplate great expenditure, long waiting and working, and a most free and unwonted response from the public. Looking at the delicate man, of deliberate speech and of thin and sallow face, browned by an Indian sun, the writer, although heartily approving of the object, regarded the scheme as a dream . . .

The writer knew the man well—morally and as a Christian and a scholar —and knew that in this respect there was the right stuff in him, but he did not know what fertility of invention, executive force and persistence and insight to perceive the golden ends of lines of business lay under that mild, quiet, modest exterior, and in that enfeebled frame. Nor did he know what wealth of versatility, life, and tact for training young ladies were combined in Mrs. Mills . . .

They bought the Benicia Seminary on October 7, 1865, for $5,000, and took control on January 1, 1866. The property consisted of three lots, a converted residence, and a cottage. The history of the school, the men who founded it, and the nine principals who successively managed it between 1852 and 1886 is summarized in Appendix F. The point of present interest is that the school was suffering from a discouraging slump—and that calls for a story, not altogether a digression.

When Miss Atkins went on her sabbatical voyage she rented the school to Miss Margaret Lammond for the school year 1863–64. Miss Atkins gave the following account of the affair:

After nine years of uninterrupted care of the institution, the state of health of the Principal admonished her that she needed rest and recreation, which she sought and found in an extended voyage to the Eastern Hemisphere. While absent, her place was supplied by Miss M. Lammond, who rented the establishment with the view of purchasing it at the close of the twelfth year. Untoward circumstances, however, chiefly arising from the long, unprecedented drought of that year, prevented the fulfillment of the negotiations on the part of Miss Lammond, and accordingly on the fifteenth day of October, 1864, Miss Atkins resumed her place as Principal . . .

Tradition, once again grooved as history, has added that Miss Lammond lacked Miss Atkins' ability, and that the school declined under her management; but the enrollment increased to 149—the highest on record to that time. There was a decline when the next academic year began, in August 1864, and the meager rainfall was a factor; but the marble style of Miss Atkins' paragraph hardly tells what really happened. Miss Atkins returned from Siam on September 6, and after twelve days of negotiation, she and Miss Lammond broke off all friendly relations. It is a fair conjecture that they disagreed about the price.

Usually the private schools had spent their advertising budgets by mid-

August and the printers of the *Alta* laid the Educational headline away until Christmas; but now they dusted it off out of season, and for a few weeks that column was acidulous.

MISS M. LAMMOND

Present Principal of Benicia Seminary

Has the pleasure to announce that she has purchased the seminary for Young Ladies known as the California Collegiate Institute.

Formerly under the control of Mrs. M. B. Swedenstierna, and will remove there with her entire corps of Superior Teachers and Professors, on Friday, October 14th.

The location of this Institute (on the suburbs of the city) commends at once, for its boarding pupils the retirement of country life, with the advantages of the finest professional talent from the city.

As Miss Lammond desires to make this a permanent institution, no efforts will be spared to make it worthy of the patronage which has been so liberally extended to her during the past four years. For further particulars Catalogues may be obtained by addressing Miss Lammond, Principal of Benicia Seminary, until October 14th, after which communications must be sent to the Collegiate Institute, corner of Silver and Third Streets, San Francisco.

Miss Atkins rejoined in a cold, third-personal tone. And whether by coincidence or an aptness for dramatic timing, a certain Colonel Monstery, Professor of Arms, at this point enriched the Educational column with word of his Fencing Academy and Sparring Rooms. He offered "Instruction in the Art of Fencing with Foil, Broadsword, Bayonet, Lance, Dagger, and Boxing. The Science of Fencing," he informed his public, "is recommended by the most eminent physicians as a complete restorer of weak and debilitated persons. Salle d'Arms. No. 522 Montgomery Street."

In announcing that she was carrying with her her full corps of "Superior Teachers and Professors," Miss Lammond seems to have been indulging in a slight overstatement such as used to be discernible in the publicity of schools and colleges eighty years ago. In the parlance of that day, a Professor was a male teacher of music or painting or foreign languages; a Teacher, merely a female who dug the stony glebe of algebra and history and Greene's *Analysis of the English Language*. Miss Lammond did indeed carry off with her two teachers—a loss more reparable, no doubt, than that of the nineteen pupils(three of them seniors) who likewise followed her to Silver Street.

Across the dim years one's eye catches a verve in Miss Lammond, a peppery irreverence. She needed no fencing master to instruct her in the immortal passado, the punto reverso; and history seems to have underrated her ability as a manager.

It was clear that Miss Atkins regretted her failure to sell to Miss Lammond; clear also that the dry season did not prevent Miss Lammond from buying in a better market, and that she had a considerable popularity with students. In any case, the Benicia Seminary was hard hit; the enrollment after Miss Lammond's exodus fell from 149 to 80—the lowest on extant record. In June 1865 Miss Atkins wrote to a kinsman, "The school has not begun to pay expenses." The enrollment when the Mills bought was a little above ninety. To the same kinsman Miss Atkins expressed deep disappointment that she had not been able to get a higher price than the Mills paid. They had very little money; during the first ten months of 1866 Miss Atkins acknowledged payments from them amounting to $3,435, noting $1,040 as "balance due on furniture." They found only thirty-eight boarding pupils and a small corps of untried teachers; and in June 1866 they had but one graduate. The school had lost patronage along the Mother Lode, but five girls entered from Hawaii when the Mills began, and six more came in the next two years. The most notable increase was from San Francisco.

The Mills added two courses in science and one in literature and increased the stint of junior and senior classes from three courses to four. Their notable improvement was to cure the rapid turnover of teachers. Between 1852 and 1865 the school had had thirty-three teachers in the "regular" courses; twenty had taught during only one year or only one term; only three had continued longer than two years. The Mills soon had three Mount Holyoke teachers on their staff, and Miss Emily S. Wilson (Mount Holyoke '61) stayed with them for eighteen years. The results were encouraging: one graduate in 1866, six in 1867, seven in 1868, ten in 1869, seventeen in 1870. (The senior classes before their time had averaged 3.5.)

Miss Atkins, not a lenient critic, visited the Benicia Seminary several times in 1866. She rated Cyrus Mills only "so-so" as a teacher, but was moved to tears by his kindness when he came to San Francisco bringing her a present from her Benicia friends. Moreover, he made his payments on the dot. She made the rounds of the Bay schools at commencement time. Naturally she found little to admire at Miss Lammond's Collegiate Institute and thought the speakers (including Leland Stanford and two bishops) too lavish in their praise. At Mrs. Blake's: "Music bad. Young Ladies overdressed." At Benicia: "Best of the season"—though she noted with asperity that the one senior dragged Mary Lyon into her essay. But Kitty Sherman "played better than anybody I have ever heard." And Mrs. Mills' friendliness quite overcame the austere former principal. In October, when Miss Atkins departed for New York, Mrs. Mills gave her a parting gift of twenty dollars.

Drawing and painting may have been on the wistful side at Benicia; but the music teachers were Germans of that group who put the teaching of music on a high level in San Francisco. J. B. Beutler, who had migrated to America during the revolution of 1848, was long remembered with affection. Under his baton the girls sang—the whole group of them—more freely than modern students do. The talents of Reinhard Schumacher, piano teacher, were more than respectable, but paradoxically the good man is remembered for his blushing self-effacement, as if protective coloration defeated its own end. He was so very shy that Mrs. Mills could never coax him to eat at the regular table. I take it that he was "off campus," as most of the music men were, and that he would be hungry after two hours on the river boat and three more of beating time and pleading *Nach einmal, bitte*—ravenous but too bashful to savor the good Mills brown bread while so many curious maidens were eyeing him. "He nearly faints if he meets a girl in her Gymnastic costume." Shy gentleman, if the gymnasium suit of 1867 did this to thee. . . . His photograph shows the most universal beard I know of in pictures: a majestic fall, a downpour of benevolence, unprofaned by French or Italian barber's bastions or militaristic upjaunts; a beard of flowing goodness, of mercy that endureth forever. So very long it was, one aches wondering whether it may not have muted the keyboard when a gusty *Weltschmerz* poured through his fingers. Be patient, good man, while beating time and pleading, hour after hour, while training those four girls in the eight-handed version of the *Overture to Zampa*. On the return trip you may find an unobserved corner of the boat saloon and munch a roll, and think of Leipsic and Vienna, and muse with heartache over the sonatas that never were finished.

It was unkind to point at you, Herr Schumacher, who wanted not to be noticed. But fate played a more ironic trick upon another man who was not allergic to attention. Tradition, smiling, raps with her gavel: "A surprise for you! We have a Mark Twain story—authentic beyond doubt." We bend forward to listen. "A story of Mark Twain at Benicia. For Mark attended the graduating exercises in 1868, and he was at his best. The situation was a 'natural': prosy little Cyrus, correct Susan, the girl graduates and their essays and all. Sarah Garretson read a prophecy, *California in 1900*, and America's prince of humorists convulsed the audience by drawling—" here Tradition adjusts her glasses and fumbles her notes—"by drawling a remark that convulsed the audience."

And is that all? Mass! You were about to say something: where did you leave off? Mark *was* there. And of course he said something. But nobody in all the world remembers what he said. The daughter of one graduate used to recall, from her mother's telling, that Mark asked, "May I kiss one of these pretty girls, Mrs. Mills?" "Certainly not." "What if I should kiss one behind the door?" And at this point the daughter's memory stops and Mark chokes in the tule fog. Tradition, like an irritated professor covering up his own blunder, scolds you, scolds me, because we cannot remember what we never knew. Tradition insists that Mark wrote about that evening: but on what page of what book?* The waiting grows numb as the arctic chill around that Boston table when Mark chaffed the silvery nobles of literature— a joke that didn't come off. This one came off—and is forgotten. Find it who can. It may exist. And if Mark failed to give Cyrus and Susan a page— well, we have in later years expected legacies that failed to materialize.

Late in October 1866 Maria Rice Isenberg, then in her twenty-fifth year, came from Hawaii to Benicia in search of health, leaving her husband and baby daughter with her mother in the Islands. She was a paying guest of the Mills for some three months, her younger sister being a student with them, and her brother William attending Oakland College School. On alternate week ends William rode horseback to Martinez and ferried over to see his sisters, and once Mrs. Isenberg visited the Townsend Taylors, who had moved to a farm "four miles out of Oakland."

Mrs. Isenberg could view the Benicia scene with a mind less preoccupied with youthful friendships than are the reminiscences of most alumnae. The enrollment of boarding pupils had risen from thirty-eight to sixty-seven in ten months. She was impressed by the happiness of the girls, "all so fresh, without that weary, tired look that school children so often have." They thronged into Mrs. Mills' sitting room after supper, or danced in the largest music room. One or two sillies wore hoop skirts which tilted up at times and exposed what grave Mrs. Isenberg thought was too much of the nether limbs. And the boys from Mr. Flatt's school would persist in airing themselves in front of the seminary, waving their handkerchieves—an aspect of male behaviorism for which Mrs. Mills had a calm and forthright remedy even before psychology invented a name for it.

Mrs. Mills told Mrs. Isenberg something about their business problems,

* The late Dixon Wecter, literary editor of the Mark Twain estate, doubted that any of the Mark Twain papers contain a reference to the Benicia commencement in 1868.

the debt that was being paid off, and confided that they were helping ten students through school. And though she came from the fruitful Islands and a home that was no longer poor, she marveled at the good food and itemized it as any student would, and wondered how Mrs. Mills managed to have baskets of pears and grapes always within the girls' reach.

> *Mr. Mills is not well but She is flying around as usual, she does the greatest amount of work I ever saw Woman accomplish. She has taken the idea that I need even more nourishment and so has a nice little Beefsteak for me every Noon. Also she gives me California Port Wine, and my cheeks are quite filled out.*

Does the regimentation, the darning, the Saturday morning inspection, when a teacher ran a white-gloved finger or handkerchief over window sill and pane, evoke a scream from the modern student? These usages were not invented by Cyrus and Susan Mills. Boys in Oakland College School were not allowed to leave the premises on Sunday except to go to church; and though Miss M. Lammond may have bitten her thumb at the Montagues, her students on Silver Street toed the line—or at least her printed rules were of the universal mint. There was hardly one respectable school or college in the country that neglected boot-camp discipline in the 1860's. One girl at Benicia who was near graduation when the Mills came, had, in the early 1860's, written to her parents about the austerity of Miss Atkins' regime when the girls were marched out to take the air:

> *Such a queer walk, no fun, no freedom, just march out two by two, still we can choose with whom we go, with a teacher leading and another behind. Sometimes we go to the hills and others to the beach. These two are best. It is very stupid when we just march around town blocks. I wish I didn't feel so like a prisoner, being guarded and watched.*

Another alumna remembered that the girls were at first surprised at Mrs. Mills' youthful animation. She was really forty, but she seemed livelier than any teacher had the right to be, as if vital feelings of delight were in themselves a good law.

On Friday evenings students and teachers brought their sewing baskets into the schoolroom, the laundered clothes were distributed—each garment plainly marked with the owner's name—and Mrs. Mills helped the youngest girls do their mending. "No girl is allowed to take home ragged clothing." It is not improbable that on those Friday evenings, and at the Saturday morning inspection of rooms, the students heard an occasional reference to

Mary Lyon. And so an old-fashioned household virtue was made habit—for a little longer.

> *Friday evening we had a grand display of Fancy Work made here this term and all laid out on clean white tables in the Dining Room . . . There were 35 Bead watch cases of almost every color of silk & velvet, Bead needle cases, Tidies, Socks, Braided Aprons & Dresses, three beautiful Dolls dressed for Christmas, Lamp Mats, Sofa cushions, a handsome Flannel shirt one girl had embroidered for her Father, Bonnets, Caps, Scarfs and Drawings. On a third table were huge platters of Cake and Apples for all of us.*

Small as the enrollment was, the school required seven music rooms; sixty percent of the students studied music, and everybody sang.

> *I have just come from morning Prayers. Mr. Mills reads a verse, then the whole school reads one and such attention is paid to reading in classes that every word of the Bible reading comes as distinctly to the ear as though spoken by one person. Then they sing, led by a small melodeon, and that is my delight. There is perfect time, no drawling, and so hearty that sometimes even upstairs in my room I have distinguished every word of the hymn.*

The rains came late that season, then the brown fields turned so bright a green they reminded Mrs. Isenberg of green moss in the Islands. In January there was snow halfway down the slopes of Diablo, with brilliant morning clouds over the mountain. Even the bleak rainy days were happy for her, with a bright fire in her room and all about her the sense of being endeared. In no other reminiscences of that school have I found so deep a tone of inner happiness. A beautiful world to remember during the brief time yet allowed her. Eleven years after her death her own daughter came to California, entrusted, of course, to Mrs. Mills. By such accretions a small school grew.

Four of the men who had founded the seminary in 1852 still lived in Benicia; one of them, the Reverend Sylvester Woodbridge, had been the leading spirit in that work. By the late 1860's the village had ebbed from his old school Presbyterian church, as life itself had left Benicia stranded. In 1868 the Reverend Charles Henry Pope came to the village as minister of the Congregational church. A Bowdoin man ('62), he had served in California for six years. One infers that the seminary teachers and students mainly attended his church; at least, Mrs. Mills transferred her membership there.

The name of still another Benicia man belongs here. Checking over the polling list for 1866, hoping to recover some of the lost relationships, I found the name *Michael Herlihy*—and I forgot the rest. In one breath the world seemed good again. Even though a second reading showed that the man listed was the father of the Michael we knew, yet Michael himself was there. Later polling lists in Alameda County gave our Michael as "born in Ireland" —yes, we knew that; a citizen by the naturalization of his father; occupation, coachman. But "coachman" tells so little. When Mrs. Mills died, Michael had served her forty-six years. He had no blarney, and no one quoted him for cleverness. When he retired in 1915 I likened him to old Adam in *As You Like It*—an age frosty yet kindly; but that similitude, though well meant, had a kind of artifice—and artifice never belonged with Michael. I reckon him at nineteen when he became trusted handy man around the stable and grounds. He served for six years in Benicia; then for forty years on the new campus he was carter and coachman, met the trains, chaperoned Catholic girls to church, and made faithful goodness a lifework. The clear face of Michael and his honest eyes are good to remember—dearer than the approval, stronger than the disapproval, of sophisticated great ones. But more of Michael hereafter.

The school was prospering. Before the end of 1866 Cyrus Mills bought two lots adjacent to the school, and in 1868 four more, to round out the property. Besides these he bought two other parcels of land in Benicia, presumably on speculation; and from 1867 on he was buying land in or near Oakland. Benicia was not the place for the permanent school he and Mrs. Mills wanted. In the early 1850's the town saw itself the future metropolis of California; it was the capital of the state for nine months, and the home port of the Pacific Mail Steamship Company for a little longer; but that glamour was gone. One notes in the reminiscences of Benicia students a warm sentiment for the old school building, but little or none for the town or the bare hills behind it. The remodeled residence and the cottages were crowded; the available town property was not inviting as a site for the new school of which Cyrus and Susan dreamed. If they moved to the country—well, those rides along the San Leandro road were vivid in their minds. They wanted the country—with room enough; Cyrus yearned to plant trees. Their good friend Eli Corwin was now preaching in Oakland; the Taylors and other friends were there. But deeper than all friendship, the Mills were learning to trust their own judgment. They now knew they could make money. Would it not be rather wonderful to build a school and equip it as a school should be? No makeshift adaptation, but something in which they could feel an honest pride?

The little man had a frail body; in the pulpit he was not the equal of Scudder or Mooar or Dwinell; still, somehow, these men liked him. The

Williams men of '44 were proud of him. Some of his western classmates reported to the class: "Mills has been prospered in this world's goods, and is using his property liberally for good. He has no children. You would all know him, but time has improved him in personal appearance." Time, gentlemen, and Susan too, perhaps? All of which was very pleasant; but what counted most was a summons back to Williams to receive an honorary doctorate in 1870. Cyrus was the second man of his class to be so honored; only the brilliant Theron H. Hawks, valedictorian of the class, had had that tribute. Another Californian, Justice John Curry of the state supreme court, had the same call that year, but history has neglected to record whether the two candidates (both Oneida County men) made the trip together. One infers they went by the new overland train; if so, that was the first time Cyrus crossed the continent, though he had been around it three times. At Williamstown he and Justice Curry found themselves in worthy company. Honorary doctorates were not passed out like greeting cards in those days, nor traded by eager executives as small boys swap marbles and stamps. The five other candidates were a headmaster, a judge of the United States circuit court, a theologian, a great surgeon, and a minister plenipotentiary. Cyrus found three of his old teachers there: John Tatlock had retired, but fiery Albert Hopkins was still teaching, and Mark Hopkins, though drooping ever so little at the shoulders, was still tall inside. Two more years of presiding and the great man could resign his office ("I retire that it may not be asked why I do not retire") and settle back on his log and really enjoy teaching, as he did until he was eighty-five.

On October 29, 1870, the Mills sold the Benicia Seminary to the Reverend Charles H. Pope, for $10,000, retaining management of the school until the end of the academic year. Their move to Alameda County had long been decided upon; five months before the sale to Pope they had begun their new buildings at Seminary Park, where the upper brooks of Lion Creek join in a sloping meadow that looks upon the South Bay.

twelve

THE FORKS OF LION CREEK

*W*HEN CYRUS AND SUSAN WENT ABOUT CHOOSING A SITE FOR their campus they had the old-fashioned trait of liking one piece of land, for its own sake, above all others. On December 25, 1867, they bought for $4,500 seven and a half acres in Oakland near the head of the estuary that later became Lake Merritt; but if they at first thought of building their school there they quickly dropped the plan: that site was too near the village of Oakland. Three months later they sold the tract to the Reverend E. B. Walsworth for $7,500. They bought four pieces of business property in or near Oakland; they had an eye to Berkeley, and bought a quarter-block there; and—either on speculation or to help a friend—they bought two acres from their classmates, the Taylors, near where the Claremont Hotel now stands. But some fondness kept drawing them back to the district above the San Leandro road, where little capes of foothills reach down upon the gentle slope that falls to the Bay. Certain farms that Robert Simson had sold from his large holdings were again for sale, and Simson himself, still owner of half a township, was at hand.

He was a forty-niner, a member of the party which included John Woodhouse Audubon, son of the ornithologist. The party went overland and by river from New York to New Orleans, then sailed to the mouth of the Rio Grande and tried to find a short cut across Mexico. Their first leader bungled and failed, and in the ordeal of death by cholera and hardship and violence, Simson and Audubon saved the remnant. After they reached the coast, it was Simson to whom Audubon entrusted two hundred drawings of South-western birds, and no fault of Simson that the ship by which he dispatched the portfolio was lost in a storm. Audubon's name gives color to the story; Simson's plain fiber carries it through.

He tried his hand at mining, but a glint of Scottish foresight in the man affected the Mills more than if he had panned out gold. From the tents and shacks of San Francisco he sized up the Contra Costa shore; twenty miles of it, from the cone of El Cerrito to a point well beyond the estuary that divides Alameda from the main shore, and from tideland to mountaintop, belonged to the four Peralta brothers. This was the great Rancho San Antonio, forty-four thousand acres in extent. There were no towns there, only a few squatters' cabins along the estuary, and at four places along the slope the adobe homes of the Peraltas and their in-laws. The east bay shore was only a country to be hurried through on the way to quick fortune.

It were romantic to credit Simson with a prophet's vision of the cities that now cover that shore, and equally false to think of him as a plunger. He seems to have had a liking for the land itself, the rising hill benches that give a sweeping view of the Bay and the Gate, and of the purple Coast Range from Los Gatos Gap to Tamalpais. He could not buy all. For three thousand dollars he bought what no one else wanted—a few thousand acres from some of the Peralta heirs—Regne, Pacheco, the Bernals. The second-oldest-and-dustiest deed book has copies of the deeds, dating from 1854, Spanish and English in alternate lines, and the boundaries as vague as romance. Grantors and grantee understood: that was sufficient. (Project Sixty-eighth Avenue from the Bay to the mountaintop: that was the brothers' line; and Simson's holdings lay on the northwesterly side of that line.

He was no promoter and had none of the cold-chisel hardness of some of the men who carved fortunes down on Broadway. He sold reasonably to other men—only he wanted room for his own home—a sheltered hill bench where the south fork of Lion Creek in its thicketed ravine used to keep a mur-mur of water even in late summer. That ravine was a wild park, with old-man live oaks that leaned uphill from the sea wind, and under them a profusion of spicy and colorful plant life. Colonel Simson planted a few groves of euca-lypts, and bordered his drive with them. One tree, felled twenty years ago by the improver, was six feet in diameter, and being solitary it made a noble picture against the lift of the hills. Do alumnae of the early '20's remember the morning when, on a knoll where eucalupts made a bronze cliff against the sky, Vachel Lindsay gave one of the happiest readings of his life? Lindsay wrote a poem (never printed) about those trees, likening them to Plutarch's men.

It is hard to be coldly objective toward Robert Simson; for many years I have spaded deep an acre he once owned, and have seen from my study windows the house he built. Its right lines make a man wonder why our own dreams have gone small. Long after he died the neglected almond and plum trees in his orchard could still manage a surprise of color in late February. In a generation of wild ambitions he avoided dramatic extremes: the kind of man, I gather, to whom men turn when, after speakers have spent their emotion, a good cause needs a chairman of ways and means. He was a trustee of Durant's and Willey's California College; and he became, through their long uphill pull, one of the steadiest friends of Cyrus and Susan Mills.

By 1868 much of the land along Lion Creek had passed from Simson to other owners—the Saillots, Dankert, Bonaparte Phillips, Edward Tompkins. I think the Mills had fancied this land ever since the autumn of '65, and had stolen back many times for another look. It were wise to try it in all weathers: February and March may overpower the judgment on a high day when stiff wind off the ocean sends white thunderheads marching along the mountain; but so may August, when ripened wild grasses are spicy with tarweed, and the live oaks look solid black in the sun glare; or December, when under a golden haze the South Bay turns to molten bronze; or a January morning, when a low ceiling of rain clouds drifts into the little canyons, and the mountains look as tall as the Cascades. Best of all, though, are early mornings when the sunlight, striking transversely along the range, reveals arches and ravines that never appear at any other time. But the weather being much the same all along the range, it must have been something imponderable that drew Cyrus and Susan back to the Simson lands: an orchard that ripened earlier than those swept by cold wind through the Gate, or the pattern of foothills that make a vale of Saillot's meadow, or maybe the neighborliness of Robert Simsom himself—until they knew "This is the place."

On July 7, 1868, they bought eighty-four acres from Alphonse and Emerie and Celine Saillot for $25,500; and on August 15, another eighty-four from John Dankert for $10,666.75. By whose tenacity, whose quiddity, was that bargain whittled to the precise six bits? But what a price: three times what the land was ever worth for farming. Had canny Cyrus lost his head?

Or did the Saillots, with Gallic cunning, make the buyers pay for their fancy? Or was there a land boom on? The Mills might say they planned a richer crop than oat hay. And there was something of a boom; the next year, Governor Henry Haight, no sentimentalist, bought seventy-nine acres from Bonaparte Phillips for $10,000. Haight's sister was the wife of Senator Edward Tompkins, and Tompkins had large holdings along the base of the range. No, Cyrus had not altogether lost his head.

For a few months the Mills weighed the qualities of the Saillot and Dankert farms. Which place should it be? They walked and climbed and viewed the land from all sides. The Saillot land gave them both forks of Lion Creek, the little hills made a vale of it, and there are certain spots on that upper forty from which the mountains seem twice as tall. And so, on March 1, 1869 they sold the Dankert land to Edward Trenor for $16,000.

On the bank of the now hidden South Fork, at a spot near the present chemistry building, stood a live oak "eighteen inches in diameter and blazed A." Four farms based their surveys from that tree, and the descriptions of boundaries in the early deeds would drive a modern surveyor frantic: "Beginning at a point on the southwesterly line of lands of B. Phillips, which point is also the northerly corner of lands of M. C. La Grange"; or "to a live-oak stump two and one-half feet in diameter on the north bank of Lion Creek, thence meandering up the center of said creek"; or "thence along Simson's northwesterly boundary" so many chains and links "to a fence-post marked L. P." One live oak six feet in diameter stood near a corner of the present hockey field. Was it as grand as that other giant wrestler that once bent its strength near the campanile? Who remembers the final moment in Ben Jonson's *The Sad Shepherd*, when Puck ran up that leaning tree and stood tiptoe?

> *Come, follow me, I'll once more be your pilot,*
> *And you shall thank me.*

(The Peraltas knew the creek as Leona, when cougars stalked deer on that meadow. The forty-niners shied away from soft Spanish words and blunted the name to Lion. Trying to recapture something that has vanished, we Spanish it once more.)

For Cyrus and Susan Mills, the planning of the new building was almost as exciting as starting for Ceylon—and much better in hand. They wanted proportion, comfort, dignity; life needed high ceilings, wide halls, reaches of open country through every window. And these matters need to be talked over so many times with Messrs. S. C. Bugbee and Son, Architects. On a

Friday night we pack our carpetbag, and long after our Miss Emily Wilson and Miss Sarah Sherman have seen their young charges to bed, we pick our way down muddy Benicia streets to the wharf and board the down-river boat—the *Antelope* or the *Yosemite;* or if this is the night for the *Chrysopolis* we go earlier, for she is always on time. (The new train never is.) Except for a few noisy gentlemen at the bar the parlor deck is quiet. We put our heads together over the plan which young Mr. Bugbee brought last week. The front hall, so, and the parlors, so; but we must have more space for Seminary Hall, a place for morning and evening prayers, as it was at Mount Holyoke. Seminary Hall is to be lived in happily, twice a day—not closed like a church.* And we must inquire further into this matter of gas lighting— safer than oil and more elegant, and Mr. Bugbee assures us we can build our own generating plant. Plumbing is expensive, but we must have running water in every room, and plenty of baths and toilets, though this means a sewer line two miles to the Bay. Quite an undertaking; Cyrus figures long on that problem. And the water problem—but see, the boat is nosing into the slip; the same nice hackman we had last time is waving to us. To the Lick House, please.

Many Saturdays in the office of Bugbee and Son. The first drawing of the front elevation is prideful: three stories, with a mansard roof—a style like that of Oakland College School only much larger; and no scroll-saw nonsense. Then on a Saturday late in May 1870 the Bugbees join us in Oak-land, and Mr. Wilber, the contractor, takes us in his carriage to our land. Tape measures and many stakes. The lupine is fading on the little hills, and the candle racemes on the buckeyes along the two brooks are about to be lighted, and the quail are rook-rooking in every oak, and—yes, let us set the building farther to the left, for North Fork has more water, and the sound of it will be close under the windows of our own suite, comforting as a psalm in the night. While Mr. Bugbee and Mr. Wilber are driving more stakes, we step off the space back of the building site and estimate how many apricot and pear and almond and fig trees there will be room for. Not nearly enough—and thinking the same thought we climb Tompkins' hill. The view is exciting: tall ships at anchor on the San Francisco side, all the South Bay with its estuaries like a map below us, and two white church spires rising above the dark green of oaks six miles away in the village of Oakland. Ten thousand dollars will buy this hill: more debt, but we must manage it. All our lives were a getting ready for this project; we must do it right. And

* Seminary Hall was in the east end of Mills Hall; for thirty-five years it was the heart of the school.

so, a few days later, they bought the thirty acres that are now called Pine Top. They now had one hundred fourteen acres,* a meadow for the dairy herd, and, best of all, they would border directly upon the home ranch of Robert Simson.

When Cyrus was dickering with Senator Tompkins an odd fact came to light: both men had been born at the same pinpoint village. Oneida County should erect a bronze marker on the site of vanished Paris. Gerrit P. Judd, Edward Tompkins, and Cyrus Mills: if every crossroad in America had done as well . . .

A woman who died in 1940 remembered how as a little girl she rode in a buggy with her father to pilot the first four-horse load of timbers from the wharf at Brooklyn,† out along the San Leandro road, then up across unfenced fields to that vale in the hills. You cannot buy such pine and redwood now; and Mr. Wilber's carpenters respected their craft. Mills Hall has been remodeled; no building on the campus requires less repair. It was nine months a-building. The *Brooklyn Home Journal* sounded trumpets over the brave enterprise, venturing only one criticism: the cupola, visible for miles, should have more color. It was a vivid blue—but not bright enough for the editor. Other papers praised the cherubs and roses with which Signori Pellegrini and Buzzi embellished the parlor walls and ceiling. Those cherubs (blossomy innocents! one must not think of them as mural figures) were long since improved away. They provoked no analysis, no pained bewilderment. Not a cherub leg was out of joint, nor could the aptest cherub spell one syllable of frustration. Clearly, they were not art.

On July 29, 1871, the *Brooklyn Home Journal* informed the world: "The gas was admitted into the building on Thursday last. . . . Messrs. Steers and Webster's busses make two trips daily to the Park. . . . Property about the institution is becoming valuable." Seminary Park, not sharply defined, was both campus and the district later called "down the Ave."; and Seminary Park Station was at the foot of that new Seminary Road. (The competing railroads along the bay shore were complicated—Seminary Park Station, Simson's Station, Melrose, Brooklyn—and the puzzled traveler had better take one of Messrs. Steers and Webster's busses—if he can find one.)

And so on a day late in July they moved from Benicia—administration, staff, manservant, maidservant, and such pupils as had stayed the summer,

---

* In 1877 they deeded fifty-five acres to the trustees; accordingly, dutiful copyists have inferred that they bought only that acreage.

† Brooklyn, once the county seat, is now lost in the district around Nineteenth Avenue and East Fourteenth Street.

as orphan girls and girls remote from home used to do. They made the hegira by train to Oakland, and then by some other train to Brooklyn—"or thereabouts." Michael Herlihy, with a man or two to help, had brought the livestock a day or so earlier, either by the old Telegraph Road or maybe through Redwood Canyon. Trust Michael to find the way that would be kindest to the cattle. And when the train arrived, Michael was on hand to pack the carryall with the oldest and the youngest. One girl used to tell us how the overflow, the foot party, walked from Brooklyn over the summer-ripe fields three good miles to "the Park," and how they shouted—ladylike, of course—when the bright cupola came into sight over the massive oaks, and how good the supper tasted that night. Everybody's first night in a shining new dormitory, and running water in every room, and if anybody woke from excitement at two, one hopes the restive soul heard the great-grandfather of Runcible, our campus owl—not boding, no fatal bellman—comforting with his three notes of the English horn. And may we hope that if Cyrus and Susan were wakeful they murmured, "Better than Batticotta, my dear. Better than Benicia or even Punahou." "We worked so many years for this. Yes, it *is* good." School opened on August 2; ten days later the *Home Journal* was urging Dr. Mills to hurry and build a second hall to accommodate the overflow.

But what a debt to carry. They had invested $55,000 of their own money —earnings of the school turned back into the school; they had received $30,000 from friends; there remained a debt of $80,000—their debt. How did that boyhood formula of yours go, Cyrus? "If there be any reasonable prospect . . ." There was some prospect; but for Cyrus and Susan, who had no persuasive "line" among the moneyed gentlemen on Montgomery Street, that prospect called for a faith that could recuperate their tired bodies and minds, many skills—day in, day out, through the years, and much prayer. Scrupulous Israel Dwinell said that the Mills paid $50,000 in interest before that debt was finally cleared.

A fortnight after school opened, the Seminary and the neighborhood began building a community church on land which Cyrus and Susan gave. (Near the corner of Seminary and Camden a large redwood marks the site of the church garden.) When the structure was half-completed there came one night a dry northeaster; not an average northeaster, a psychopathic tantrum; this one mounted to a crazy rage wherein the reeling stars clung to the taffrail. When such a wind comes, dwellers along Leona Heights suffer a martyr's pride that nowhere else along the Contra Costa range is that howl-ing maniac quite so malevolent as when he whoops down the little canyon of Lion Creek—that pleasant vale that Cyrus and Susan chose! And on that October night in '71 he laid the new church flat. Like the termites of Batticotta he did not believe Paley's *Evidences*.

They rebuilt Divinity Church, and for several years the school and the neighbors worshipped there. Then the organization failed, land and building reverted to the Mills, and the wooden Gothic was recarpentered into a sort of dwelling where, during the last twenty years of her life, Miss Jane Tolman lived with her books and pictures and her memory of one trip to Europe. The loft above the tall rooms still kept the sky-blue church ceiling, flecked with gold and silver stars—big stars, little stars; and the roof girders were doweled with Puritan stoutness, enough to fortify whole city blocks of such bungalows as now cover the land. "Now thou dost ill to say the gallows is built stronger than the church: argal . . ."

The wind that leveled the church may have quickened Cyrus' bent for planting tall trees to weatherfend his vale; windbreaks on Pine Top and all around the Saillot and Tompkins land. Who first planted eucalyptus in California, and when, is a question to start graybeards arguing hotly about their grandsires. Cyrus was not the first, by many years; but he and Robert Simson were the first in their neighborhood. Aromatic gray cones, minute seeds in flats, then nursery rows, and perhaps by '73 the woolly gray whiplings were ready for open ground. Pines, too, and many acacias; easy to start acacias, harder to stop them. One would like to have been on hand some dripping-shiny January morning when the first acacia burst overnight into its incredible fountain of yellow bloom. Other trees, too: a few elms, enough Monterey cypress, some hawthorne, a few palms, an olive or two on a dry hilltop. In 1875, when Cyrus made a trip to Japan, he brought back many Japanese ornamentals—but these it would now be hard to identify. One only knows that the Oval as it was forty years ago had such a rightness, one forgot it was planned. Eucalypts are out of favor now, and the gardeners grumble when a mild northeaster litters the ground with bark and moon-sickle leaves; but the mustiest campus tempers grow aromatic after the first autumn rains make all the air stinging-sweet from that alien tree, and those treetops against a twilight sky know a beauty that will never be out of fashion.

How many students and teachers did the Mills bring with them from Benicia? Catalogues of Benicia Seminary for the Mills' last year and for Pope's period are lacking. The catalogue for 1870 lists eleven teachers (besides the Mills), four of whom accompanied them to Seminary Park. Alumnae records of Benicia show that ten students graduated during Pope's three years, a number equaling the average for Miss Atkins' time but lower than that during the Mills' administration. It is a fair inference that Pope retained as large an enrollment as the Mills inherited when they bought the Benicia school.

In the first year in their new school the Mills had twenty teachers. Three were Mount Holyoke graduates: and from 1866 until her retirement in 1909, Mrs. Mills appointed twenty-seven Mount Holyoke women to her staff. Cyrus was principal, but she made most of the appointments. When the going was rough, when spirit and vitality lagged, her trusted remedy was to add more of the Mary Lyon tradition. Three more of that faculty were her own Benicia graduates—never too many, but always a leavening.

In the fall of 1872 came another Mount Holyoke woman, Cynthia K. Goulding, who was destined to become during her long service—well down into Dean Ege's time—almost a Dean Ege. There is a thread of tradition that Mrs. Mills had known Miss Goulding in Ware; and it must be granted that Mrs. Mills in some instances created minor positions for pensioners, but Miss Goulding was no pensioner. One who knew her says that she was "as New England as baked beans, and as puckery as a not quite ripe persimmon, but she was a darling." She had come to Mount Holyoke shortly after Mary Lyon's death, but the genius of that forceful woman had so stamped itself upon her successors that Miss Goulding learned from them the plodding discipline upon which the genius of a more original leader has always to depend. For a quarter of a century she was Mrs. Mills' right hand.

In the music department the catalogues of the '70's sounded of Leipsic and Vienna; besides Herr Schumacher (and his beard) and animated Mr. Beutler, the Germans and Austrians fairly swarmed: Ernst Hartmann, Frederic Katzenbach, Emil Steinle, Otto Linden, Edward Hohfeld, Otto Seyd, and Ferdinand Zellner (who continued well on into Louis Lisser's time). In 1874 came Alfred Kelleher from the Royal Academy of London, who for eighteen years made ours a singing campus. There were no music majors; music was an accomplishment, rarely a vocation. In 1873, out of a total enrollment of 270 students, 214 studied piano and 51 studied singing. It was Alfred Kelleher who found and brought out Emma Wixon, who, as Emma Nevada, brought romantic recognition to the little college.

Those were the happy days, when the new University of California, no larger than Mills, admitted no women, and propinquity had its way as eagles in the air. President Daniel Coit Gilman and his entire senior class attended concerts at Mills, not as conferring a favor, and all the men at Cal were not

too many for a dance. A happy Amherst-and-Mount-Holyoke balance, with
no disparity to mar the manner; the University *Echo* could praise the Mills
Quarterly, both being journalistic babes; and all the Seminary could attend
an oratorical contest at Berkeley and the *Quarterly* could note: "The prize
was awarded to Mr. Josiah Royce, of Oakland, and we tender him our sincere
congratulations." (Did Professor Royce, weighing the cosmos in Harvard
Yard, remember?) Days when the great Tom Hill—he of the acre-vast
canvases—was a campus visitor and benefactor; and when another painter
trudged to the Oval with a picture under his arm: before collectors heard of
him, Susan Mills believed in William Keith.

A world of happy newness: a Washington's Birthday when all the Seminary
hiked up the old logging road and over the summit (three hundred feet higher
than the Mount Holyoke range) and down to Redwood Canyon; and when
a before-breakfast climb to Pansy Hill could tally off the required daily eight
turns around the Oval. (Pansy Hill is still there—miles nearer than the Top
of the Mark—but no student finds it, and the dainty gold-brown flowers and
the silvery-blue wild irises that grew in the wet meadow under the hill have
been improved away.) Eight turns daily around the Oval, but (the *Quarterly*
notes) students made an average gain of seven pounds in the first term. A day
to write home about, when the seniors and juniors rode in carryalls, and in-
spected Washington College (at Irvington) and the Normal at San Jose,
and found Notre Dame Convent friendly; and, coming late and hungry to
Santa Clara, had a gracious welcome from Father Varsi, who first served a
delicious lunch and then showed them his laboratories. Another day, lasting
into late evening, when Mrs. Mills took the whole flock to admire the new
Palace Hotel. With our own eyes we saw the handsomest teams, in silver-
trimmed harness, drive round the interior court, while top-hatted gentlemen
and ladies with seven rows of ruffles looked down(we with them) from the
seven galleries; and the view from the top—words cannot describe it, but
words (in the *Quarterly*) did their brave best. An evening (this was in '72)
when Dr. Mills was arriving home from a business trip to the east coast, and
every window in Seminary Hall, and even the cupola, was illuminated so
brightly that passengers on the westbound overland approaching Melrose
stared and asked excited questions. And a morning when all of the older girls
who had no demerit marks were chaperoned down to Melrose Station, their
arms full of wreaths and bouquets, and the eastbound overland train stopped
to allow them to sing their compliments to a crowned king—a real monarch—
King Kalakaua of Hawaii, whom the Mills had known when he was a shaveling

prince.* His majesty made a speech from the rear platform—right in Melrose. Ah, but those were the happy days.

And happy little *Quarterly*, so lady-prim, yet so alive with untaught joy. It could hold up its head with the best. Naïve? But so were the exchanges. The Vassar *Miscellany* had its lead article on "Sobriety," the Santa Clara *Owl* its "Make Hay While the Sun Shines," the University of Virginia *Magazine* its "Thoughts on Thought." The fillers—puns and quoted howlers and clipped items—in the *Quarterly* were (to borrow from the modern hall-song) " respected"; even so, one filler leaves the modern reader stunned. Casually, the *Quarterly* notes, "The national debt is being paid at the rate of $2.50 a minute."

Now all these matters needed to be contrived by a lively imagination. Cyrus, while paying interest to the bankers, was slowly defaulting to a more implacable creditor. Those years in Ceylon were about to foreclose on him; while by a strange law of compensation Susan, who had been nearest death in Ceylon, became an inexhaustible well of energy and the last mainstay of her own family. Deacon John Tolman died in Ware in 1868; his wife, Submit, in 1873. Julia Tolman, after long and exacting service at Mount Holyoke, married a distant cousin, Lucius Tolman. For several years they were art dealers and importers in Boston; then, frail in health, they came in 1871 to Seminary Park, where he was to assist Cyrus Mills in the business affairs of the school; but he died four days after the new school opened, and his widow, returning to Roxbury, followed him within a few months. (She gave her small estate for the benefit of Mount Holyoke teachers.) To the end of their days, Susan Mills felt a big-sisterly responsibility toward her last sister, Jane. Living side by side, they lived in different worlds. Miss Tolman should have lived on Beacon Street, an amateur of paintings and bindings, with an income that provided a yearly trip to Florence—a life wherein religion was a decorous adjunct to culture. With a critic's mind, it was her lot to wonder at, but never fully to understand, Susan's wanting to mother all creation, her quick adaptiveness, her genius for deriving from religion a beauty that surpassed the aesthetic. Even so, the older sister was (some say) a little afraid of Jane.

Together Cyrus and Susan were paying other debts not in the bankers' files. Back in the late '60's they heard that Thomas H. Rouse (Williams '47), who married one of Leavitt Hallock's twin daughters, needed a milder climate; and so they helped him find a pulpit in California and made a place for him

* On his return from Europe King Kalakaua was guest of honor at a tea on the campus. One Southern lady, all aquiver to meet a real king, was terribly put out and bolted from the line when she found he was a colored man.

as a teacher at Benicia. Of course his daughters graduated from the Seminary; later, one of them wrote "Fires of Wisdom." The Mills taught the daughters of Dr. Henry M. Scudder; and when he moved on to Chicago they turned to Daniel W. Poor, son of Daniel the mystic of Ceylon—and of course Anna Poor graduated. Someone should count in the old catalogues the daughters of Williams and Mount Holyoke and Ceylon and Hawaiian Island friends who found, in the suite nearest the brook, a welcome deep-rooted in old loyalties. A few years after the period of this chapter came a daughter of Isaac Hurd, in whose home in Madras the Mills had lived for seven months while waiting permission to return to America. Helen Hurd, born some years after the Madras days, never forgot her wonder that Mrs. Mills, at first meeting, seemed to have known her always.

And this was no armchair kindness, tearful with resignation. When Susan Mills was eighty a man wrote to her recalling a memory of his youth. He had ridden along the range past Joaquin Miller's and down to the campus, and there he had seen her riding a spirited horse. "You were so fearless, and you were such a slender little bit of a woman . . . and there sat you, 'having the time of your life.' And then you let him go—and it was 'Go!' How you did streak it down that road, and left nothing behind but the dust and my sighs of envy." They say that when she read that letter she assured the sedate scholar-women around her that she could very easily mount and gallop again.

thirteen

"OUR PLANS AND OUR HOPES"

CATALOGUES OF HOPEFUL LITTLE COLLEGES WEAR THEIR company manners, their starched English. Like wistful applicants—which they are—they stress no shortcomings but solemnly declare their heavenward aims. Cyrus Mills did not fiddle easily in that style. In the catalogue of 1872 he stated his case in not too big a voice:

The aim in the building of the Institution at Seminary Park, Brooklyn, has been the establishment of a Christian Female Seminary of high order on a permanent basis.

Many of the States of our Union have made, through their Legislatures, generous donations for colleges and universities for young men; but the daughters of the land have been left, in their higher education, to the efforts and benefactions of private individuals. Hence few of our Female Seminaries, however excellent, have any principle of perpetual life, but change with the proprietors, or die with the founders.

Though the Mills Seminary, for the present, is private property, the hope and purpose is, to make it a permanent institution. It is the desire of the

190

proprietor, as well as those who have so generously aided him in the work, that it shall be so arranged and eventually so endowed, that, like Mount Holyoke, or Vassar, it shall be self-supporting. The hope is, that it will add to its resources and appliances until it shall become in every respect all that can be desired, and depend upon no individual life, but continue to be a fountain of knowledge and blessed influence, long after those who have aided in the enterprise have finished their work upon earth.

A few years later he put the matter even more simply:

Believing that in no way could more be accomplished for the good of this Coast, and for the cause of CHRIST, than by the proper education of the young women, it was the aim of the founders, from the first, to seek to lay the foundation for a permanent institution of the highest order

The emphasis is his; and the reserved little gentleman meant what he said.

For a while he and Mrs. Mills debated the idea of giving the school to the state as Willey and Durant had done with theirs. But the state could easily find legal obstacles to daily chapel. On great occasions the university audience did indeed, as a concession to decorum, sing a hymn and have some minister offer prayer; but hymn and prayer had an awkward unfamiliarity, like a Latin quotation by a speaker who is trying to show off. When Cyrus and Susan Mills had been at the brink of death for a cause they believed in, they hadn't "offered" prayer—they had prayed. He and Susan had made youthful blunders, mistaking the letter, the formula, for the spirit until life captured them from many sides; and still the spirit became more than ever a consuming eagerness in behalf of mankind. They had seen the terrible cruelty and fear and despair of India, and knew better than stay-at-homes the power of that strange gospel story to lift men from the dust. Allow religion to subside into an occasional adjunct to decorum and culture, and a time might come when a nation would be hard put to it to compose and vitalize a code of ethics strong enough to save its precious culture and make life livable. Let the state educate differently; they would hold fast to their convictions.

When they incorporated the school in 1877 they had a well-ripened plan. They could not afford figurehead trustees, mere patron names; and though they needed endowment, it is clear that they chose no man on that original board for his wealth, for none was wealthy. Experience had taught them tolerance; to guard against sectarianism they stipulated that not more than one-third of the trustees should belong to any one denomination. Statistics are not portraits, but they may help a little to outline the group of early trustees.

Not counting the Mills themselves (Cyrus serving until his death in 1884, Mrs. Mills succeeding him) , fifty-five men and five women served successively as trustees between 1877 and Mrs. Mills' retirement in 1909. There were a few misfits; in the troubled late '80's there was one dismissal, and three resigned in active dissent; because of removal to distant posts, the terms of minister members were shorter than the average; but the chart shows an impressive degree of tenure. Warren Olney's thirty-five years—far beyond 1909—still constitute a record; but four men served for twenty years or longer, and several for twelve years. Of the sixty, twenty-four were ministers. Only five of the sixty could be considered wealthy. To call them "typical" early Californians were only a blurred generalization; they were interestingly varied individuals. A few of the sixty refuse to be evoked from the shades, and a few more yawned and retired early. But because the twelve who sat with Cyrus Mills in 1877 and the ten successors who were elected before his death all reflect his judgment and something of his affection, let us meet some—not a confusing too many—of the men "by whom and their successors it [the college] is to be forever held for the specific purpose of educating young women."

Oldest and (I think) dearest in friendship was Israel E. Dwinell. His tenderness and tact affected his colleagues, yet no man among them had stronger moral courage. Even in the muted impersonal pages of the minutes one finds his scrupulous honor, correcting a too-sweeping statement, and his punctiliousness—when compelled to be absent he always sent a statement of the reasons. As a farm boy in Vermont he had earned a superior education in the hard way, and he never lost sympathy with humble persons. He had liked Cyrus Mills from their first acquaintance at U.T.S. in 1846. After his call from Sacramento to Oakland, his long association with the Pacific Theological Seminary gave him a period of service on the Board longer than that of any other minister.

The first president of the Board was James Eells, sixth clergyman in his family in direct descent, father to son. Here again, as with the Claps and Howes, one has to conclude there is something in a family, all the long way from John the beehive-maker of Dorchester and Windsor. James Eells, father of this James, was a frontier missionary in Oneida County, New York, at that period when life was sowing a generous handful of superior seed in Oneida. James the missionary helped found Hamilton College, with whose history the family name is interwoven much as the Dewey name is with Williams. The Reverend Cushing Eells, of a collateral line, founded Whitman College at Walla Walla. Like Israel Dwinell, our trustee James won a superior education in the hard way, and became, in time, one of the best-loved ministers in Cleveland, in Brooklyn, in San Francisco, and Oakland. Like Dwinell, he had a genius for drawing and holding large and intelligent congregations. Such men, using no spectacular methods, exercised a leadership comparable to that of the great Puritan preachers—even greater, in that the response was not regimented. Dr. Eells removed to Cincinnati in 1879, and taught in Lane Theological Seminary until his death.

When we focus upon the "typical" forty-niner he often turns out to be a disappointingly decent citizen, running a sawmill or selling hardware. Mayor A. J. Bryant of San Francisco and Robert Simson were two of the forty-niners on the Board. Their laconic soundness and lack of photogenic appeal were counterbalanced by another forty-niner, J. O. Eldridge, who during the windy decades enjoyed the title, "Prince of Auctioneers." One gathers from the *Alta* that those were the days of real auctions, when sales were of cargo size and the hammer fell with a heartier thump than it now does over *objets d'art* in the pretty studios on Sutter Street. Eldridge was a partner of Henry Newhall, who helped the versatile Peter Donohue promote and build the San Francisco–San Jose railroad. A purposeful—one might say, a professional—optimist, Eldridge saw that Cyrus Mills needed a publicity agent. Long after he had rapped his final "gone," stories trailed after him: how he had button-holed frock coats on Montgomery Street and on the ferry *Contra Costa*, selling this worthy cause. Not in astronomical figures; but Israel Dwinell said that Eldridge raised twenty thousand dollars for the school.

The two lawyers on the Board were Ebenezer Sawyer and Henry H. Haight. Sawyer had been judge of the fourth district court for six years; and Henry Haight (Yale '44) was governor of California in 1869–71. His friendship with the Mills began when they were buying the Saillot land, and was deepened by his daughter Janet's happiness as a student at the Seminary. Haight's untimely death in 1878 deprived the Board of one of its best members.

It is hard to be coldly objective toward William Meek, the one orchardist on the Board. In the epic of the covered wagon his deed is liable to be crowded out by more spectacular things. In April 1847 he and Henderson Lewelling, his neighbor cousin in Iowa, loaded their ox-wagons with choice nursery trees, planted in tubs and buckets, and started to Oregon. Six months of hard labor and daily concern which only a grower of trees can appreciate. At some places on the desert plateau they had to carry water by hand as much as a mile to keep their little trees alive. On the bank of the Willamette a few miles south of Portland they established a nursery and multiplied rootstocks and budded them for other pioneers. In 1859 William Meek moved to California, planted orchards around San Lorenzo, and built a reservoir in the hills. How did he and Cyrus Mills come to know each other? Cyrus probably bought his first fruit trees from Meek, and the two unloquacious men recognized in each other the qualities for which an orchardist calls some trees "good doers." We are glad you were on the Board, William Meek. Many a parable, homely and perennial as those in the gospels, was in your mind. You knew that young trees do best when they are loved; and you, a good judge, liked Cyrus and Susan. When we are choked with dusty words and too-glossy words, it is good to think of you on the high plateau, laboring to keep something alive, and of the other days when you trudged up and down the new orchard rows and with the magic of your hands gave pliant young trees the symmetry men wondered at in after years.

Soon after the incorporation, three other men, not quite forty-niners, joined the Board. James P. Pierce, of Santa Clara, had been a hydraulic miner in Yuba County, had built a part of the sea wall along the San Francisco water front, and had been a lumberman in the Santa Cruz and the Siskiyou mountains. His twenty years of service to the school grew, it seems, from a deep respect rather than any earlier and personal affection. His picture shows him with white spade-beard, a firm mouth not apt at pretty compliments, eyes that met you squarely but with no "unconscious arrogance of conscious power"; a man not likely to be patient with verbiage or quirks of temperament but who would take time to see justice done. He was more instant at affairs of the Board than some men who lived nearer; he gave real money when givers were few; and no man did more to steady the ship during the troubled years.

David Hewes missed being a forty-niner by a month or two but made up for it by working overtime. Earning his way through Yale, he tried a vacation venture as book agent, and did so well that his publisher gave him a general agency which netted the sophomore an incredible $3,000. This he invested in sheet-iron houses which he shipped around the Horn. By 1852 he had made a fortune as builder and merchant in Sacramento, lost it overnight by fire, and was back in San Francisco, poor as the next man. Looking around him, he perceived sand dunes and hollows, and an owner who wanted his lot leveled. The former book agent considered: one shovel, one wheelbarrow, one Chinaman: Q.E.D. Other lots—whole blocks of sand hills; more shovels and barrows and Chinamen; then mules and scrapers and wagons; then a huge ordnance of jeep-sturdy little engines and trains of dump cars, and steam shovels, and brigades of unrefined men, leveling the hills on both sides of

Market as far as the present Civic Center, and filling in acres of mud flats: until that generation, not unused to Homeric exploits, coined a thwacking name for the Welshman—"Steam-Paddy" Hewes. It was he who took a handful of nuggets to a goldsmith and ordered the making and engraving of the Last Spike and had it ready for the meeting of East and West at Promontory Point in May 1869. All of which makes him, surely, the expected figure of the whooping, hard-fisted and not too ethical forty-niner? You insist?

He was one of the wistfulest, bashfulest, most self-effacing gentlemen I have ever met. When Mrs. Mills was eighty-five and he eighty-eight, he came from his orange ranch in the south to pay her one more visit. (They say he never forgot to send her flowers at Christmas and on her birthday.) To see and hear the two of them in her little dining room; the old-school courtesy, the tender deference, the bubbling laughter, as if mere youths of thirty to sixty could not possibly understand the delicious savor of life. Now that their work was done, they seemed to see things in a delightfully clear perspective. Let Achievement be introduced and turn its profile to the best advantage; let Administration speak of its mighty problems—of personnel, of new areas of effort, of co-ordination of many-sided activities: their smiling old eyes said, "What an enormous and important sand hill, my dear! And you made it all by yourself?"

Fevered men and women wondered why, with a chance to make a huge fortune, David Hewes stopped contracting at noon: but no—an orange grove near Whittier seemed nicer, and why spoil the long afternoon in strained effort to outdo the bonanza kings? Academic mendicants, not able to conceive unmercenary friendship, calculated the possibilities of the man, and were baffled by the strange delight he and Susan Mills found in one another. He had given money during his comparatively brief term as trustee, before he retired; later he gave the chimes for El Campanile; and I wonder how many persons who first heard them at the Chicago Fair in '93 again heard them boom over the Oval. But mayn't one like a man for himself? I have kept back until last one point in the story. What were the books which, after a few words with that Yale sophomore, thrifty New England housewives simply had to buy? One was *Peter Parley's Merry Museum*; the other, *Mother's Assistant*.

Justice Milton H. Myrick once listed eight distinguished Californians whom he knew—including a bishop, another justice of the state supreme court, a cabinet member and a mere general—all of whom were born in his home county: Oneida, of course. Indeed, Judge Myrick's wide acquaintance-ship and his frank delight in it might be read as vanity, mere busyness, in another man; but he was too girthy for that. Term it rather the assurance which grew from discovering that he too could make his way easily through a crowded world, that there was no occasion to be overawed by "front," and that the magic lay somehow in the Oneida County water. He was the happy man of the world, not given to overplaying the poor-boy-makes-good theme. At ten he learned to set type on his clerical father's small newspaper; at nineteen he braved New York City with twenty-five cents and a fund of self-possession. While he was working on the *American Whig Review*, it is said that he set type for the first printing of "The Raven"—a prophylactic experience; and as a young reporter he met N. P. Willis, Bayard Taylor, Fenimore Cooper, Washington Irving, and Horace Greeley himself. He studied law, came to California in '54, was a newsman in San Francisco and knew Thomas Starr King; then he started his own paper in Shasta, where he knew Martin Kellogg, General Bidwell, and the family of John Brown of Osawatomie.

Established as a lawyer in San Francisco in 1866, he was for a time a partner of Judge Sawyer. He was probate judge from 1871 to 1879, and then associate judge on the supreme court from 1881 until 1887. His volume, *Probate Reports*, is still assigned reading in the law schools. Among the trustees whom Cyrus Mills chose, Judge Myrick was the most urbane, shrewd in understanding the idiosyncrasies and crotchets of humanity, mastering hard situations by his own poise. His goodness was not the gospel compassion of Israel Dwinell, but rather a world-ripened benevolence permeated by humor. He was president of the Board during the most troubled period; with him in the chair, and James Pierce, Israel Dwinell, laconic Robert Simson, and astute Warren Olney around the table, a blustering dissident might learn too late (as one did) that there were men west of the Hudson.

Dr. Joseph H. Wythe, Cyrus Mills' physician, was an inspector of hospitals in and around Washington during the Civil War, and organized a large hospital in Alexandria. With a versatility not uncommon in his day he was also an ordained and spirited minister. Coming to the West Coast, he was president of Willamette University for three years; later he was professor of histology in Lane Hospital, precursor of the Stanford Medical School. In the '80's the vocabulary of psychology had not become the parlous catch-phrases of whosoever guesses, but the little doctor's acute perception and sympathetic understanding reveal him a good psychologist before the time. Israel Dwinell left the most revealing interpretation of Cyrus Mills; but if we judged by his remembered conversations with his intimates, Dr. Wythe could have interpreted Mills best in terms more significant to our generation, and his devotion was warmer than mere praise. In the case of another and very different man—as will appear—Dr. Wythe's charitable allowances indicate again the clinical mind. It was he who gave the good small telescope and built the little observatory that stood on Prospect Hill on the site of Ethel Moore Hall. In a transition period when older things were forgotten, the telescope disappeared, prized more by thieves than by heirs of learning.

Among the many letters wherein descendants of these early trustees speak of them, none is more beautiful than the one written about Leroy H. Briggs, for it speaks not of achievement but of being. He had risen from private to command a regiment in the Civil War. One day (in '78, was it not?) Mrs. Mills sent for his daughter to come to the parlors, and there a stocky, taciturn man laid his hand on her shoulder and said, "You are the little daughter of a very brave soldier." Stevenson rated Grant's considerateness toward Lee in the surrender scene the perfection of courtesy; but R.L.S. is out of fashion now, and the General more so—though not in the memory of that little girl. Indeed, does one recall many speeches of praise, spoken on any campus, that are better bonds at face value? The daughter remembers her father's gift of enjoyment: he could quote Shakespeare by the hour, not as exhibition of his own memory but of Shakespeare's memorableness. He was a lively amateur of astronomy, a wizard with plants, "a philosophical soul with a Christ-like spirit." Can our current rediscovery of the humanities hope to accomplish more?

One man I may point out without knowing more than the externals of his story. John Hemphill, a spirited Irish Presbyterian preacher, came to America to solicit funds for his church, and so captivated his audiences that he was competed for, and practically drafted to stay on. He succeeded the Reverend Charles Wadsworth in the pastorate of Calvary Presbyterian Church in San Francisco.

Youngest of the Board at the time of Cyrus Mills' death was Rodney L. Tabor, another Williams and U.T.S. man, whose devotion to Dr. and Mrs. Mills was singularly filial. As minister of a church in Alameda he brought Josiah Keep to Mrs. Mills' attention; and Tabor himself succeeded Cyrus Mills as teacher of moral philosophy until his own untimely death. Among Mrs. Mills' keepsakes is a volume of photographs—campus views, many tree-bordered paths and woodland vistas now hard to identify—the work of Rodney L. Tabor.

At the time of the incorporation, five trustees—Sawyer, Haight, Bryant, Eldridge, and Bray—had daughters who were alumnae of the Seminary, and James Eells' daughter graduated later from the college. I have not counted the several daughters and nieces of other trustees who attended the school after the incorporation; but no board in modern times has known, and been known by, the school more intimately. They were men of extraordinary breadth of experience, whose judgment was likely to be original. They knew the dignity of labor. Every man of the twenty-two who served before Cyrus Mills' death had made his way from some state east of the Mississippi to a degree of authority, and mostly to a deep-rooted identity of interest, in California.

The school was incorporated as "Mills Seminary-College," a title due to be changed with a reincorporation in 1885 when steps were taken to make it really a college. Cyrus and Susan Mills deeded to the trustees fifty-five acres of their hundred and fourteen, including mainly the upper reaches of the Saillot land and all the buildings. The original cost of the property they gave was $150,000; added improvements and natural increment brought the value of the gift well above that figure. The rest of the land they kept as an anchor to windward, for they had no assured expectation of a livelihood from the school in their old age. They had paid off $50,000 of debt. One condition of the transfer, due to become of exaggerated importance in certain minds, was that the trustees arranged for the Mills to continue financial and practical control of the school by leasing it to them for five years. The lease was re-newed at the end of that term, by request of the Board; and after Cyrus Mills' death, Mrs. Mills' conveyance of additional properties to the Board required an extension of that lease in October 1886. It is not known who originated the idea of the lease; Judge Sawyer and ex-Governor Haight drafted it, and statements made by certain trustees in 1886 indicate that the Board devised the plan. Evidently the trustees were convinced that the Mills could and would manage the school, both practically and educationally, better than any one else could do, and that those two were committed to give their all to the institution—a trust that was fulfilled to the letter. In their original gift they had amply fulfilled their obligation to the donors of the $30,000 which they had received. The school was no longer theirs, and in the minds of the men who knew them best there was no doubt that their faithful stewardship would continue. Any supposition that the trustees, by means of the lease, merely marked time and evaded responsibility, is wide of the mark. The minutes prove, over and over again, that the Board exercised not only due care of the business details but a personal regard for the teachers and the human relation-ships of the school. Indeed, so far as the records show, all was carried on as if the lease never existed. I cannot judge to what extent, if any, responsibility for the remaining debt was a considered factor in the arrangement.

One thing is certain: Cyrus Mills still felt a personal responsibility for that debt. He had not foreseen—few men could have foreseen—the growing competition from free public high schools which made the Seminary less profitable after the middle 1870's. The future of the institution lay in developing as rapidly as possible into full college caliber—a problem that became acute in the next two decades. But to him the immediate thing was the clearing of that debt, and to that he set his tired energies. He had long admired and deferred to his wife's superior genius in managing students and selecting teachers and keeping the big household healthy and happy. His land investments in Alameda County and elsewhere had encouraged him to trust his own canny judgment of investments. He could and would pay off that debt; he might even do, singlehanded, what he could not ask wealthier men to do: endow the college amply.

In 1882, while buying properties in southern California, he organized the Pomona Land and Water Company to develop the townsite of Pomona; and besides, he bought fifteen pieces of real estate in Los Angeles and San Diego counties, ranging from a city lot to ranches of several hundred acres. Incomplete as the venture was, he cleared in two years all the remaining debt but $7,000, which was paid by James Pierce, William H. Hyde (of Ware), and Mrs. M. S. Percy of Oakland. It was the opinion of such men as James Pierce and A. J. Bryant that, had he lived, he would have accomplished his aim of a liberal endowment. Without his shrewd judgment the venture made less than he had hoped, but it was not a loss.

In March 1884 an injury to his right arm aggravated the old ailments that had taxed his health ever since his years in Ceylon; pyaemia set in, and on April 19 Dr. Wythe and two other surgeons amputated the arm. For a few hours the case appeared hopeful, but early on the following morning—a Sunday morning—Dr. Mills died. He and Mrs. Mills had long planned together to build a cottage for their old age on the little knoll two hundred yards southwest of the "live-oak eighteen inches in diameter and blazed A." They had named the knoll Sunnyside; and now she chose it as the place for his grave.

It is ironical that men should measure him by the amount of his estate. Since the incorporation he and Mrs. Mills had deeded thirty more acres to the trustees, and had added buildings and equipment. One San Francisco newspaper "estimated"—sheer guess—that he had begun at Benicia with "perhaps not more than $20,000." The business items in Mary Atkins' diary for 1866 show clearly that he had begun with less than $5,000. At thirty-seven he had known the humiliation of having to ask the Mission Board to supplement a little his sick-leave pittance of thirty-three dollars a month. At the end, whatever satisfaction he may have felt in having proved his self-dependence was as nothing compared to the fulfillment of his and his wife's dream.

His holographic will was drawn in March 1882. His writing, once clear, had become feeble. (For easier reading I have standardized the punctuation.)

> *I, Cyrus T. Mills, of Mills Seminary, Alameda Co., Cal., do deliberately and of my own free will make this my last will and testament.*
>
> *I bequeath to my niece, Addie E. Mills, three thousand dollars, and to my niece, Issie Mills, five hundred dollars.* I bequeath to the President and Board of Trustees of Mills Seminary College one third of my property personal and real. All the balance of my property of every kind I bequeath to my wife, Susan T. Mills, and I request her to carry out our plans for endowing three scholarships, one in Williams College, Mass., one in Mount Holyoke Seminary, and one in Jaffna College, Ceylon. I also request her, after reserving what she may deem necessary for her own use and comfort, to convey the balance for the endowment of Mills Seminary College. I also request the Trustees of said Institution to hold it forever free from debt, to make it thoroughly Christian but not sectarian, to maintain a high moral and literary standard and thus realize in the fullest measure our plans and our hopes . . .*

[Here follows the usual revoking of former wills, and the appointment of his wife as executrix without bond.]

And the man himself? He left no book, no dissertation. Upon only a few occasions—one being in Tremont Temple, Boston—had he broken through that "want of address" which umpirical Dr. Robinson noted, and moved his audience by uttering a plain truth which went against the official grain. I have heard that in his later years when a guest at assembly had spoken unusually well Cyrus sometimes repeated the main points in the speech—an unique failing. They say he was uncomfortable when, as president, he had to admonish the students. It was improper for Mary Lyon to say grace if a man was present; Mrs. Mills felt that way about admonitions, yet he obviously hated the job, for she could turn the sting into laughter and he never could. He knew he was not clever, but he may have taken Oneida comfort from knowing that he had the fewer erratic splurges to varnish over, and no strain of histrionics to keep his public applausive. With little gift of charm there was less danger of overestimating and depending upon that tricky ally. Being sensitive, he had learned, if not at Plainfield, surely all the way from Batticotta to the Oval,

---

* The two nieces were daughters of his deceased brother, Giles. Both had attended the Seminary, and Adeline had graduated in 1873.

youth's propensity for singling out a teacher's absurd mannerisms and scrawling these upon the side wall where they outlast all nobler inscriptions. His humility was knit with such dry independence that his want of dramatic color is canceled by the quiet dignity of human nature.*

And he could never forget what those Williams men had done for him. An awkward country boy with no inherited right, no preordained claim to culture, and no clowning humor to mask his want, he had dared Williamstown. Mark and Albert Hopkins had withheld nothing. With superior minds, both, they had not a grain of academic snobbery. And what would Cyrus Mills have been without them? He knew the answer; and he, in turn, could never deny opportunity to other youths. The best men in his class had, as it were, adopted the school he and Mrs. Mills founded. Back in '74, when his ailing arm kept him from writing, Mrs. Mills had reported for both of them to the thirtieth reunion of his class, and had given them explicit directions how to reach the Melrose station if they ever came west! He was looking forward with ardor to the fortieth reunion in August '84; and now the class wrote to her with a feeling far deeper than perfunctory sorrow. They spoke of his "uprightness and courtesy, the unaffected piety and sweet charity which marked his college life and gave a charm to his steady perseverance in all his class duties and to his ripening scholarship"; and they were well informed of his later success. Of the last four survivors of that class, three—Theron H. Hawks, William B. Rice, and Marshall Wilcox—continued to correspond with Mrs. Mills, and had her as a guest, to the end. And the steady approval and affection of Mark Hopkins† was, to Cyrus, the dearest approval of all— all but one.

Cheated of his own childhood, he had one charm not in the academic record. Once during a daylong train ride from Los Angeles to Oakland, busy Judge Sawyer fumed because he could not draw Cyrus' attention to a weighty conference, because Cyrus was playing all day with two engaging small boys. And one gentlewoman remembers her own delight when, at five, she heard he was coming for a visit: there would be droll stories and rhymes and all the by-play of a fancy that was wholly at ease in company of a child.

Did he and Susan love each other? One witness used to say, "Humph! he just pecked her cheek when he kissed." But another woman, one of those who knew Mrs. Mills best, abolishes that pertness: "I watched by her bedside

---

* I am reminded belatedly that he introduced archery to the campus. And where did he learn that?

† Mrs. Mills gave $50,000 to endow the Mark Hopkins Chair of Moral Philosophy in Mills College, as a memorial to that great teacher.

when she was near death from pneumonia, twenty years after Dr. Mills died. You should have seen her face light with joy when the whispered talk turned back to him. 'My dear used to say' thus and so; or, 'My dear was so fond of' this or that thing. No, they simply adored each other." What matters which was the vine and which the tree? "Here the I's end and the we's begin," and so it was down to that final "our plans and our hopes."

His final achievement—who knows?—may be to make us ashamed that we have done so little.

Under these genial skies, unhindered by the extremes of an inauspicious climate, less fettered by tyrannical customs, here where bounteous nature all the year long pours forth her treasures in unparalleled variety and inexhaustible profusion, here where the light of America confronts the light of Asia as the golden west glides into the purple east, it needs but the highest education to produce a society not less rich in intellect and far nobler in morals than that of ancient Greece in her palmiest age, and to realize, not in external nature alone, but in the spiritual beauty and grandeur also, the fulfillment of Shelley's prophetic vision—

> *A brighter Hellas rears its mountains*
> *From waves serener far.*
> *A new Peneus rolls its fountains*
> *Against the morning star.*

The platform ached with trustees and prominent clergymen and educators, and a governor was almost present. Governor Stoneman was on the campus the evening before, but as no speech by him is recorded, one infers that he did not stay over for the great day. Shadowed by notables, Mrs. Mills listened anxiously. The chief speaker was obviously in favor of all good things: clean government, many reforms; "we shall find a solution of the harassing questions connected with international relations, civil service reform, silver coinage, paper currency, free trade and protective tariff, freedom of the ballot, the Monroe doctrine, prohibition or license, what to do with the Chinese, what to do with the Mormons, what to do with the Indians, what to do with the monopolies, what to do with ecclesiasticism, and innumerable other momentous issues sure to arise." Above all, he championed educated woman as homemaker, wife, and mother; the world needed "a large number of gifted women for companionship with gifted men." Mrs. Mills could take no exception, but she reflected drily that her girls had heard from many visiting male speakers the same formula. The speaker praised "the far-seeing sagacity, the unwearied toil, the sleepless vigilance, the unselfish devotion, the perfect consecration" of the Mills, and spoke nobly of what they had done. Had done: yes, she must readjust her tenses. His eloquence had a smoother flow than Miss Lyon's hearty, impromptu talks; more color than that of any speaker she could remember, from nice old Mr. Condit and Levi Spaulding and the Island men down to Dr. Eells and Dr. Dwinell. An eloquence that covered the map with dizzying problems. She couldn't exactly say it was not a religious eloquence, for he praised the church and the Bible and good morals —and yet it wasn't Scriptural. Plenty of quotations from poets—but only two lines from *Paradise Lost*. Even Martha Vincent's ode had not been quite right.

Martha had likened Cyrus Mills to Elijah, and of course Elijah's mantle was bound to fall upon Elisha; but Susan had never liked Elisha as a good Christian should, for one of the first things he did, wearing his inherited mantle, was to call two she-bears to devour some little children who had offended his precious dignity. Dear me, if she and Cyrus had been that touchy! Anyway, Cyrus was not Elijah: he was only Cyrus, patient and humble, needing to be encouraged and yet far braver than most people had ever supposed; and it were wiser not to pitch the song of praise too high. It did not hurt her to be omitted from the program; she couldn't have borne it to speak this day. Besides, if she was any judge, the program was plenty long enough.* But there! She blamed herself for this slight mistrust. Through all their years together she and Cyrus had planned and worked to build a school, and then to transform it into a college. And this new president had educational scope and breadth—ever so many recommenders had assured her of that—and she must do her full share to help him. The trustees were generous; they had passed a resolution allowing her to choose any three rooms she wanted, or they would build her a separate cottage on the campus and provide her with servants. She would keep the familiar rooms nearest the brook, the rooms she and Cyrus had chosen when—when they needed nobody's permission. But there again! Better soothe her mind with that passage from Proverbs 3, which the girls had read so well to open the program: "Happy is the man that findeth wisdom, and the man that getteth understanding." A good passage, though she still preferred Psalms. Proverbs (except the chapter about King Lemuel's mother) sounded as though written by a shrewd Ben Franklin; Psalms, as if all mankind opened their hearts like children. And now at last it is almost over; John Swett has spoken,† and Professor Howison is speaking.‡ She hopes the Chinaboys will manage, in spite of the delay, to serve an exceptionally good lunch, for the new president and his wife and her sisters are still tired from their journey, and a nice lunch will gentle their frayed nerves.

* The record fills thirty-five pages, nearly twenty thousand words, even omitting one prayer and one speech.

† Fifty years ago no public school teacher in California would have supposed the time would ever come when it would be necessary to identify John Swett. At teachers' gatherings he was a sturdy independent who drew young men unto him by hickory flavor, an unimitative John the Baptist with a sense of humor. He spoke sparingly, not as one parading for position; he had caught long ago from a diet of locusts and wild honey a primitive passion for teaching.

‡ Professor George Howison, a newcomer at the University of California in 1885, lived to be a venerable landmark in the philosophy department of President Wheeler's time.

Mills College would feel hurt if these guests from Boston found the campus wanting in hospitality.

The day was Saturday, October 24, 1885. The new president was Homer Baxter Sprague (1829–1918), Yale 1852. He had practiced law and had taught in high schools; he had fought in the Civil War, rising to brevet colonel; he had been a legislator in Connecticut, a teacher for two years at Cornell and, since 1876, headmaster of the Girls' High School in Boston. He had received the Ph.D. degree from New York University in 1874.

When he, with his wife, the youngest of their four children, and two sisters and a niece of Mrs. Sprague, arrived on the coast, a committee of five trustees, accompanied by a reporter from the *Oakland Tribune*, met the party at Benicia. The *Tribune* man wrote, "Dr. Sprague wore a gray suit. He is of average height and is of a stout, compact, build. He is an Anglo-Saxon type." With which Rembrandtian portrait we shall try to be content. "Don't put in anything about my being a prominent man," the new executive protested. "That is all bosh. I am not a prominent man." Despite this self-depreciation the reporter contrived to gather a considerable part of the plenteous data which later filled a sketch (not one of the briefest) in *Who's Who*. At Sixteenth Street the party entered carriages and, in freshman parlance, were whirled away to the campus, where they found the Oval decorated with "WELCOME" spelled in golden flowers. There was a reception.

The story of the next thirteen months need not be told in calendared detail. A year and a day after Dr. Sprague's inauguration the trustees requested his resignation, and upon his refusal they declared his office vacant. In November 1886 he published a lengthy pamphlet, *To My Friends,* and in December the Board published a reply. Various committee reports on the case were lost in the San Francisco fire, but one important report is quoted at some length in Dr. Sprague's pamphlet. Omitting the trivia and accepting the stipulated points, the story comes down to this:

Sprague came well recommended, and he had much ability. The trustees had sent the Reverend C. D. Barrows east to prospect for candidates, and he was impressed with the prestige of some of Sprague's backers, President Daniel C. Gilman of Johns Hopkins and President Andrew D. White of Cornell among them. Their letters being lost, there is no way of judging how the balance swung between good wishes for Sprague's preferment and their critical judgment of his fitness for the job. Sprague and Gilman had been classmates at Yale (1852) and White was a year behind them. As an undergraduate Sprague had been the most brilliant man in his class, winning all manner of prizes for composition and oratory, and had been valedictorian.

But now thirty-three years had passed; how much of Gilman's and White's commendation was a carryover of undergraduate friendship, qualified perhaps with kindly regret that youthful eloquence had not ripened into a hardier fruit? White had had Sprague for two years on his faculty at Cornell. Gilman, as president of the University of California before going to Johns Hopkins, should have known whether his old classmate was adaptable to the conditions at Mills Seminary-College. Or was this new presidency but a consolation prize? From Sprague's own account, a certain Major Henry C. Dane had been the real go-between. Dane had known something of Mills Seminary, and he had (it seems) known Sprague in the army. Take for what it is worth the fact that before Sprague arrived on the coast he announced Dane as one of his new faculty, though there is no record that Dane ever taught or lectured in the school. Sprague and the trustees corresponded for six months, and at one point the Board invited him to visit the Seminary and satisfy himself as to its needs—an offer which he waived and which they had been wiser to insist upon. Far too much was taken for granted on both sides.

The arrangement gave him executive control of education, appointment of teachers, establishment of a college curriculum, the voluble duties of speaking in public and the privilege of hoping for endowment. Mrs. Mills was to continue as "Lady Principal" (dean of students), household manager, and comptroller. She had succeeded her husband as a member of the Board, and as treasurer of that body she was strictly accountable. Any amused supposition that the trustees were puppets in her hands is flatly wrong; the trustees did not slur their duty. Her function as business manager was covered by the lease that has been discussed in Chapter XIII. Under that lease the Mills had cleared the school of heavy debt, and she was regularly turning whatever profit accrued back into the school.

It has been represented that in her reluctance to yield power and prestige she hampered President Sprague. The minutes of the trustees give no evidence of this, nor does his own pamphlet. He tells that she feared he was appointing too many men teachers, and too many Episcopalians (there being already five from that church); but he adds that "she yielded gracefully." He wanted to drum up more day students, to help pay the bills; she disapproved. She wanted to have girls in residence; the school could do more for them in that way.

One amusing item turned upon an old rule that required graduates not to dress expensively at commencement. In March 1886 Mrs. Mills went for a visit to friendly Honolulu, and during her absence some of the seniors rebelled over what they felt was an arbitrary interpretation of that rule by the president. When Mrs. Mills returned, the girls appealed to her; and she—it would be just like her!—pleaded privately with Mrs. Sprague to intercede for the girls. Instead, Mrs. Sprague told her husband "on" Mrs. Mills. In his angry pamphlet he cited this plea as an undermining, not merely of morale, but of morals. As between president and dean, who should decide whether a dress is unduly expensive? He mentioned no further conflicts of opinion as between him and Mrs. Mills, and he seems to have omitted nothing.

There was as yet no college class, and the hoped-for freshmen in the fall of '86 would face a severe regimen in the classics: Livy, Tacitus and Horace, Homer, Herodotus and Plato—with not a molecule of science. One of the president's policies sounds fantastic. In his inaugural he advised "drawing into the schools at least a clear majority of the young, and by liberal premiums holding them there until they become wise, patriotic, conscientious." A casual reader would hardly suppose he meant premiums of money—but that is exactly what he did mean. He early announced that he had raised $700, to be equally divided as a bonus among freshman intrants the next year, the student to repay her bonus if she withdrew before graduation.

Even before his bitter quarrel with the trustees, he was unhappy here. Being a proud man, he could not fail to notice that after the generous spread of publicity during his first weeks the papers ignored him. A man who knew him in Berkeley a few years after his term at Mills, writes: "Dr. Sprague had a formal manner, which to many persons seemed at times stiff and even haughty." An alumna, later a teacher, writes:

> *I remember that he was conventional, stuffy, and uninteresting. He seemed to lack the spark of originality that makes a speaker attractive. His evening prayer was always the same, I can even now repeat parts of it. When he spoke to his audience he had a peculiar habit of rolling his eyes here, there, and everywhere, instead of looking at his audience.*

There is a still earlier witness who had been a student at Cornell long ago. He enjoyed a variety of men and subjects, and he wrote with tempered judgment:

> *In the English Literature courses I enjoyed the fine and sympathetic readings of Hiram Corson, but systematic instruction had failed to "strike its gait." As to that, I remember the very first lecture I heard at Cornell. This was by Corson's predecessor, Colonel Homer B. Sprague, then an ambitious young man with a fine war record and the special glory of having escaped from Libby Prison. Sprague began: "James Thomson was born at Ednam, near Kelso on the river Tweed in Roxburgh County, Scot-*

land," *continuing with further details which we faithfully noted down. We soon learned, however, that all such matters were to be found in the handy compendium from which they were probably gleaned.*

Another of Sprague's courses, it is only fair to say, was more illuminating. It dealt with word roots which we had to dig out for ourselves. Our first task dealt with the sentence, "We do not expect savage sarcasm from the apostles."

That student was David Starr Jordan.

The only evidence I find upon Sprague's teaching at Mills is a complaint from the trustees that he was doing so little. He protested that his illness in April was due to overwork, partly the arduous labor of composing his inaugural address in October. Later, at the University of North Dakota, his sophomore class in English read during the year thirty-eight stanzas of the first canto of *The Faerie Queene*, all of *Julius Caesar*, and the first three acts of *Macbeth*.

His bitter quarrel with the trustees grew from an issue too fundamental to be compromised. In August 1886 he demanded complete financial control of the college, household and plant management, and life tenure; and these demands the Board was not willing to grant. Those trustees are forgotten now; but the little college survived only because real men were on the Board when most needed. The Board had its usual proportion: six ministers, two judges, and six business and professional men. Rodney L. Tabor, a fine-spirited and scholarly minister (a Williams man) died midyear before the trouble broke. His successor was Senator James G. Fair—a strange sequence. Fair was hardly a devout patron of the humanities nor an encourager of monastic ideals, but even his enemies admitted that he was not purblind in judging people, or an easy man to bluff. He may not have regarded his seat on the Board as paramount to his more colorful interests, but to his credit he gave a certain level-eyed attention to Mills College during its greatest need. But the members who carried the main weight in the case were the veterans Judge Myrick, Dr. I. E. Dwinell, former mayor A. J. Bryant, Robert Simson, James Pierce of Santa Clara, and Dr. J. H. Wythe. The college has never had more devoted trustees. The new secretary of the Board, Warren Olney, was destined to serve the college for thirty-five years, the longest term on record. Mrs. Mills had chosen him as her attorney after her husband's death, and she became an adoptive mother to the Olney family. The Sprague affair brought out the complementary abilities of her mind and Olney's.

For two months the trustees tried conciliation; a complete break would injure the school and the president; but once thoroughly angry, Sprague threw both considerations to the wind. He chiefly attacked the lease under which Mrs. Mills managed the business affairs. The Board rejoined: "It was at our request and because of our entire confidence in her that we requested her to take the lease and the responsibility and cares connected with it. We have not found the slightest occasion for criticism. Mrs. Mills has done not merely what she agreed to do, but far more." Sprague protested that the lease was fraudulent, and that he had never dreamt of its existence when he accepted the position; but it had been publicized repeatedly, and careful Warren Olney's files proved that Sprague had been well informed. In fine, he made no objection to the lease until he demanded powers far greater than those it conferred.

His temper out of control, his pamphlet became a scatter-gun of spite. "I shall publish a statement that will make some of you feel pretty cheap." Nothing had been right—not even the committee of welcome. "I continually objected to this Barnum-like show business,* but was constantly told that such things were necessary in California." Only two teachers, he said, were fully competent; Josiah Keep, then beginning his long career at Mills, was but half-competent. To say and to unsay in the same breath put a strain upon the man's rationalizing:

> *While I yield to none in my reverence and admiration of the wonderful skill, energy, fidelity and consecration with which Mrs. Mills has carried on the work of the school, and while I believe that multitudes whom she has trained here will for time and eternity regard her with tender love and warm gratitude, I yet feel it my duty . . .*

One verbal missile let us keep. He called the proprietor of a very nice shop in Oakland "a mono-hippic milliner." A student who bought her hats there was upset over the possible connotation; she followed the composition teacher's advice, "See dictionary,"—and got no comfort thereby.

Three teachers resigned in sympathy with Dr. Sprague, one being John M. Chase, a Cornell man whom he had appointed.

A strange autointoxication of words, with no energy left for the doing, but only enough to scold his helpers because they could not build Athens in a day and without a blueprint. He could not do spade work. Better men—Willey,

---

* On the welcoming committee were Israel E. Dwinell, Rodney L. Tabor, and Francis A. Horton, three of the best-loved ministers in California in that or any other period. All three were memorable for fine-spirited gentleness. A fourth member was A. J. Bryant, who, though once a mayor, was not a geyser. The fifth man, Palmer, does not come to my mind: was he five Barnums?

Woodbridge, Brayton, Durant—had worked with cruder material on a frontier and had not blamed the conditions.*

Dr. Sprague was elected president of the University of North Dakota in October 1887. That institution, founded in 1885 and combining both seminary and college, had a faculty of six. Under his administration the school grew; the first class graduated in 1889, and he was getting on well until some tactless ineptitude in a speech he made at a banquet of legislators provoked them to slash the university's budget. In January 1891, with the election of a United States Senator coming up in the legislature, the old excitement took him, and he issued a campaign document which ran in part:

> . . . *while I would like to be senator . . . To get it I can engage in no fight, no scramble, no intrigue, and no bargain; I shall neglect no present duty, make no speeches, curry favor with no politician, countenance no corruption, solicit no votes, pull no wires, promise no offices, pay no money, fling no mud, tell no lies.*

Apparently to his surprise he got no vote, and he promptly resigned in midterm; but he listed among his achievements in *Who's Who*, "strongly supported for U.S. Senator, N. Dakota." A Dakota alumna, an admirer of President Sprague, gives a livelier picture of him than the *Tribune* man's "Anglo-Saxon type." She writes: "The University was situated about two miles west of the city, and once a day he walked both ways. He was dignified and used a cane. It always seemed to me that he made the best use of a cane of anyone I had known."

Soon after he resigned from North Dakota Dr. Sprague returned to California and started a school for boys in Berkeley—the Peralta School, located near the former residence of Domingo Peralta. He coined for the school a motto—*Per alta ad altiora*. The venture lasted about two years.

Vale, vir eloquens et superbe, ascende cum baculo per alta ad altiora ad immortalitatem.

Dr. Charles Carroll Stratton (1833–1910) succeeded Dr. Sprague as president of Mills College in June 1887 but was not inaugurated until the following May. The story of his administration has been told with painful caution; but to varnish it over is to ignore the hardest problem Mrs. Mills ever had to face.

Stratton's father had pioneered in Oregon in 1852. The young man en-

---

* I have not traced the story through the New England papers, but the trustees' rejoinder to Sprague's angry pamphlet implies that the college was severely criticized in Boston.

tered Willamette University in 1855 and graduated in 1858. He was ordained in the Methodist church and, circuit-rider fashion, held successive posts in Oregon and at Salt Lake City, and was transferred to San Jose in 1874. Because of his success as preacher and organizer he was elected president of the University of the Pacific (then at San Jose) in 1877, and served for ten years. He had a hearty way of meeting people on their own ground, and did much to carry the struggling denominational college against the growing competition of state colleges and high schools. It is said that he was approached by Governor Stanford with an offer of the presidency of Stanford University, but this I have to doubt—though "approach" is an elastic word. Stratton had been friendly with the Mills; he tried to mediate in the Sprague affair, and Mrs. Mills asked his counsel in that crisis.

His inauguration was simple; no one wanted another symphonic overture; and though he too had the reputation of a silver tongue he spoke more as a bustling superintendent of schools with a flair for statistics than as a college president. He argued the need of colleges that would foster religion, and pleaded for tax exemption of such institutions. He lacked Sprague's academic and classical background—and neither man had a tithe of the Mills' respect for science—but he felt no condescension toward the work that needed to be done. His audience doubtless caught the overtone when an alumna (no poet, this time) said, "We are glad that you believe in California and in her sons and daughters."

Dr. Stratton put his hand to improve the physical plant, his main achievement being the building of College Hall—that underprivileged half sister of Mills Hall. Science Hall was begun in his time, and he also engineered the dam that impounds Lake Aliso. In the third year of his administration, Divinity Church was remodeled for a residence, and the president's family lived there.

With no fanfare he got the college classes going and established a workable curriculum. (The first college class, five in number, graduated in 1889.) In the fall of 1889 a committee of trustees under the energetic leadership of a new member, Dr. J. K. McLean, drew a new plan for faculty and department organization—the beginning of specialization by teachers. None of Stratton's appointees continued long enough to prove their caliber. There was an encouraging increase in enrollment, but something was wrong, some incompatibility felt rather than defined. The theoretical division of authority between president and lady principal was becoming blurred, and teachers and students could not remain neutral. The issue was, I think, one of deep-rooted sympathies. Users of the word "spiritual" are blamed for vagueness, but teachers and students sensed the spiritual difference between Dr. Stratton and Mrs. Mills. One alumna recalls a sermon in which Stratton extolled Turkish girls who allowed themselves to be sold into harems for the benefit of their financially distressed fathers—a question which Mrs. Mills felt was wide of the gospel. Still another alumna, writing (I am sure) without malice and making no comment upon gross scandal, remembers that she felt hurt and ashamed hearing President Stratton quote more than once his favorite aphorism:

With gas and brass and backers too
A smart man ought to wiggle through.

What the dissension would have come to is mere guess. Before it came to a head on general issues it was short-circuited by a rude fact.

In January 1890 three faculty women complained to Mrs. Mills and then to the Board that President Stratton had pressed amatory attentions upon them. The Board referred the matter to a committee: Giles H. Gray, Dr. J. K. McLean, and L. H. Briggs. Colonel Briggs had been on the Board for nine years, while Gray, a son of the Nathaniel Gray who gave money toward building Science Hall, was a new member. Also new was Dr. John Knox McLean (1834–1914), who with fiery volubility became chief defender of Stratton. Brought up on a farm in upstate New York, he had his college work at Union (with Phi Beta Kappa) and his theological course at Princeton, and had had three live pastorates in New England and Illinois before coming to Oakland in 1872. Here he succeeded Dr. George Mooar (Williams '51) as minister of the First Congregational Church, where he served for twenty-three years, and then became president of the Pacific Theological Seminary (later the Pacific School of Religion), holding that post until he retired in 1912. Dr. Mooar had been one of the closest friends of Cyrus Mills; I cannot find that Mills in his shy way opened his heart to McLean, or that McLean with his sweeping energy perceived the worth of Mills. It was upon Mrs. Mills' motion that he was elected a trustee in 1889, and if he used toward her a less adulatory outspokenness than others, she might sensibly reflect that he did not apostrophize her as a saint in one breath and damn her in the next with howevers. Dr. McLean had a powerful influence upon public opinion in northern California, and once he let himself go in the Stratton affair, controversy fitted him like the grip of a Covenanter's sword. If one may judge from the copious interviews in the papers, Dr. McLean allowed the vehemence of argument to sweep him along until discomfiting his opponents became a greater object than the elusive truth of the original question. (In gentler parentheses, he was a scholarly trout fisherman, a warm friend of the poet Sill, whom he companioned on trips to Mount Shasta; and his paternal ancestors came from the Isle of Mull, where they must have known Red Fergus. How could Dr. McLean be other than a spirited man?)

The prim minutes of the Board are reticent, and stenographic reports of the statements of the three complaining teachers have disappeared. Just what the committee reported to the Board, no one knows; but at the March meeting the Board advised that, for the good of the college, the matter be dropped. Trustee Briggs denounced the report of his own committee as whitewash, and it came out later that President Stratton had brushed the charges aside as being a conspiracy to make his position untenable. Still later he was quoted by the press as claiming the charges were made to win advancement for the plaintiffs —a claim that sounds too incredible. One has to be cautious of inference, but it appears that the complaints did not charge gross immorality, and that committeemen Gray and McLean regarded the affair as being not very serious, while Colonel Briggs and the other trustees felt that the president had showed at least a poor sense of decorum. Later on, after the storm broke, the trustees put themselves on cautious record regarding the March meeting: "No vote as to exoneration or condemnation was had, nor any collective expression of opinion thereon." Merely, for the good of the college let the matter be dropped.

The central figures may have tried to hush the story, but a small campus has psychic radar, and in April the newspapers got word of it. In fairness, the reporters were not half as wicked as they might have been. Mrs. Mills and the teachers declined to be interviewed, and Dr. Stratton had been wiser to follow their example, for he was no match for the reporters. *Enter Rumour, painted full of tongues.* Old scandals were hinted and denied. Osculation became a topic for forums. One headline ran:

> *Some Kisses are Iniquitous and Some are Innocuous—*
> *Some Innocent and Some Guilty!*

Most of the students refused to attend church when Dr. Stratton preached. Seminary girls, forgetting they were ladies, poured into a mob, made a little coffin (black, hexagonal, grisly as the Dance of Death), tacked a photograph of President Stratton on the lid, marched it around the Oval and up and down the woodland paths, then toted it to the trash grate and burned it, but not until after one foreseeing young Maenad had taken a picture of it, a copy of which is now a collector's item. Gentlewomen once members of that Klan assure us the episode was shocking, simply shocking. Then they chuckle.

On May 8 the president resigned. Regardless of guilt or innocence, his usefulness was gone. Immediately Trustees Gray, McLean, and Wythe resigned from the Board. (Dr. J. H. Wythe, both physician and clergyman, was once president of Willamette, where Stratton graduated, and had preceded Stratton as president of the University of the Pacific.) Three teachers resigned, all being Dr. Stratton's appointees; the remaining twenty were loyal to Mills, and the tone of a resolution they signed sounds like more than bread-and-butter loyalty. One senior student went home—for the week end. Dr. Stratton asked for and was granted a hearing by a jury of Methodist clergymen, but as Mrs. Mills and the complaining teachers declined to appear before that body, the brethren voted "Innocent" and admonished the college to treat its presidents better. One trustee declared in the press that Stratton's friends had bargained that he would resign in March if the charges were hushed; this was denied.

After sixty years who can retry the case? It was *The Ring and the Book* once more, were there only a Browning to tell it. Was there a black conspiracy against a good man's reputation? But the plaintiffs also had reputations. Between 1866 and 1890 about three hundred teachers came, taught for a time, and went. They are now only names on a chart, their faces indistinct. Only a few of their students in 1890 still live, and memories fail. It is something of a miracle, then, to justify Browning's imagination, that one of those three plaintiffs is still remembered out of the ghostly blur. She was a Mills alumna, and she still lives in the memory of a few, with noble dignity and beauty. Gentlemen of the Board—both factions, your compromise, "neither exoneration nor condemnation," had a flaw. It was a painful dilemma, but compromise cured nothing. Was President Stratton a wronged gentleman? Or the sort of man upon whom a women's college puts a dangerous strain? Fifty-odd years after the affair the daughter of one of Stratton's defenders stated that her father had shielded him not because he thought him innocent but because as a clergyman he would be cruelly punished anyway. A Scottish verdict satisfies no one. This Old Yellow Book is closed with the conviction that certain competent witnesses were not summoned.

On May 8 the trustees elected Mrs. Mills president of the college. She was sixty-four years old. The Board had chosen Sprague upon the recommendation of eastern men. That would become a familiar story through the years: distant men, confident that they knew what the small college needed, or stretching ethical obligation to boost the preferment of a friend. But she herself had chosen Stratton. That realization shocked her, made her over-cautious; yet henceforth she would have to trust her own judgment more than ever. Each man had praised her and Cyrus to the skies, then each had promptly schemed to bundle her off to Europe so that he might have a free hand to make of the school something very different from what she and Cyrus had wanted. The one man's pride made him haughty toward western students and teachers. Halfway around the world, she and Cyrus had been patient; the joy lay in discovering something fine in humble youth. And one needed the friendship of common men, to build anything. Would Dr. Sprague have won for the college better friends than the trustees whom he held in contempt? And the other man had given the lie to three young women whom she knew and trusted as her own daughters.

She was eager for the school to become a real college: might it not do that without losing the spirit that had been so happy during the good years? As to her judgment of teachers, Josiah Keep, her own last appointee, was worth all the interim appointees put together. Years ago, she and Cyrus had considered giving their school to the state, as Willey and Brayton and Durant had done. The university had raised the standard, as men say, but it had lost something, too. She could bear to be told that her school needed improving, but why tell it so unkindly? Mark Hopkins had never scorned what she and Cyrus had done. They had guarded against sectarianism; the Mount Holyoke of her youth would have thought it strange that she could bring together girls of every faith—Protestant, Catholic, Jew—all learning the friendliness that has no need to argue tolerance. Did it hurt them, or lower the standard of scholarship, to read a chapter and sing a hymn together twice daily? She had learned long ago that preparing souls for the last Judgment is a sorry business; but how could any real teacher see boys and girls bewildered by the mystery of life and not want to help them? No, let the small college remain small rather than lose the very purpose of its being.

But the sickening publicity of the Stratton affair—the good name of her teachers, her own and Cyrus' name, tittered by gossip. Compromise to avoid scandal had only brought worse scandal. Let people criticize her for interfering, how could she be silent and allow any man brashly to ruin the gift she and Cyrus had given?

The story of the two men presidents became a sealed chapter. Their names were omitted from the historical sketch of the college; and a teacher might become a veteran before hearing, in asterisks of voice, that there had ever been such men. Mrs. Mills became shrewd, jealous, in her appointment of teachers; and as never before, she turned, in the early '90's, to Mount Holyoke women.

fifteen

"OLD-FASHIONED EYES,
NOT EASY TO SURPRISE . . ."

WISER FOR THE STRATTON AFFAIR, PROMPTED BY MRS. MILLS, THE gentlemen of the Board elected two women trustees to look under the academic rugs, and a visiting committee of alumnae to be careful. There were, in all, five women trustees before Mrs. Mills retired, three of whom were alumnae.

She had no intention of continuing long at the helm, for she made a prompt effort to find a new president—a woman, this time. She had saved her school, and she had a rare insight into the qualities of teachers, but her respect for the term "college" caused her to underestimate her own ability. Her effort to find a successor never got into the papers; the present account is derived mainly from one former teacher whose knowledge of the affair and whose later experience in education command the highest respect.

In the fall of 1891 Dr. Marietta Kies came to the college as vice-principal, but really as a probationer to the presidency. Graduated from Mount Holyoke in 1881, she was one of the first alumnae to earn a doctorate degree, working in psychology under William T. Harris at the University of Michigan. She had taught well at Mount Holyoke and at Colorado College, and she

217

combined the traditional Mount Holyoke seriousness with a comprehension of new standards in education and especially of modern psychology. Mrs. Mills had thought it prudent not to let some of her intimates know her plans regarding Dr. Kies, and it appears that when Miss Jane Tolman and Miss Mary Ellis (Mount Holoke '55) discovered that authority was in danger of passing into other hands they contrived obstacles which Mrs. Mills and Miss Kies thought insurmountable. Mrs. Mills could be valiant enough against alien opponents, yet less than brave against persons who pleaded old claims upon her. Miss Ellis had taught many years at Mount Holyoke and Grinnell, and had come to Mills as to a retirement home. She and Miss Tolman had been colleagues at Mount Holyoke for six years, both had been to Europe (as Mrs. Mills had not), and Miss Ellis had even seen Egypt and the Holy Land. The two dissidents may have felt that if Rome and the pyramids gathered prestige with the centuries there was no reason to replace Upham's *Mental Philosophy* (in two volumes) by this upstart Psychology with its doctorate degree from Michigan. Mrs. Mills has been criticized for her reluctance to yield authority; in this case she may have been too reluctant to exercise it. Dr. Kies withdrew after one year.

Many colleges and some universities maintained academy departments until well into the 1890's, though conceding that these would have to be closed; and certainly such an adjunct as the preparatory department (grammar grades) at Mills was doomed. But the lower schools were paying the heavy deficit of the college proper. Besides, more and still more friends wanted their daughters, younger than seminary years, to be with Mrs. Mills, and how could she refuse? Poor lambs. There was that little girl from Nevada who had never seen a real tree until her train neared Truckee, and had never touched one until she found on the campus a live oak that was created simply to be climbed, and of course some literalist caught her and read Rule 23, and the child was in tears. To be sent back to Nevada for climbing a tree! Then Mrs. Mills heard of it and—yes, it *is* a most inviting tree and—when I was a girl in Enosburg there was such a nice apple tree in Uncle Levi Nichols' orchard and—it's a silly rule that can't be waived for a human hunger. Or that other little girl, so very homesick, who cried herself to sleep every night until Mrs. Mills heard of that, too, and had the young one in to sleep with her until the campus became less strange. (The Nevada girl told us her story, nearly twenty years later; and the homesick child told hers to an alumna a few years ago. Each remembered the kindness as a great event in her life.) Still, the university pundits and the progressive young teachers said the lower schools must go. To prepare for a theoretical greater good you had to repress your lifelong habit of doing an immediate good.

Between 1890 and 1895 Mrs. Mills appointed eleven Mount Holyoke women to the faculty, and others from Carleton, Earlham, Wooster, Wellesley, and the University of Minnesota. Between 1896 and 1908 she appointed six more teachers from Mount Holyoke, and others from Cornell, Chicago, Stanford, and California. In matters of scholarship she acceded to their judgment, but in her heart she still clung to the old relationship wherein a mediocre student might be humanly as dear as one with straight A's. Mary Lyon had sent a host of young women into the world, not to select disciples too exquisitely but to give young people what they needed. That was the democracy of education, and the young teachers' insistence upon selectiveness and specialization disturbed Mrs. Mills. She had taught for forty years—and the veteran is not always wrong. Many of her new teachers had never been used to the old-fashioned faculty prayer meeting, and misdoubted their colleagues were worth praying for; others saw a meaning in Mrs. Mills' concern for their inner happiness, and in the hospitality that amazed them with its forethought and ease. One young teacher who understood the situation was Mary Browning Henderson (Mrs. William McPherson). Appreciating Mrs. Mills' cautiousness after the Sprague and Stratton affairs, Miss Henderson during her two terms of service (1890–94 and 1905–08) persuaded her more by kindness and by her own good teaching than others were able to do by sharper insistence. Gradually the standard of scholarship was raised. One argument stirred Mrs. Mills like trumpets: Mills College must "make" the accredited list.

Not all the good teachers were new. She had called Josiah Keep in 1885. Setting the house to rights after the Stratton regime, she sent Professor Keep on a tour of eastern colleges to observe improved laboratories, and until 1900 he carried most of the science courses. Young teachers with a glimpse of specialization thought it absurd that one man should undertake so much. (In 1879 when David Starr Jordan went to Indiana University as professor of natural history he was expected to—and did—teach Zoology, Botany, Geology, and Physiology.) Professor Keep was one of that host of teachers who, in small colleges, taught faithfully what other men discovered and what every student needed to know. In one field—the shells of the Pacific Coast—he had his modest prestige and wrote his book. "Contented if he might enjoy"—and there were many things to enjoy: the small telescope which Dr. Wythe gave; the trails to Redwood Canyon, and field trips to Marin; an occasional venture into the High Sierra, and a revel of discovery, each summer, along the coves and beaches of Pacific Grove. Not least, his faith in an old story whose simplicity made the world a happier place than it is now.

Louis Lisser became head of the music department in 1880. He was thirty, fresh from the Royal Academy of Arts and Music in Berlin, and for thirty years more he was a real leader in the musical life of San Francisco and gave his department at the college high prestige. In time he gathered around him younger teachers—Weber and Schneider and Biggerstaff—whom he had trained and sent abroad. I have heard Mrs. Mills say that he offered to lease the music department at a rental far above its revenue; he wanted to make of it an independent school of music, but she preferred to keep it as an adjunct to a liberal education, and her refusal never diminished their strong mutual respect and affection. One still remembers the vitality that charged the air when Dr. Lisser entered any room. He and his oldest assistant, Julius Rehn Weber, were snowy and rosy and so well groomed you were sure they had been gone over with silver polish and chamois each morning.

And if the room was charged with vitality before, it broke into prismed joy when Giuseppe Cadenasso entered. It won't do to say he walked like an emperor, for he couldn't to save him have thrown the most disagreeable Christian to the lions nor have frowned long enough to compose a single stoic aphorism. There was nothing of divided personality in him, no wrestling with dark angels, and he never confused the relative importances of himself and God. But he did indeed walk like a man who owns the color-happy earth, in unspoiled joy, a Turner glory pinpointing his tweeds and suffusing his tie. What more could he ask than to find still another bronze cliff of eucalypts to paint towering against the hills, or to watch with remembering eyes over the marshes an afternoon sky "of meadow-bloom wind-moving"? To Mrs. Mills he was, in spite of his silvery halo, only a boy to be admonished with a finger-shake; he must not let those Bohemian Club loafers rob him of so much precious time. In a certain small painting (just a potboiler, he called it) a cathedral grove like the one at Aliso looms massive in shadows, and a cloaked Dante figure stands lost in wonder. I think it is himself, too humbly honest to attempt an explanation, but only to wonder and enjoy.

Miss Clara K. Wittenmeyer ('74) exemplified the tendency of a satellite to continue forever in its prescribed orbit. Somebody has to record absences and check demerits—and she loved it. Joining the faculty in 1891 she had a hand with the preparatory classes and seminary. In 1915 she edited and published *The Susan Lincoln Mills Memory Book*, a birthday album of daily readings, good placer diggings of anecdote. The harmless little book was so saturated with Victorian emotions it antagonized certain critics, and doubtless it was tiresome; but it was hardly programmed flattery, for Mrs. Mills had been dead three years.

Miss Fannie A. Madison was not, as some supposed, a relative of either Cyrus or Susan Mills, but among the women whom Mrs. Mills in her old age thought of as daughters Miss Madison was her right hand. After graduating (1897) she began a service of more than forty years in one function or another—secretary, bursar, purchasing agent, treasurer, accountant: the title of her office did not matter; her name was a guaranty that the duty would be done with integrity and uneffusive kindness. When academic big talk had spent itself her dry-worded common sense was what we could live by. She knew that things have to be paid for and that vanity costs too much in money and character. She knew by heart the unpublished generosities of Mrs. Mills, knew too that many were never repaid, and yet she was no cynic. For thirty-five years after Mrs. Mills' death Fannie Madison's memory was the last repository of fact and story of an earlier day. But come, this sounds like honorary degrees . . .

During the first World War Miss Madison caught the fever of beekeeping —a restful hobby, she thought. The temptation may have come to her with the gift of a crock of slow-ripened eucalyptus honey, spicy and so thick it would hardly ooze from the broken comb; or it may have come on a mild winter afternoon when in the garden of Tolman House she watched laden bees coasting down to the hive porches with the long gliding swing of skaters. Anyway, she borrowed and read the bee-Scriptures of Amos Root, and of Dadant of Spoonriver; and bought a beginner's outfit: two colonies, extra supers, veil and gloves and smoker and hive tool, with all else that goes with that dream ritual. It would be glorious: honey—eucalyptus honey—to give away to all the nice persons on campus. There were then twice as many great eucalypts within a mile of the Oval, and in that first season every tree fairly exerted itself to draw virtue from the earth and hold it ready for Miss Madison's bees. The dish ran away with the spoon.

It was too good to last. Next year her overpeopled colonies took to swarming. She bought more equipment—it was a pity to let so many swarms escape. The honey flow stopped suddenly, bee tempers grew mean, the hives were heavy lifting for a woman, and the stings did hurt. She was not easily defeated. She moved them and moved them; the treeless ridge where the road now runs to Ethel Moore Hall was like a government housing project with hives; but after four years she was wise enough to know she had been unwise, and a beekeepers' supply house salvaged the remnants of the dream.

There was another newcomer in the '90's, a country school teacher who wanted to be a doctor. She did not ask for help, but Mrs. Mills gave her room and board on the campus during her course at Lane Cooper. The Chinaboys got up an hour early to serve her breakfast; and a few persons remember seeing her trudge off in the dark for a walk of nearly two miles to get a train for the ferry. Dr. Mariana Bertola earned her high place in medicine and surgery, and became a physician of souls as well. She was college physician for many years, and Mrs. Mills opened her inmost heart to her as (I think) to no other person now living.

At first faculty meeting in the fall of '95 there was a new young woman from Western College at Oxford, Ohio. Even Mrs. Mills with her insight could not have guessed what a prize she had drawn; for that young teacher was to become known to generations as Hettie Belle Ege—Dean Ege (pronounced a-gee; *a* as in aye (forever); *g* as in grand and good; accent on the *a*). A small college is poor indeed if it has not at least one teacher who becomes a beloved legend, a figure of gentle or even fantastic caricature around whom apocrypha grow. But there are no apocryphal stories about Dean Ege, and so dear she was by natural right, there was no mimicking stroke of caricature. Except to Mills alumnae, she was hardly known beyond the campus; her serene strength was never depleted by the demands of fame. She seemed immune to the occupational malady of teachers' nerves, the martyr complex. And was an official ever less officious? Most young teachers regard the small-college post as a steppingstone and the colleague who stays as cursed with inertia or cowardice—as he often is. But the stayer may be that independent soul to whom the small college is world enough, wherein there is no such blurred decimal-point anomaly as "the average student." Dean Ege loved to teach: and so—and only so—the small college justifies its dubious claim of an advantage in personal contact between teacher and student. There may be no advantage whatsoever; that contact may be stultifying, a dawdling waste, or sheer poison. To know Dean Ege was a wholesome experience.

Her coming was most timely. She understood the depth and beauty of Mrs. Mills' ideals, and with her own warm heart and tender humor it required no policy, no effort, to give herself to the venerable president and to steady younger teachers until they felt a similar devotion. One of the best teachers I have known, long since retired, writes: "I have rarely seen such *esprit de corps* and such real devotion as among the faculty of that period."

Dean Ege was not considered a brilliant speaker, but she could bring to this shifting, self-vexing world of words a curative Euclidian honesty. She used words for the rarest purpose known in the academic world: to express thought simply. Still she knew the beauty of words. Once she stopped by my desk on some errand, glanced at but did not open my worn Shakespeare, and her face lighted with a memory. When she was twelve her father took her to her first play—Edwin Booth and Lawrence Barrett in *Othello*. They were alternating, night about, between hero and villain, and it was Booth's night to play the Moor. "I had never known before how beautiful English words can be. That was more than fifty years ago," she said, "but I can still hear Booth's voice reading:

> *'This to hear*
> *Would Desdemona seriously incline.'* "

Twice the college has been in grave peril. Between 1885 and 1890 Mrs. Mills saved it. Between 1914 and 1916 Dean Ege, as acting president, kept a lost battalion of teachers and students together. Had she been less noble and warmhearted, morale would have been lost. Never have I seen teachers and students so completely inspired by selfless devotion. A priceless secret in the history of those two years, could we but find it.

One man did more than any other to overcome Mrs. Mills' reluctance about dropping the lower schools. At some time in the early '90's she met David Starr Jordan. It is said that Warren Olney brought that about; and of the innumerable good things he did, that was one of the happiest. Jordan was no easy man to please, but he knew a better measuring instrument than the academic yardstick. No other university president saw at first hand—as a man, not an executive—so much of his country and of the world. He knew the regional colors of America with an artist's insight, and his mind was peopled with men and women as diverse and right as the glacial gouges and eroded cliffs and mesas and valleys he knew so well. As a young man he had known two Mount Holyoke teachers in the group whom Agassiz taught on Penikese. And though Jordan's religious faith was light-years beyond the Biblical literalness of Mary Lyon's, their natures had strong traits in common: education was not a catering to pained gentility; both could heartily improvise ways and means to learning, and their democracy was original.

As a boy, Jordan had noted that maple trees grew best where a terminal moraine crossed his father's cold hill farm in western New York. Maple land was the richest crop land. He recognized in Mrs. Mills those qualities, old as Roger Clap's day, that had made men and women deep-rooted and strong—a beauty never seen by arrogant eyes. His vast dry humor was a solvent; and though he seemed unemotional and certainly was undramatic, his tenderness was deep. From the first, Mrs. Mills trusted him, and their delight in one another became proverbial. I like to remember one sentence he wrote to her: "You will let me use the good old word *revere* when I think or speak of you."

To see them as partners in academic procession on the Mills campus—he, slow-moving giant, she, small and quick with vivacity. Or that day in the Greek Theatre at Berkeley when Theodore Roosevelt spoke—"I *took* Panama!" The stage needed all its concrete strength not to sag under the weight of eminence: senators and governors and justices, generals and admirals, educators and men who hoped to be mayor. So long was the procession, the orchestra had to repeat "*The March of the Priests*" until men who had never carried a tune began to recognize something vaguely familiar in the sounds: perhaps they were about to master "America" at last. And then, when "Old Davey" entered with Mrs. Mills, all became simple and right again.

Judge Myrick and Robert Simson had retired from the Board. Israel Dwinell died in June 1890, his death hastened (so his friends believed) by the Stratton affair. There would never be another just like him, but there were young ministers who were like Rodney Tabor in filial devotion. William W. Scudder, son (by a second marriage) of the man whose baby daughter Mrs. Mills had kept alive in Ceylon in 1849, was trustee; and Leavitt Hallock, son of Cyrus Mills' benefactor in Plainfield, was college pastor for several years. The last pioneer on the Board was Captain Charles Nelson, who had been river boatman, shipbuilder, and lumberman. His great house with its ten acres of garden was a landmark down the Avenue. With Warren Olney's seasoned legal mind, and with Charles R. Brown and Raymond C. Brooks among the ministers, the Board had not deteriorated. In 1896 Colonel George C. Edwards began a service that was to continue almost as long as Warren Olney's. One of the Old Guard at the University of California, he had the warmest sympathy for the small college. His father had been a missionary among the Indians, his mother a Mount Holyoke alumna, and his sister a graduate of Mills. He was a gentleman indeed, in whom was no guile; idolized by generations of university students, yet none ever presumed to colloquialize him; and to the last he remembered with devotion the founders of Mills College.

From around 1900 on, the years were like the last chapters of an old-fashioned story where misunderstandings are cleared up and messengers keep coming with good news. Dr. J. K. McLean, willing to be forgiven the animus of the Stratton affair, came to the campus again; and Dr. E. R. Dille, one of the Methodist jury in that unhappy case, was friendly now. These two reconciliations go deeper than a mere happy ending. Dr. McLean was not the kind of man who would think by a gesture of affable condescension to heal a wound he had given. There would be through the years plenty of affable, or even amused, condescension from lesser men toward Mrs. Mills, but Dr. McLean carried austere nobility like a banner in a cynical world.

Can anybody remember a time when there was not at least one pensioner and at least one permanent nonpaying guest? Missionaries and their families with no place to go; old friends, helpless now; daughters and nieces of someone she had known. Some of them needed above all else a few months of unreproving quiet after defeat. Mrs. Mills did not speak in the terms of psychology; she remembered Madras and Coimbatoor, and the months in New England when she and Cyrus were broken in body and purse and were considered failures.

> *The lines are fallen unto me in goodly places;*
> *Yea, I have a goodly heritage.*

In '95 Mrs. Mills' class met at South Hadley for their fiftieth anniversary —a russet-apple gathering for youth to envy. But the proudest day came in 1901 when Mount Holyoke called her to receive an honorary doctorate. Alma Mater had not been lavish with ribbons; its first doctorate (D.C.L.) was given to President McKinley in '99. Now it gave the Litt.D. to three alumnae: Susan Tolman Mills ('45), Julia E. Ward ('57), and Mary A. Evans ('60). *Keep back thy servant from presumptuous sins*—but the gown and hood and gold tassel *were* handsome; one could rightly feel that Miss Lyon would have approved, and all the girls of '45 could share the honor. Hadn't they all known, away back in '42, that they were a good class? Besides, the Mills seniors had worn scholars' gowns since '96; it would do them and their young teachers good to see a few velvet stripes on her sleeves. In 1870 when Cyrus got his doctorate at Williams, Samuel Damon had pithily remarked in *The Friend* that Mrs. Mills deserved one also. But not before Cyrus, Brother Damon; Cyrus had the greater need of encouragement. But now—well, the doctorate was very nice.

And then on November 18, 1905, the academic world united in doing a very gracious thing, and almost spontaneously—though good Louis Lisser nudged the collective elbow and pointed to the calendar: the eightieth birthday of a still active college president. Universities and colleges, ivied tower and raw brick, for once agreed about something; and *not* to join in the felicitations imperiled one's Who-ness. Letters and telegrams poured in, and Dr. Lisser mounted them in a huge album. Gilman of Johns Hopkins, Hadley of Yale, Schurman of Cornell, Angell of Michigan, Harper of Chicago, G. Stanley Hall of Clark, Nicholas Murray Butler himself, Booker T. Washington, Tucker of Dartmouth, Hyde of Bowdoin, Faunce of Brown, Thwing of Western Reserve, Kane of Washington, Henry Hopkins (son of Mark) of Williams, Miss Hazard of Wellesley, Miss Thomas of Bryn Mawr, the entire faculty of Amherst, and a chorus of others. A nostalgic aht: there were giants on the earth. G. Stanley Hall wrote that he was joining the New England alumnae in their celebration. Charles Custis Harrison of the University of Pennsylvania was especially gracious; he spoke of Cyrus Mills too (as a few others had done), and he remarked to Louis Lisser: "It is a pleasure to us, also, to send this letter of commemoration through yourself, because you are so active in the intellectual life of San Francisco." All the way from the American Embassy in London came the official card of Whitelaw Reid with a personal message. Henry Van Dyke wrote: "When I saw you at Mills College last Spring, I understood the secret of your escape from the benumbing spell of old age." The trustees of Punahou (many of the good old names—Alexander and Judd and Thurston and Cooke and Dole) testified: "She met and overcame obstacles with equanimity; she accomplished a great work with poor facilities; she drew her inspiration from the dull routine of a busy life."

Of course the Berkeley men responded: President Wheeler (composing always as for marble tablets); Henry Morse Stephens, suave and courtly; Hugo Schilling, with a mind and manner to go with his beautiful copperplate hand; Professor Howison, himself venerable; and greathearted Elmer E. Brown, who wrote her a real poem. Thomas R. Bacon simply could not express himself in cap-and-gown language: "Everyone knew that you could keep a good school, but everyone (almost) denied that you could make a college for women. And you have done it. You have done it in the face of suspicion, opposition, and the competition of free co-education."

From the Hights the Poet of the Sierra gathered himself—beard, boots and all—in a mighty period. "For my part, Madam, let me congratulate the State"—which he did at some length. And little Cyril Damon sent from Hawaii "eighty kisses and one to grow on," and drew them, full count—circles, which (the highest authorities agree) are more difficult than crosses and much more loving.

Of course there was a program. Professor Gayley, in behalf of the University of California, spoke grandly as few men could do; and John M. Stillman, one of the Stanford Old Guard, gave his tribute. (The gentle face and voice of Stillman: Stanford men and women of my day would be moved by the least word of his.) And there was a reception, and if your grandmother was a bluestocking in the City or in Oakland or Berkeley you may learn from her calling card in the big album whether she received on first and third Wednesdays or on alternate Fridays.

It is true that Princeton's formal regrets were coolish as constitutional law; but Dr. Lisser had only one downright refusal—or at least he imbedded but one in amber:

> DEAR SIR: *Your note of October 17th is at hand. I regret that I do not know enough about the work of Mills College and Seminary to justify me in writing the congratulatory letter which you ask of me. I have never been in California but once, and then for no long time, and, moreover, although I have been long engaged in the work of education, I have had little to do with the education of women. My own children were all sons, and Harvard University has not admitted women students.*
>
> *Regretting that I cannot serve you, I am,*
>
> *Very truly yours,*
CHARLES W. ELIOT.

Two nonacademic letters I have kept until last. The miners of Grass Valley wrote: "This from the men who have in the past 10 years felt the good of your gentle words in times of adversity." This letter was accompanied by a check for $130, to be applied toward completing the gymnasium. I wonder whether she ever heard those men sing their old Cornish chapel songs:

> *Our souls are in His mighty hand*
> *And He will keep us still*

or that counting song of the twelve mystical emblems:

> *"Come and I will sing you"*—
> *"What will you sing me?"*
> *"I will sing you Twelve O"*—
> *"What is your Twelve O?"*
>
> *"Twelve is the Twelve Apostles" . . .*

The writer of the next letter had been chief cook—forever, it seemed. Old at the time of writing, he was soon to return to China. The students had happy cause to remember Yep Wo.

MILLS COLLEGE nov. 17, 1905.

MY DEAR FRIEND
  MRS. S. L. MILLS
I am Thankful that Yours so kindness and
Treats me Faith always for I am never Forget.
 but now I wish Your to joy Happiness
Many More as today and Hope God Will Bless Your
Enjoy and Comfortable for Ever
Your Farithful Friend
YEP WO

Though her good friends, Mr. and Mrs. F. M. Smith, had persuaded the quarry railway to add the K-Leona car to its rolling stock ("rolling" is euphemistic), and blobs of settlement formed along that line, there were only a few houses within a mile of the campus. The capes of hills were still wild grassland, Pansy Hill was colorful in April, and botany implied a love of flowers. There were trillium and scarlet columbine in the dense ravine of South Fork, whole crops of mariposas on the oat ridges, and mimulus and scarlet wild fuchsia where the narrow wagon road climbed past Robert Simson's gate. When Cyrus and Susan began here in '71 they had to keep a dairy herd and poultry or go without milk and eggs; and Mrs. Mills had continued to enlarge these thrifty accessories. Boys raided the orchard, of course, and Michael Herlihy had to hurry and find his star and chase them out; and when Michael's legs were too old, trust John Weston, the plant foreman, or Alexander Moore, the farmer, to safeguard the domain.

Feeding the quail became a ritual, an informal Lord's Supper. While the campus was still in the country and free from cats, the tangled wildgrass plots were a safe nesting place for the crested pretties, and in winter the acacia thickets on Sunnyside and Prospect were a whir of wings at nightfall. Knowing they were loved, the shy runaways lost all fear, and came to the Oval each evening to be fed. You could see Mrs. Mills, at least a hundred quail crowding around her, scattering a pan of grain. And how many times, along some path, she waited while anxious parents baby-talked their downy "motes of gold" from one wild seed harvest to another.

In '98 when convalescent soldiers were badly cared for she furnished a rest home on the campus for them—no time to wait for other organization. (The veterans named one of their auxiliary posts for her.) And after the earthquake in 1906, not only teachers who lived in the City but many alumnae as well came with their families for refuge. Besides, Yep Wo and Yang were favorably known in Chinatown. In the considered judgment of Grant Avenue and Dupont Street, there may well have been some doubt about American Christianity, but none as to the goodness of the lady whom Yep Wo and Yang served; and cousins and their wives and little ones and their singing birds came to the campus and were fed.

The banks closed after the quake, but the conductor of the K-Leona car brought his Monday's cash to Mrs. Mills and would take no receipt; and Michael Herlihy handed her fifty dollars toward emergency needs. She could report to her eastern friends that the college had received only superficial damage. The new campanile, given by Mr. and Mrs. F. M. Smith, was unscathed; Science Hall was sound; and as for Mills Hall, Mr. Wilber's carpenters had not skimped on timbers and square-wrought nails. She was tenderly thankful also because the portrait bust of her husband had not been damaged.

Doing good to human beings was second nature, requiring no formal restatement of social obligations. In her old age she spent no effort trying to pack all beliefs and exceptions into one portable creed. The universe was too big for that; there was no false humility in the Eighth Psalm:

> *When I consider thy heavens, the work of thy fingers,*
> *The moon and the stars which thou hast ordained,*
> *What is man, that thou art mindful of him . . .*

Isabel Raney Mowry, who had the strange experience in this next story, assures me that only two other persons, Mrs. Mills and another teacher, ever knew of this incident until she herself revealed it a few years ago. As Isabel Raney, she taught music at the college in the early '90's, the youngest teacher on the faculty, and because of her youth and friendliness she was a favorite with Mrs. Mills. Miss Raney's father, a veteran of the Civil War, lived in the Napa Valley. There had developed between him and his daughter a deep spiritual sympathy. She had visited him about a week before this incident, and knew that he planned to march with the veterans on Washington's Birthday.

The first call bell rang at 6:30. She was lying in drowsy half-consciousness, wondering whether the bell had rung, when she heard a knock at her door, and called, "Come in." It was her father. Surprised with joy she sprang out of bed and hurried to clasp his hands, which were icy cold. He said, "Dear, I am dying, and there is one thing I must tell you before I go." He gave her his message (which remains a secret) and faded away. She hurried to the room of an older teacher and told her what had happened. The older woman tried to quiet her—it must have been a dream—soothed her as best she could, and at the seven o'clock bell they went down to breakfast.

As they were leaving the dining room, Mrs. Mills, standing in the corridor, nodded to Miss Raney that she wished to speak with her. "My dear, I have sorrowful news for you." Miss Raney said, "Yes, I know. My father died at 6:30 this morning." Mrs. Mills said, "The telegram stated 6:35. But who told you? I gave strict orders that no one should tell you until after breakfast." They went to Mrs. Mills' rooms, and the girl told her what had happened. She expected the older woman to be incredulous, but Mrs. Mills said: "Yes, I understand. I saw strange things in India. There are stranger things in the universe than the wisest man knows."

Past the eightieth birthday, the problem of finding a successor to Mrs. Mills pressed harder upon the trustees, of whom Dr. Charles R. Brown was president. There is no warrant for supposing that the Board would have given rubber-stamp approval to a nominee of hers, regardless of fitness, but they did value her wishes. She was ironically familiar with wistful candidates who, disposing themselves in the best light, waited for the proposal while their friends dropped hintless hints. One more Mount Holyoke woman came as a sojourner, but the audition was not favorable. Finally the choice fell upon Dr. Luella Clay Carson, professor of rhetoric and dean of women at the University of Oregon. From girlhood Miss Carson had felt a filial warmth toward Mr. and Mrs. Mills. She had entered the preparatory (grammar) department at Benicia in 1870, moved on to Mills Seminary for the year 1871, and had completed her schooling in Portland. Not a college graduate, she had a deep, perhaps an extravagant, respect for the prestige of scholarship and degrees. She had a lively interest in what other colleges were doing and what other educators were saying, and was eager to make Mills College well known. She was inaugurated in the fall of 1909.

For Mrs. Mills, it was good to be free. Back in 1901 she had given the college $200,000, the balance of the estate with increment, reserving only enough to provide the personal gifts she would want to make and to take care of her pensioners. The college was established at last. These nice young teachers had an admirable knack of observing how things were done in the best colleges; their catalogues had been ladylike and correct. Faithful Fannie Madison had taken over the main burden of business, leaving Mrs. Mills more time to see her friends and to keep an eye on Barney—Barney Barry, the universal mother's wandering boy.

Barney came to Mills, a displaced person, after the earthquake; and Barney was what Mrs. Mills forever needed, a middle-aged boy to be prayed over and admonished and forgiven. He was droll but shy, no hand at Hibernian wisecracks, wistful and tenderhearted, as one who accepts the certainty that whatever he does will appear mildly absurd. It won't do to say Mrs. Mills could never be hoaxed, but there was no hoaxing from the likes of Barney; his very failings were so abject. He could withstand the inner pressure for half a year, then he went off the deep end. A week would pass, then John Weston or one of his men would go find the wanderer, sick and sickhearted, in lodging house or hospital; and Mrs. Mills would write him another of the pleading letters that, in time, made up the "Barney" anthology. A few excerpts give the tone of those letters:

My Dear Barney—*Michael is going down to see you, and I will write*

this for him to take to you. I am sorry for you, sorry that you are yield-
ing to temptation, sorry that you met with such an accident. The only
wonder is that you were not killed. You fell about twelve feet. Dr. Ber-
tola told me she was afraid you would have a stiff wrist, as there was a
compound fracture . . . You are good to others, but you must be good
to yourself, and pray God to help you be a strong man for the right . . .

When she was starting on her last trip to Honolulu, she wrote:

MY DEAR BARNEY—*I am sorry to go away and leave all my friends and*
you among them . . . I am old and shall not live a great while, but while
I live you belong to me. Be especially helpful to Miss Madison, Mrs. Smith
and Miss Wittenmeyer . . . Look out for Michael, who is old and not
very well . . . I pray many times a day for you as for my very own . . .

After Mrs. Mills died, Miss Madison with one or another of the older teachers
interceded for Barney after a fall. Eventually he went back to Ireland for a
visit, and died there.

In 1908 Mrs. Mills had Miss Alice Jones paint a portrait of Mary Lyon
from a daguerreotype—a poor original, for no daguerrean had ever caught
the eagerness of that face, and the painter could only suggest the womanly
dignity. Then in 1911 a group of students and teachers insisted that Mrs.
Mills sit for a portrait. It is said there was some rivalry between the two
sororities then active in the college for the honor of presenting the portrait,
and (so quickly is history overgrown with hearsay) it is even said that two
rival portraits were sketched; but that detail, like the sororities, is drifted
over with oblivion. The core of the story, well authenticated, leads to the art
colony on Russian Hill in San Francisco and to the small Swedenborgian
church—"the Lyon Street Society of the New Church"—and its venerated
minister, the Reverend Joseph Worcester, so warm a friend of William Keith
that Keith's friends said the painter was a Worcesterian though not a Swedenborgian. That little church had Keith landscapes on its walls before most
churches were ready to believe that a landscape without saints may be holy.
One member of that small society was the portrait painter, Mary C. Richardson. (Another member was a Mills teacher, though her fellowship in the
church and her friendship with Mrs. Richardson are not relevant to the making
of Mrs. Mills' portrait, but only to the background of the story.) No salesmanship was needed, and Mrs. Richardson painted the portrait. One well-
informed person remembers that Mrs. Richardson preferred the three-quarters
profile because she greatly admired the strong contour of Mrs. Mills' head.

How good is the portrait? Photographers nearly always made Mrs. Mills self-conscious; is there any trace of that in the painting? One person who knew Mrs. Mills and also knows the picture wonders whether the painter intended to intimate a fondness for power. Is there any pose, any self-prompted attitudinizing, on the part of the subject, as if she had just passed a full-length mirror on her way to the sitting?

> *What majesty is in her gait? Remember,*
> *If e'er thou look'dst on majesty.*

Let me, like the man who saw Shelley plain, forget the rest. The face in the portrait is tired, the eyes and mind dim on something in the distance; but in life, never until the last two or three months were those eyes turned away, nor can I remember many faces more transparent of feeling. She could not draw a curtain over her heart.

Well, now that they had her picture she could relax and earn her salt by teaching one more class. (She taught ethics for two years after she retired.) Maybe the registrar would be thinking she gave too many A's and B's, but the girls were nice girls and she refused to worry about conforming to the grade curve. Dr. Carson's first catalogue puzzled her a little with its talk about the strategic position of the college in the Education of the Womanhood of this New West. She and Cyrus had built the school where they did because they liked Leona Creek; now it seemed they had been strategic too—which was comforting. And these new maps of Dr. Carson's with radiating lines showing how far it was to Wenatchee and Boise and Pendleton and Winnemucca—maybe a good way of attracting students, but in her experience there were stronger attractions than mileage. Dr. Carson's talks sounded enthusiastic but vague, like her own girlhood thoughts about saving the world. Once in the field, somehow she had found so many things to do she had little time for theory.

She hoped the campus would never be spoiled. Forty years, now, since Cyrus had planned the landscaping, and the years had justified his imagination. Visitors driving up the Avenue turned in at the tree-bordered bridge,* and there, in a breath, was the Oval, every tree, every shrub around it, a part of a balanced picture; and if the Rose Porch was in bloom! No wonder that alumnae and strangers alike exclaimed over that view. "My dear" had been a real landscape artist. She would never tire of the shaded paths, the familiar surprise at each turning, each rustic bridge asking for time to enjoy the sun-mottled water. Going from one place to another was not a matter of speed

* That main entrance crossed South Brook (now buried in a conduit) south of the library, and entered the Oval between the library and the campanile.

alone but also of time for accompanying thoughts. She had been able to out-walk any girl; now somebody always wanted to accompany her. If she went around Mills Hall to see that everything was neat, Yang would have the most plausible excuses for keeping a few steps behind her. She and Ida Anderson (her maid) could take one of the easier walks—the winding path from the left of the campanile, past the bee tree and the remnant of the live oak once blazed "A," cross the footbridge, and go pay a call on sister Jane. The garden of "Tolman House" was formal: a tall privet hedge hid it from the road, and low box hedges outlined the walks and flower beds and the big rose garden like prim stitches of a sampler. On the return, by leaning a little on Ida's arm, she could manage the easy climb to Sunnyside. The arbor had grown so that it screened the benches into privacy—a nice place for students to come and sit with their sweethearts. And why not? Their happiness was a better tribute than funereal faces.

In the summer of 1910 she and Ida went to Honolulu. The First Families had intermarried until each couple were descended eight ways from somebody she had taught, and the Frears and Damons and Alexanders and Doles "passed her around like cake" and would have worn her out with kindness—but wear *her* out? Still, one had to use common sense. Visiting at Stockton in 1911, when an alumna slipped her hand under Mrs. Mills' elbow, she avowed: "My dear, I am not feeble. I am only cautious." And when another alumna of twenty-five years back came to the campus, the lively memory flashed: "You will want to see your old room"; and without consulting a record book she led the way to it.

1912. Not so many walks now; two or three each day to see that Barney was keeping the paths neat. It was activity enough to sit at her window and look across the Oval to the bridge, to see if friends were coming. The acacias bordering the bridge made a sharp silhouette of some fancied picture—for-gotten now. In the summer, to Honolulu again, with Ida. When college opened and teachers came in to pay their devotion, she was eager with ques-tions. And yet the twilight was falling. Professor Keep was gone, a year ago; and sister Jane had died in April. Last year on her birthday she had walked into the big dining room and spoken for ten minutes; this year she rode in her wheelchair, and somehow the words would not come.

She died on Thursday, December 12. The following Sunday was one of the mildest days of that Indian summer which, after rain, may turn into spring overnight. The ridgy-barked eucalyptus at the left of the Science Hall bridge as you go from the Oval to Lisser was heavy with bloom, and the bees' sound was more beautiful than any line ever written about Hymettus or Innisfree. In Lisser Hall the girls sang Mrs. Mills' favorite hymn, "Guide me, O thou great Jehovah," and one remembers their faces when they turned down the path on the way to Sunnyside. Four of the bearers I remember: John Weston, Alexander Moore the plowman, Barney Barry, and Michael, white-haired and frail but not to be denied. We had seen the passing of the Last Puritan, in the noblest sense of that term.

The path from the K-Leona station crossed the site of the Art Building, then followed the creek bank to the Oval. There was a small grove of tallest eucalypts along that path, the noble columns never marred. Each morning during the last three years of his service (after Mrs. Mills died) Michael Herlihy raked and swept the floor of that grove as if it were a temple. The superintendent may have contrived that chore so that the frail old man would not feel hurt, or Michael may have invented it for an inner need. Do I make too much of Michael? He is a surveyor's mark by which we may estimate the changes in time, in culture.

The college has been put upon the map. But the map is bordered with isothermal lines, storm pressures converging and ominous; and the weather appears to be out of control. Can democracy save the world, or itself? We offer courses and attend conferences upon that problem. We visualize world movements, masses of men, and many of these masses do not feel democratic. But in order to keep ourselves on the academic map, we are almost distracted with a multiplicity of interests. Our teachers drive themselves to make what we call "important contributions to scholarship," prized in proportion to their publicity values; and heaven knows we labor to be aesthetic. But no miners now remember "the good of our gentle words in times of adversity." The sickening truth is that labor distrusts colleges like ours and all that they stand for. We cajole the gardener, the electrician, and the carpenter; they could make us acutely uncomfortable. But the man himself, as a man?

Michael and Mrs. Mills found somehow a solution: a deep and religious respect for the dignity of human nature. She could not wrong you, Michael, for the Bible had taught her from girlhood that it is wrong to snub even the humblest human being or to tyrannize over him, however smoothly; and you, attending your church faithfully, were an unfailing well of kindness. Religious tolerance? It seems to have been no problem with you and her. Cynics might guess that she blarneyed you because she too liked service; but no, if anything had cheapened your manhood she would have grieved; and of all of those near to her you were bravest with your "No" when her impulsiveness was in danger of leading her to a wrong decision.

You were not colorful, Michael. Your sayings furnished no amusing stories for a hostess to relate to her guests. But no man I have known was more of a man, for a' that. The best poets have tried to tell us this, but we are scholars. You had something that our generation has lost; it was not political theory, and (to save our pained gentility) we must not call it cultural. There seems to be no other term for it than the distrusted term, spiritual beauty. She helped that beauty to grow because you were quite as dear and important in her old-fashioned eyes as if you had had a dozen doctorates. Your clear face and eyes, the wistful smile and the morning greetings that passed, are very good to remember.

The religion expressed in her diary and journal at Mount Holyoke was often literal with primitive dread. Who could have foreseen how greatly she would change? One thoughtful person says: she remained a conservative in theology but became broadly liberal in religion; but even that does not explain all. As the years passed, something led her to select precisely the most spiritual parts of the Bible and quietly ignore the rest. Instinct was truer than scholarship. In her later years she seems never to have quoted any passage of hurt or angry psychology—the "enemy" or "persecution" psalms—but to have gone like a homing bird to the poems of spiritual renewal and compassion. One earnest, troubled writer urges us to form and make effective "an ethic to replace the religious myth." To her, it was no myth. Her faith was as old and as deep-rooted as Captain Roger Clap's—and that was as old as the wonder and reverence in man. She knew the sense of internationalism long before it became our slogan. Isaiah had taught her that. Ceylon and its aftermath would have made a cynic of a weaker person; but sickness and seeming defeat and the ineptitudes of bad management only confirmed her faith in that inner resource which she called God. The habit of the busy hands allowed her no time to speculate on what might be if t'other thing was or wasn't. Indefinable as her religion may have been, that habit of the busy hands was a part of it. While she lived she kept most of the teachers and students fairly together in her own faith that there is a spiritual power in the world, stronger than man but not indifferent to him. Eager as she was to have the college recognized, I think she would never have surrendered that faith for the dubious satisfaction of conforming to the times.

We cannot turn the clock back: is that equivalent to saying we can never regain a lost faith? I am thinking of the rillets of pennies and dimes and quarters that flowed into foreign missions, and of the ill-trained, pathetically eager young missionaries who went to the remote beachheads, and of their failures, the meager harvest in most fields. And then I think of a contrast so ironic it sickens the heart: the cost of one tank, one bomber, and a million youths in arms at our cloudy command, trying to do by force what love failed to do. God forgive us! We need humility.

The girl of sixteen who entered Mount Holyoke in 1842 had already discovered an unfailing well-spring of spiritual power: that poem, the most exciting (I believe) of all poems that ever got into our language—the book we call Isaiah. All hope is in that poem, all humility, compassion for all mankind. Reading that wholeheartedly at sixteen, one could never be complacent again nor idle nor cynical. Culture alone would never satisfy that impassioned heart. After the worst defeat, the bitterest despair, broken mankind must begin once more to rise from the dust.

Appendix A

DEACON SAMUEL TOLMAN'S HOLLOW CANE

Besides town and church records and the wills, there is the homely source book on Tolman history, an account written in 1830 by Deacon Samuel Tolman (5), whose father was Johnson Tolman (4), younger brother of Aquila (4) and therefore son of Samuel (3). This Deacon Samuel, aged seventy-five, had lived all his life at Stoughton, once a part of Dorchester, and on land acquired by the first Thomas Tolman. He wrote this account for his cousin, Desire Tolman, Mrs. Mills' grandfather.

Deacon Samuel wrote out of a full and circumstantial memory. His spelling and syntax were homespun, but he was shrewdly accurate on practically every point that can be checked by other evidence. A part of what he told had already appeared in the books of Roger Clap and James Blake, but much more had come to him in well-seasoned family tradition. He had evidently read Blake's book, but not Roger Clap's.

A copy of Deacon Samuel's story was in Mrs. Mills' possession for many years, and at least three copies were made from it, in some of which well-meaning copyists ironed out the Deacon's verbal errors—and half the flavor.

Deacon Samuel was quite certain that the first Thomas Tolman came over on the *Mary and John;* he did not know that ship by name, but says it was a ship of "four hundred tun," and proceeds to tell about the landing, with some details not in Clap's *Memoirs.* He tells how Thomas Tolman "came on the shore, where he built him a house near the north side of the crick which runs across the turnpike about a quarter of a mile north of Neponset Bridge; which place was never sold, but is now in the familey. In the year 1636, they bought the land of the Indians, which contained Dorchester, Milton, Canton, Stoughton, Sharon, and Foxburrow; which old deed I now have in the house . . .

"Samuel, my grandfather, was born in 1676; and Nov. 21st, 1704, he married Expearance Clap, he being 28 and she 21; She was the daughter of Desire Clap, youngest son of Roger Clap; who for many years was captain of the Castle, and wrote a book that was printed—an advice to his children."

Deacon Samuel remembered a certain great-uncle as a mean man who kept the Deacon's father out of an inheritance of land, until God sent a "large

237

rattelsnake" as a warning. The uncle repented, "and before sunrise next morning he went and sold my father his wright.

"It may seem needless that I have written so much about the land; but I suppose it seames more to me; it being the place where I was born and whare I now live, and have lived these 75 years and 6 months . . .

"I have got the whole history in the house, which I have written with my own hand, on a sheet of parchment, and to have it kept secure, I have bought me a cane, for which I gave seven dollars, on the first day of January, 1824, which is hollow. I unscrew the top and put in the History, and then unscrew the middle and in the lower part I put in the old Indian deed, and my great-grandfather's will . . . "

God rest you well, Deacon Samuel. You were not a caricature. There were still many men like you in 1830. And your cane—could we find it—should be placed with other honest antiques in the Old State House in Boston.

Appendix B

WILL OF THE FIRST THOMAS TOLMAN

In the Name of God Amen: The twenty-fift of ye Third moneth in the yeare of our Lord One thousand six hundred Eighty Eight I Thomas Tolman Senr of Dorchester in the Collony of the Massachusets in New England being now through the great Goodness & Mercy of God praised be his name, entred into the Eightyeth yeare of my Age, but of good & sound memory & waiting dayly for my great change, which I trust & believe shall through the Electing love of God & the Redeeming Grace of Christ my only Lord & Saviour be most welcome & happy to mee I Do make constitute & declare this my last will & Testament in manner & forme following: Revoking & hereby makeing voyd all former & other will & wills by me at any time made:

And first of all my will is that my body be decently buryed (if God permit) by the care of my Executrs hereafter named. Next I doe will that all my just debts to every man be duely & Speedily paid—Item unto my Eldest son Thomas Tolman I give & confirme my present Dwelling house & barne to be his with the halfe Acre of land it stands upon as all Land Meadows & Upland that I gave him at his marriage & that his deeds make mention of. Moreover that six Acres wc I bough since his Marriage of Jonathan Birch to him his heires & Assignes for ever: Provided alwayes & it is my will & appointment That he my son Thomas he his heires Exectrs Administrs shall and do pay as followeth: that is to say, to my daughter Sarah Leadbetter the sume of fifteen pounds, & to my daughter Rebekah Tucker the like sume of fifteen pounds in good current country pay at such reasonable price as it may pass between man & man: only my will is that my daughter Rebekah be first paid; because she may need it more. . . . Item I give to my son Thomas my Great Chub Axe Item unto my son John Tolman I give & confirm all the Meadows & upland that his deeds from me make mention of, to be his with the buildings that is thereon, to be to him his heires & Assignes for ever . . . Also my wearing Apparel I give unto my two sons woolen & linnen Equally to be divided between them. But I will that my son John shall have my Iron hoopes & boxes that may be upon my wheeles that shall be left for I have given my son Thomas a new sett of Iron hoopes heretofore & to my daughter Hannah Lion I give my best bed I usually lie upon with the best paire of sheets & the best furniture belonging to it & bedstead & to my daughter Rebecca Tucker my second best bed with ye second best appurtenances thereto belonging: And I will that she my daughter shall have my lesser Kettle of Brass & Hannah my Daughter the biggest. As for my pewter my will is that my Daughter Mary shall have one of the biggest pewter platters & Sarah Leadbetter the other biggest & Hannah my Daughter the third best & Rebecca my daughter the fourth, & the rest of my moveable household Stuff to be lovingly divided between my three Daughters, Sarah, Hannah & Rebecca, & my old brass pott I give to my son John, & my part of the Iron barr or Crow, & I make & constitute my two Sonnes Thomas & John to my Executrs. And further my will is that there be no demanding of any Debt that any of my children thinke I owe any of them or if any paper be found what I have done for them, be all quitt, this I write that peace & love be continued amongst my dear children. Only if I dy before James Tucker pay me Ten pound in money of New England that then my will is that he the said James Tucker shall pay or cause to be paid to Isaac Ryalls two Eldest daughters Ruth and Mary five pound apiece in current money of New England if it be to be had if not then to pay in current pay at money price as indifferent men shall judge, if you cannot agree amongst yourselves, & my will is yt ye said James Tucker doing this shall have up his bond of Eighteen pound that I lent him & the remainder of what he borrowed I give to his wife Rebecca my daughter in part of her portion beside what I have already Specifyed & this I ordain as my Last will & Testament. In Witness whereof I have sett to my hand & seal this 29 of Octo. 1688

Thomas Tolman

Senior   Seale

Peter Thacher
John Danforth
James Blake

Feb 5 1691

Thomas Tolman Jr. presented this will
for probate

A few items from the inventory of Abraham Howe's estate, evaluated in pounds, shillings, and pence;

About 12 bushels of Indian corne and 4 bushels of Rye unthrashed	01	18	00
A beetle & 3 wedges, an old broad axe a hamer and an old spade		06	00
About 24 bushels of Apples; about 5 bushls Turneps	01	09	00
5 bb Cider the casks at 10 per bb	02	10	00
Biefe salted for winter provision 24 s Butter 3 s	01	07	00
A pair of braces and whiptrees Chaines and a frow		07	00
An old warming pan and an old pr of tramels		04	00
All his wearing clothes woolen and linen	05	00	00
A fowleing piece and an old backsword	01	10	00

Appendix C

WE LOOK AT A FAVORITE OF KING CHARLES

There is a legend that Thomas Tolman of Dorchester was a descendant of Sir Thomas Tolman of Lincolnshire, who is said to have commanded a Puritan regiment at Marston Moor. The story goes that in a cavalry charge Sir Thomas unhorsed a young cavalier who turned out to be his own nephew— "a favorite of King Charles." According to the legend, Sir Thomas spared his nephew and helped him escape to France, and at the Restoration the nephew persuaded Charles II not to confiscate the Puritan uncle's estate. One version has it that the uncle himself then became "a favorite of King Charles"; and most versions proceed to hint the Tolman lineage back to the time of Egbert the Saxon (825).

This story originated around 1890, when a mysterious old gentleman who purported to be of the Lincolnshire house told the germ of it to a very distant Chicago cousin of Mrs. Mills; and that cousin's written account is the sole source of the legend as it has developed in Mills literature. Let us listen to it a second time. The word "descendant" is cracked in the ring. If the wheel-wright (born in Dorset in 1608) was a descendant of the Lincolnshire knight (who led a cavalry charge in 1644 and became a court favorite in 1660), he was a son. The time scheme forbids any remoter degree of descent. The wheelwright's grandsire would have been in his eighties at the time of Marston Moor, and a ripe hundred at the Restoration. A son, then, or no descendant. But how came a landed knight of Lincolnshire to have a yeoman son learning the wheelwright's trade in faraway Dorset? Burke, the best authority on English genealogy, could find no connection between the Tolmans of Lincoln-shire and those of Dorset, and neither the mysterious old gentleman nor the Chicago cousin suggested any way of bridging that gap—no parish or probate records, no documents of any kind. Indeed, neither of them avowed any belief that the wheelwright *was* a descendant of the knight: merely, both were Tolmans. They implied a little, and their readers inferred a great deal too much. Romantic wish became conclusive fact.

The Chicago cousin did not claim to have traced the Tolman lineage back to A.D. 825. He wrote: "The earliest record of the name that I have found is of a Sir Thomas Tolman, grand Almoner of Egbert the Saxon." He did not say where he found that remarkable anachronism, and his readers were not critical. The old English gentleman ignored Egbert the Saxon, but in com-pensation he gave the Lincolnshire Tolmans (*ergo* all Tolmans) an unbroken succession of landed estates and knighthood clear back to the Saxon conquest (449). That aged and wandering Tom Sawyer had a pleasant way with his-tory. One more flight and we'd find the original Thomas Tolman cupbearer to Beowulf.

Goodman Thomas Tolman, the wheelwright of Dorchester, was "no mas-ter, sir, but a poor man's son." All this traipsing around after kings' favorites leads to no godly end. And if that cavalry charge at Marston Moor escaped the attention of coldly methodical historians (as it appears to have done), we may take the greater comfort from the Psalmist's admonition, *A horse is a vain thing.*

Appendix D

EMILY DICKINSON AT MOUNT HOLYOKE

Emily Dickinson's year at Mount Holyoke (1847–48) has, like some other sectors of her story, been discolored with apocrypha. In his excellent biography, *This Was a Poet*, George F. Whicher has been careful to know and understand the seminary. Commending his work I touch mainly upon that part of Emily's experience that pertains to Susan Tolman; and if I hear a more personal and tender overtone than Professor Whicher finds in the soul-saving anxiety of Susan's missionary journal, my vantage point has been explained in the first pages of Chapter III. That journal, which at first reading seemed "but gray wind over a grave," became humanized with glints of color as I came to know the persons she named in her private record of devotions. In 1847 there was no stigma of failure upon prospective missionaries and their Mount Holyoke wives.

Most biographers have made Emily Dickinson too mature in that year. She was only sixteen when she entered Mount Holyoke, and though certainly better than mediocre she was, judged by her extant letters, naïvely youthful, natural but shy, unaware of future brilliance, a nice child of sixteen-turning-seventeen discovering how friendly the school could be. Remember too that in that same October Susan Tolman was still only twenty-one, and that she had been, ever since she was sixteen, under the powerful impact of Mary Lyon. Susan's faith was never half-hearted, and if her missionary journal, recording from week to week the tension of a religious revival, sounds overanxious, the anxiety may have come from a warmhearted solicitude for the well-being and happiness of others.

All of Emily's extant letters of that year were written to two persons: to her brother Austin, and these are bantering and whimsical with small by-play of annoyances; the others, to her dearest girl-friend, Abiah Root, are deep with inner revelation.

Everything is pleasant and happy here and I think I could be no happier at any other school away from home. Things seem more like home than I had anticipated and the teachers are all very kind and affectionate to us. They call on us frequently and urge us to return their calls and when we do, we always receive a cordial welcome . . . Miss Lyon and all the

*teachers seem to consult our comfort and happiness in everything they do
. . . When I left home I did not think I should find a companion or dear
friend in all the multitude. I expected to find rough and uncultivated manners, and to be sure I have found some of that stamp, but on the whole,
there is much ease and grace and a desire to make one another happy,
which delights and at the same time surprises me very much.*

*My domestic work is not difficult and consists in carrying the knives and
forks from the first tier tables at morning and noon and at night washing
and wiping the same quantity of knives.**

This was written early in the school year; nothing in her later letters indicates
any change in her feelings toward Mount Holyoke. On January 17 she wrote
to Abiah, "I love this Seminary, and all its teachers are bound strongly to my
heart by ties of affection. There are many sweet girls here." In February
she caricatured to Austin Miss Lyon's disapproval of valentines, and twice
she winked at him about Miss Whitman's magisterial fussiness. Once she
commented upon the boredom of paraphrasing Pope—as who wouldn't!
Aside from this the teaching seems to have challenged her mind. Two inci-
dents showed some degree of reserve: she did not attend the circus(and oh,
Ringmaster of the Universe, Emily should have ridden the elephant), nor did
she take part in Mountain Day. In the spring her family, alarmed by a busy-
body's gossip about her health, brought her home for a few weeks against her
tearful protest, but she returned and completed the year's work. But her father
had decided she should not continue for a second year, and his word was more
rigid law than any rule imposed at Mount Holyoke. She had been happy at
South Hadley; but she may well have overestimated the permanence of those
new friendships. Why labor to read some unhappy omen into her own words?

Now across this well-verified account Martha Dickinson Bianchi, Emily's
niece and biographer, has obtruded an after-dinner yarn that Mary Lyon
ordered her students to observe Christmas as a day of fasting and prayer, and
that Emily rebelled and went home, being restored later to good standing.
There is simply no truth in that story. A day of fasting and prayer (incidentally not Christmas but the day before) was requested of the village church
by an Amherst minister temporarily supplying in South Hadley. Any student
was free, without blame, not to share in the observance. No school in New
England had a Christmas vacation, and Mary Lyon never ordered anyone
to fast and pray. Emily's own unabridged letter to Abiah Root makes it clear

* The letter, preserved in the alumnae archives of the Mount Holyoke Library, has
been published in *A Hundred Years of Mount Holyoke College,* by Arthur C. Cole
(Yale University Press, 1940), Appendix I, pp. 391–93.

that she had not visited her home at any time between Thanksgiving and January 17. To bolster the apocryphal yarn Mrs. Bianchi omitted from her version of that letter all of Emily's happiness and all the details that flatly disprove the story of rebellion.*

Another garbled story, harder to trace to its origin though it seems to have a grain of truth, runs in effect that Miss Lyon asked all the unconverted who wished to become Christians to rise; and that when the negative vote was called for, Emily made a dramatic exit. Susan Tolman's missionary newsletter makes it clear that through several weeks of a quiet but intense revival Mary Lyon used beautiful tact toward girls who were not ready to accept religious faith. She had private meetings in her own room for those who wished to attend, and she encouraged girls to communicate with her by sealed notes dropped in her private box. The story of a melodramatic exit from the pressure of a public meeting hardly fits into that background, nor into the natures of Mary Lyon and Emily Dickinson. It would have required no great spiritual courage to resist the distorted ogress of the myth; it took much courage to dissent from a faith held by so many friendly persons. In an oral statement made to a friend Emily indicated that at some meeting she disappointed either Miss Lyon or some other person by her inability or unreadiness to accept the offered religion. The problem she faced at South Hadley confronted her in Amherst—and everywhere. Two letters she wrote to Abiah Root after the revival reveal her inner hurt because she had found no peace; both letters are humble and deeply serious.

Nowhere in her journal did Susan Tolman name Emily Dickinson, though there can be no doubt she was concerned for the younger girl. Sarah Jane Anderson, a senior who was closely observant of Emily, was one of Susan's best friends. Miss Anderson's father, the everywhere-at-once Secretary of the Mission Board in Boston, was already laboring to enlist Miss Tolman for the foreign field.

In her letters Emily names, besides Miss Lyon and Miss Whitman, only one teacher—Rebecca Fiske, an Amherst woman. Must we then let Susan and Emily live for more than half a year† in the same hall, see each other unseeingly, and go their opposite ways without even a gossamer thread to connect them? Merely a few reiterations from the younger girl, "I like all my teachers," and from the older one a glance at an elusive but anonymous "impenitent." Well, there was at least one gossamer thread. The office of

---

* That letter should be read in its complete form in *The Letters of Emily Dickinson,* edited by Mabel Loomis Todd (1931).

† Susan Tolman withdrew as a teacher in April 1848 to prepare as a missionary.

records, with its files and photostats, had not been invented; but Emily's letters name some of the courses she took, and Susan's not-all-somber missionary journal names some of the courses she taught that year. Being an enthusiastic teacher, she indulged in much shop talk when writing about the March midyear public orals. There were two sections of the choir; Emily rehearsed in one of them, and Susan Tolman had charge of both. It was a pity the younger girl had already taken botany and made an herbarium in the Amherst academy, for that was Susan's best course; but she did have physiology with Miss Tolman. Only a textbook course, I'm afraid. There is one other possible but tenuous reference. In mid-February Emily wrote to her brother: "One of our teachers, who is engaged, received a visit from her intended quite unexpectedly yesterday afternoon, and she has gone to her home to show him, I opine, and will be absent until Saturday." The reference fits Susan Tolman better than any other teacher, though her intended had visited Ware several months earlier.

Did either woman remember the other after many years? I have found no evidence. It is unlikely that Mrs. Mills ever heard of Emily as a poet. The fact that three small volumes of Emily Dickinson's poems were published between 1890 and 1896 should not be argued too strongly. Emily was discovered as Whitman was discovered by poetry lovers everywhere only with that great revival of poetry that began around 1912. And it is still more unlikely that the recluse of Amherst ever knew that the demure, dutiful teacher sailed far across the "everywhere of silver" on ships with gallant names, and thridded Madras and Jaffna and the Cape and Panama and Punahou and Yerba Buena like topazes set in a silver chain. Comparison can't adjust itself to such different dimensions. Each of the two had her own way of taking a high excitement from beautiful rhythmic words, and many a person has borne witness that Mrs. Mills' prayers, rich with the King James English, were the most beautiful they ever heard. There was a common ground between them, could they but have known it: Squire Dickinson would have no bread but of Emily's baking, and Susan's bread was a savory persuasion toward goodness. But they never really knew each other, more's the pity, and the loss was not more than half on Susan's side. Could Emily in her solitude but have known the Bethesda pool of compassion in her former teacher's heart . . .

Appendix E

CYRUS MILLS' BROTHERS

William and Mary Mills are buried in some old cemetery near Lenox; their graves are probably unmarked; and because of the gaps in frontier records I have been unable to learn when they died.

David Mills graduated from Williams in 1841, and from Princeton Theological Seminary in 1845. He was ordained a Presbyterian minister in that year, was married soon after, and had small pastorates in southeastern Pennsylvania for ten or twelve years. Around 1858 his religious eccentricities caused his withdrawal from the ministry. He died at Hammonton, New Jersey, in 1881. He left three sons and a daughter, and has several living descendants. A niece wrote of him: "David was a fanatic on religious subjects and a great trial to Uncle Cyrus." In the meager data furnished by David in the archives of the Princeton Theological Seminary he makes no mention of parents or brothers, but furnished the important point of the family's origin in Hillsborough County, New Hampshire.

I have no proof that Giles Mills was the youngest of the three brothers, but local tradition so places him, and Cyrus' tender regard for Giles and his children would bear out that impression. Two of Giles' daughters—Adeline and Isadore Mills—were educated free at Benicia and at Seminary Park. Adeline Mills (Titus) stated that her father Giles went to college; and though I have been unable to find a record of him from Hamilton College eastward, there is no reason to doubt her statement. He may have withdrawn from college on account of early marriage. He died at Sycamore, Illinois, about 1860.

Giles Mills married Nancy Van Epps, and they had three daughters. The oldest, Emma, married Charles Seidel, a captain in the Union army; their daughter was the Mrs. Susan Smith whom older alumnae remember. Miss Fannie Madison's mother was a sister of Nancy Van Epps; and Miss Madison, though not related to either Cyrus or Susan Mills, became by affection and faithful service an adoptive daughter of Mrs. Mills.

Giles Mills' family having been separated by his untimely death, his daughter, Adeline Mills Titus, was able to give, in her last years, only fragments of tradition about the early years of the three brothers. She wrote that her uncle Cyrus was helped through college by a wealthy manufacturer of Ware; but she must have confused what she had heard, for there is no other indication that Cyrus knew anybody in Ware until he met Susan Tolman, and it is clear that he earned his way by teaching and with some help from the Hallock family. Mrs. Titus gave, however, a very clear account of the brothers' being brought up by the good Aunt Rebecca, and of Cyrus' care of that aunt in her old age. Mrs. Titus knew this part of the story from her own memory.

Appendix F

THE YOUNG LADIES' SEMINARY OF BENICIA

The school was founded in the summer of 1852 by Benicia citizens led by two Presbyterian ministers — Sylvester Woodbridge, Jr., of Benicia, and Samuel H. Willey, whose field was northern California in general. Coming before the Gold Rush, they were two of the first four Protestant ministers to settle in California, and though Woodbridge was Old Style Presbyterian and Willey was New Style, they were friends and both were notable founders of schools and churches. The citizens elected nine Benicia men as trustees, Woodbridge being the only trustee with a college education and the only teacher. (Willey appears to have had little to do with the school after its founding, though he with three other men founded in Oakland the college that eventually became the University of California.) Six of the nine trustees resigned within two years, three successors were elected, and the Board consisted of six when it finally disbanded in January 1855. Woodbridge, one of the three trustees who served throughout the life of the Board, continued as minister in Benicia until 1869. His three daughters graduated from the Seminary, and Mary (the oldest) married Paul Pioda, who taught music and modern languages in the Seminary for many years and finally bought and managed the school in 1883. In 1878 when a notable reunion of alumnae and former teachers was held, Woodbridge gave an account of the first years of the school—an interpretation more authentic than the usual tradition.

By correspondence with Governor Slade of Vermont the trustees engaged Susan A. Lord as principal, and she, with two assistants—the Misses Georgia A. and Frances A. Allen—opened the school in August 1852. At the end of the school year Miss Lord resigned the principalship to marry a certain Judge Wells "in the northern part of the state." Mrs. Wells was not present at the reunion in 1878, though it was implied that she was living. During the second year Miss Jemima N. Hudson was principal. In 1854 she married Thomas J. Nevins, first superintendent of schools in San Francisco, and she continued teaching in that city for twenty years. She attended the alumnae reunion in Benicia in 1878.

In September 1854 Mary Atkins (Oberlin '45) became principal. The evidence is quite conflicting as to her purpose in coming to California. Two writers have conjectured a lengthy correspondence between her and the Benicia trustees—a plausible piece of guesswork without a basis of fact. Her enigmatical letters to her family seem to indicate that she and her traveling companion, Miss Pettit, undertook the journey on a sudden impulse of adventure with no definite object. According to Major Edward Sherman's reminiscences (see the March and June numbers of the *Quarterly* of the California Historical Society, 1945) Miss Atkins had never heard of the Benicia Seminary until Sherman himself told her about the school while she was on the voyage from Panama to San Francisco. There is need of a critical evaluation of the Mary Atkins legend, overgrown as it is with guesswork and the unverified fumblings of rememberers.* In any case, Mary Atkins did not found the Young Ladies' Seminary of Benicia. Repeatedly in her catalogues she stated that it was founded in 1852; and she did not appear upon the scene until the fall of 1854.

In January 1855 the trustees transferred full control of the school to Mary Atkins, and dissolved. According to Woodbridge's account in 1878, the school had often been near bankruptcy in its first years. The trustees are not on record as having owned any property; apparently they had rented the school building (a remodeled residence), and it appears that they gave Miss Atkins the good will of the business as a worthy cause but a dubious value. In 1857 she bought the school building and lot, and in the next two years two adjoining lots—an investment of $2,495. She also built a dormitory cottage, the cost of which is not known. In one of her moods of depression, in 1857, she wanted to sell the school to anyone who would buy, or even to give it away, but was persuaded by one of her teachers, Mrs. A. A. Haskell, to take a short vacation and to think better of the affair. In October 1858 she wrote to her father that she was clearing $500 a month. The earliest catalogue

* There were three Pacific Mail steamers on the Panama-Pacific run in the summer of 1854. In a letter to Mrs. Mills in 1910, Major Sherman said that he, with Mary Atkins and her friend, made that voyage on the *Oregon*. In his reminiscences in the *California Historical Quarterly* he said they came on the *Panama*. But the passenger lists in *The Alta Californian* show that the Major and the ladies came on the steamship *California*, arriving in San Francisco September 19, 1854.

I have seen (for the year ending in June 1859) shows an enrollment of 111, including seminary and lower grades.

In the late summer or early fall of 1863 she rented the school for a year to Miss Margaret Lammond, with some sort of agreement to sell to Miss Lammond at the end of that period. Whether there was a contract to buy, or only an option, is not clear. Miss Atkins returned from a voyage to Japan, China, and Siam on September 6, 1864. For twelve days she and Miss Lammond negotiated, and then Miss Lammond declined to buy the school, though she retained possession of it until October 14. It is perilous to call a conjecture more than a conjecture, but the fact that Miss Lammond immediately bought another school in San Francisco and removed there on October 15, taking with her nineteen students, negates the theory that an unseasonable drouth was to blame. Rather, the disagreement would seem to have turned upon the price. (On September 18, 1866, nearly a year after she had sold the school to Cyrus T. Mills, Miss Atkins recorded in her diary: "Two years ago decided to take back my school [from Miss Lamond]. Fatal day!")

On October 7, 1865, Miss Atkins sold the Seminary to Cyrus T. Mills for $5,000, he and Mrs. Mills taking charge of it on January 1, 1866. The story of their practical success during the five and a half years of their ownership has been told in Chapter XI. On October 29, 1870, they sold the school to the Reverend Charles H. Pope for $10,000. He, a Bowdoin man and pastor of the Congregational church in Benicia, took control of the school in the summer of 1871 and conducted it for three years. On March 16, 1874, he sold the Seminary to two businessmen of Benicia, Daniel N. Hastings and Edward Wolfskill, for $20,000. It seems a fair conjecture that they bought the school as an investment; had it been a losing venture Pope could hardly have exacted so high a price from men who knew the conditions—and Hastings had been a trustee of the Seminary back in 1854; his resignation from the Board would imply that he was not minded to underwrite a losing venture.

By some sort of rental or lease the new owners gave control of the school to Miss Mary E. Snell. She made notable improvements in the curriculum and lengthened the course to four years. She was principal until June 1878, when she withdrew to open her own school in Oakland. I have found no catalogue for Pope's time, and only one for Miss Snell's; however, the number of graduates during their respective periods would indicate about the same enrollment as during Miss Atkins' ownership.

In the autumn of 1866 Mary Atkins returned to her former home in Ohio. She traveled in Europe between February and October 1867, then taught in Cleveland from the fall of 1868 until March 28, 1869, when she married John

Lynch, who had been a student in her classes in the Oberlin Academy in 1847. He had gone to Louisiana after the Civil War, and was an officeholder there through 1876. In 1877 he and his wife were living in Santa Barbara, California, and in 1878, when Miss Snell's departure left the Benicia Young Ladies' Seminary without a head, Mary Atkins Lynch made some sort of agreement with the owners and once more became principal. Edward Wolfskill had sold his share in the property to Andrew Goodyear, and in 1879 Hastings and Goodyear sold the school to Mrs. Lynch for $8,000. In his biographical sketch (in the Bancroft Library) Hastings claimed that he had spent more than $20,000 in supporting the school. The transactions that are of legal record show a partnership capital loss of $12,000. He may have sacrificed something in 1879 to encourage Mrs. Lynch and to foster civic culture.

During her first period of ownership Miss Atkins' ups and downs of feeling toward the school were extreme. Her second period of ownership was marked by a tired autumn joy. In October 1878 the alumnae of the school, meeting to organize an alumnae association, had welcomed her return with a kindness that permeated her reserved but hungry nature; and a large body of alumnae, from all periods, had joined in presenting her with a fine microscope. After her prolonged wandering, she was home at last; the school was now her jealously guarded possession, her personal trust. Her feeling toward it as a continuing entity is expressed in a paragraph which she repeated in her last catalogues:

HONOR TO WHOM HONOR IS DUE

The list of all the students who have graduated from the Young Ladies' Seminary of Benicia, is published in this Catalogue simply to preserve the history of the school, but with no intention or desire to deprive the Rev. C. T. Mills, D.D. and Mrs. Mills, the Rev. C. H. Pope, and Miss Mary E. Snell, of the honors justly due them for their earnest efforts in behalf of those who graduated during their respective administrations of the affairs of the Institution.

Her last will, drawn upon her deathbed, reveals her pathetic wish that the school might be perpetuated:

I, Mary Atkins Lynch, now residing in Benicia, in the state of California, being of sound mind and memory but at present being ill in health and considering the uncertainty of life, do make and declare this to be my last will and testament, that is to say:

The Seminary at Benicia, known and called "The Young Ladies Semin-

ary," *has been for many years under my care and I have expected to place it on a permanent basis for the education of Young Ladies, but being now too unwell to make the necessary and proper provisions therefor, I now make this my last will with the view to making other provisions to carry out my desires when I recover, but if I do not then this shall be my last will.*

My Executrix and Executor hereinafter named shall continue to conduct and carry on said Seminary as now organized until the end of the present term and as long thereafter as they may be able to do so, using my Seminary property for that purpose, and I order and direct them to make the best provisions in their power, to continue said Seminary, including the Seminary property, as a permanent institution for the education of Young Ladies, and if they make any disposition of the Seminary property for educational purposes they shall make easy terms of sale to any purchaser or purchasers by giving long time for payment which they may extend to five years, and a low rate of interest. Upon a final sale and disposition of said property the proceeds therefor and the proceeds of all other property owned by me shall go to my heirs at law, except that my jewelry and personal effects not used for educational purposes shall be given to my friends and relatives hereafter named by me either verbally or in writing, or if not named by me then as my Executors may think best, which shall be given as a remembrance from me. Provided that my neice (sic) Mary Atkins Fowler shall have one-third of said proceeds which I give to her, that is to say if said property shall be sold as heretofore stated, when the proceeds shall be realized and collected, one-third shall be paid over to my said neice as her own.

I hereby revoke all former wills made by me.

I hereby nominate and appoint my neice Mary Atkins Fowler Executrix and my husband John Lynch Executor of this my last will and testament and they shall not be required to give any bonds, and they shall have the necessary power to carry into effect the provisions of this will without any order of any court.

She had deferred too long; her dream of permanence was a belated wish rather than a plan. In her last extremity she could think of no one—no group —to whom she could with assurance entrust the future of her school, and her main hope was doomed to frustration. Her estate was divided, one-third to her favorite grandniece, one-third to her husband, and the remainder equally between her brother and four sisters.

Her executors managed the school after her death (September 14, 1882) until June 1883. In April 1883 John Lynch resigned as executor and bought the school for $13,000. A month later he sold it to Paul Pioda for $6,000 "and other valuable consideration." It is a fair inference that in selling to Pioda at a reduced price Lynch was trying to carry out his wife's urgent wish that the school be perpetuated as a memorial to her. Pioda and his wife, the former Mary Woodbridge, conducted the school until it finally closed in 1886.

Appendix G

"FOR I AM NEVER FORGET"

Here are some of the little stories about her. Many others have been lost. If these are not recorded now, they too, after another decade, will be forgotten.

The Chinaboys. Yep Wo retired a few years before my time. For thirty years he had ruled the kitchen, and besides his main skill he devised a pleasant usage out of the goodness of his heart. At the beginning of each year he went to Mrs. Mills and got a certain list; and each girl was served on her birthday with a magnificent cake—no two identical. They say that the expectation, the bringing-in, the craning to see what magic of icing and candy hearts Yep Wo had devised this time, were simply too exciting. When his long service was over and he was departing for China, Mrs. Mills had him on the rostrum at prayers as a visiting dignitary.

Yang, who succeeded him as dean of the Oriental servants, had earned his responsibility by merit of character and many years. Yang had full charge of hiring and training new Chinaboys, and no executive was ever more careful. He himself, as head waiter, served Mrs. Mills and her guests in the little dining room. He was spare of body, his fine face not that impenetrable mask attributed by story writers to all Chinese. He was composed and poised, but his face was transparent with feeling, and he adored Mrs. Mills. He too was growing old, and had booked his passage home when she lay in the coma of her last illness. A strange nurse twice refused Yang's request to be allowed to enter the sickroom. A third refusal, and he quietly came in anyway, sat long by the bedside, stroking Mrs. Mills' hand.

There was no summer school in those days; and the Chinaboys, too valuable to be disbanded, spent quiet weeks in polishing every windowpane and waxing every panel and bannister. Calm hours when, observing the paraphernalia of Western learning, one could discuss with one's co-workers the eventual cosmic acceptance, the All-in-Allness of Time. They were doing the library. Miss Sawyer had left it immaculate, but with soft cloths one could remove imaginary dust from the shelves, and conversationally silken-dust the covers and ends and edges of books, some of which contained pictures worth unhurried inspection and sociable comment. So very many books. Apprentice boys who had attended high school ventured information as to the incredible variety and wealth of subject matter, but maturity had its reservations. And maturity, with an eye to the aesthetic, was pained by one thing. Miss Sawyer was a wonderful lady—*but*—why this obvious disregard for artistic principle? She was overworked, her helpers were careless: that could be the only explanation. Summer was summer: time to correct the librarian's oversight and—not too obtrusively—plant the seed of beauty. And so they shelved all the big red books together, then the middle-sized red books, then the little red books; all the big green books, the middle-sized. . . . It was beautiful. And as art should do, it aroused emotion.

In the early '70's, Anna Sawyer and Janet Haight were roommates—Judge Sawyer's and Governor Haight's daughters. When I knew them they were silvery ladies who must set a good example; but in trustable company they reverted at a thought: Miss Sawyer impish and irreverent, Miss Haight, a trustee, beaming approval. Miss Sawyer was tiny, and the child that hides in the heart of many a student found in her, as little children did, the story-book image of the fairy godmother. That great crown of beautiful white hair, the warm eyes sparkling with mischief or tender with compassion. By some magic her pretty clothes could make-believe into a fairy's cape and hood; and accompanying a tallish walker across the reading room her feet played the right-hand triple notes of the "Moonlight Sonata"—but with gaiety. And who remembers the college picnic when, to the percussion of handclaps, she jigged a "Turkey in the Straw" that set the most doctorish foot a-tapping? She should have kept a children's library: you follow a winding path through a forest of Rackham trees, cross a rustic toll bridge (the fee a silver penny, and an acorn for luxury tax), and there in an open glade you find a madrone tree that learned the First Psalm by heart. Climb to the second story, and there's the door. You have to remember the right rhyme when you knock. You have forgotten it through so many Importances? We are very sorry. You must say the right rhyme.

Titania could make faces at any ogre, but she had a pitiful fear of dogs. Now Teddy was the dog emeritus of Mrs. Mills' last years, and Teddy would have nipped no mortal who bore the recommendation of a minister. But dignified though he was, Teddy may have simulated a stage growl, a poor actor's effort to get into character. Miss Sawyer would flee, and Mrs. Mills

254 *The Story of Cyrus and Susan Mills*

would remark, between pathos and laughter, "I don't see nearly as much of Anna Sawyer as I'd like to."

Because Teddy was of some breed that I miscall White Angora, I keep fancying all his predecessors to have looked like him: a Scotty size and build but with tiptilted nose, wavy Angora fleece, the black eyes peering through a chaparral of eyebrows and whiskers. "Thy hair is as a flock of goats that appear from Mount Gilead." A chemistry student had wiled one white-fleeced predecessor into the laboratory, whence he emerged scarlet as the Unmentionable Lady in Revelation (17:5). That was too much for Mrs. Mills' patience. After all, a dog has his right, even as a clouted beggar in Jaffna, not to be made ridiculous. It is told that the dyer had hard work to be forgiven; also that she became a notable civic leader and a pillar in the church.

Somewhere along the line there were two dogs at once, who mayn't have been fleecy white, but I can't rid my mind of that Angora prettiness. Now, one dog alone might, on occasion, be allowed to attend prayers, and would indeed be expected to be present at family worship in the parlor; but two dogs, and at public prayers in Seminary Hall—no! Each morning, each evening, they were shut up while their mistress led the service. Women who knew Mrs. Mills differ about many points of her personality, but all agree that her prayers were beautiful and moving. (One witness used to wish the blessing at Sunday morning breakfast were shorter, because the milk toast— one of Yep Wo's choicest *objets d'art*—pleaded to be taken piping hot.) But to our dogs. One morning even the devoutest ears heard a scrabble of paws at the door which swung open. Around the rear, up the aisle, racing feet; up two steps onto the rostrum, one teacher and another opening eyes and grabbing at the air. Mrs. Mills, her eyes closed, continued her reverent talk with God; but when the two gay naughties began leaping and begging, one at either side, she calmly reached down, got each sinner by the scruff of his neck, straightened up with a relaxed Gideon's fleece in each hand, and, with unhurried dignity—each phrase tuned to the rhythms of David and Isaiah and Paul—finished her prayer.

The teapots. Mrs. Mills herself started the collection in Ceylon and India, and augmented it during her later travels. Then one alumna after another caught the spirit, and sent back from Europe, or the Near East, or the Orient, more teapots; and still other alumnae remembered it when attending auctions or dispersing heirlooms in the attic. And so the collection grew, with teapots of every mood, quaint, fat with humor, dainty, tiny, some with association value, and many graced with real ceramic beauty and pedigree. When the collection was nearing the two hundred mark, the head of the house of

Nathan-Dohrmann asked for the special privilege of giving the two-hundredth, and remarked that his gift was the finest collector's item he had ever owned. And so the collection grew, and alumnae always hurried to the cabinets in the parlors of Mills Hall, each eager to find her own contribution and to admire once more some favorite piece. There were more than eight hundred teapots in the collection when Mrs. Mills died.

Besides her other aptitudes, Dean Ege was a good basketball coach. Mrs. Mills was delighted: now we could show the university something. When the Berkeley girls came to our campus she served lunches so lavish, a cynic may have suspected a foxy method of making 'em sleepy and scant of breath. And always—always—our own players were to be calm, poised. "Now Genevieve, if you must miss a throw, overshoot the basket. When your throw is short, it's simply too hard on our nerves." Was the game going against us? Run, somebody, and tell Professor Keep to—not to fudge, certainly not that—but to call time as soon as he can ethically do so. And then that day at Berkeley when our team walked over the university girls. We must *not* yield to unladylike excitement. The final whistle blew. Down from the bleachers, like a flushed partridge, sped Mrs. Mills (aged seventy-seven), seized the ball, embraced the Mills captain, and then, still clasping the ball with a righteous joy of one of the fighting psalms, led captain and team around the court.

There was no tearoom on the campus in her day. But if you had a letdown feeling when studying for an examination, you dropped past the corridor that leads to the dining room, and there would be a table with pitchers of milk and platters of brown bread. You helped yourself. There was no charge. And still, as in the Punahou days, Mrs. Mills could say: "After teaching the Science class, I went into the kitchen and baked fourteen pies for dinner."

Here is the recipe for Mills brown bread: but does any alumna bake, in these times?

MILLS BROWN BREAD
(for two loaves)

1 cup New Orleans molasses (black), stirred into 1½ cups of hot water
1½ cups of yeast
Equal parts of white and graham flour, a little salt
Make the batter thinner than for white bread
When well risen, knead lightly into loaves. Keep in a warm place. Let it rise quickly the second time, and bake with moderate heat.
[The loaf was about half the size of a modern baker's "small" loaf. It sliced clean, not crumbly. And it was purely personal, not a generalized

address to an imagined public. The yeast was, of course, homemade, and the baker must know whether his own yeast is good.]

Once a girl was summoned to Mrs. Mills' rooms to explain some escapade. She was shivering, really frightened. "My dear, you have a chill. Come right in here and swallow this." And "this" was a glass of invalid port—with no Mission Board to add a nauseous gr-r-r-r. It would be tantalizing to know which one of the early vintners in the Napa Valley put his old-world skill, his heirloom recipe, into that bottle; or maybe it bore the label of Antonio Mattei, whose vine rows over in the hot valley pointed to the snowy Sierra, and whose port and muscatel and angelica were sacramental indeed.

Many Thou-shalt-nots of the 1840's had given way to kindness. Old-timers remember her happiness at the Washington's Birthday dances, when half the girls were Georges in blue and silver coats, knee breeches and silver-buckled shoes, and the other half the prettiest Marthas, with powdered hair and courtly manners. The secret of her "escape from the benumbing spell of age" was her perennial enjoyment of youth. She liked pretty clothes, on others as on herself; had her dresses made at the City of Paris. The poverty of the 1850's was past; she could have nice things.

One teacher who was especially dear to Mrs. Mills in her last years remembers going with her on a business trip to the City. When they entered the Crocker Bank, officials who usually waited to be approached left their desks, hurried into the lobby, and surrounded her. Mere business apple-polish? No, she was no longer treasurer, and the college account was in another bank; but she was Mrs. Mills.

A shopping trip to the City—that was another matter. A teacher and (as a special treat) a senior or two would be invited to come along. Coming along was fairly simple while the expedition continued on train and ferry and cab; but once on the pavement, youth's legs were never enough. Off Mrs. Mills would go like a lady quail in April, half a block ahead of the accompanists, who tried to keep up without running; and by nightfall the followers had—one might say—been around.

Or the time when Luther Burbank came to inspect the campus and, guided by Mrs. Mills, had surely—surely—seen every tree and shrub from the camphor tree in Tolman House garden to the newest red-flowering dwarf eucalyptus, and was sinking exhausted into a deep chair, when suddenly she remembered one more plant—maybe one of the exotics brought by Cyrus from Japan in 1875. Up and out she hurried, while the Wizard tenderly felt of his legs, poor man, and sighed and followed, wishing to heaven he had gone in for a more sedentary subject.

A guest speaker was holding forth—and holding. The students simulated attention, but Mrs. Mills knew expertly the moment when bored decorum would begin to fidget and rustle. Tiptoeing toward the speaker she stage-whispered: "Your train leaves sooner than you realize. And you'd better make your closing prayer short."

Nothing escaped Mrs. Mills' eye. She irritated younger women by sending them on some errand about the grounds, and when they arrived she'd be there already, seeing the thing done. That day, for example, when Andrew Carnegie came to inspect the new library. He must have arrived early (it was not like her to forget courtesy)—but where was Mrs. Mills? Secretaries, young teachers, athletic students, Chinaboys—everybody ran in all directions; till somebody found her up by the dairy barn, the train of her handsome City of Paris gown draped over her arm, conferring with John Weston (Mr. Weston, if you please) about some problem of animal husbandry.

Noon in the little dining room. Grace before meat. Yang brings for the main course one of her pet curry dishes, which is a favorite all 'round. Mr. Weber beams rosily; Dr. Lisser benevolates. Enter Mr. Cadenasso—Mister, not Professor. Today his happiness has extraordinary uncontainability. Boyishly, among friends, he tells: he has sold two paintings. Nobody is vulgar enough to ask the price, but nice-boyishly he tells: for a thousand dollars. One painting of the cathedral grove at the lake; the other, of the trees in the arroyo near Pansy Hill. Dr. Carson congratulates the college upon the publicity value of this broad cultural achievement. The rest of us congratulate Caddy. Mrs. Mills fairly glows, but she remembers that Caddy, like Barney Barry, needs firm mothering. "Have you deposited that check?" Well, no; not yet. It is such a nice check to take out of the pocket and reread. "See that you deposit it the first thing tomorrow. Now remember. *You* know." After lunch she steers him to her parlor. Later, on the K-Leona car he reveals the substance of that interview—a motherly strapping about clearing off certain debts and not allowing any of the art-colony loafers to lay their hands on one cent of that money. For this hour he is resolute: first thing tomorrow morning. Then his eyes twinkle. "Anyway, I'd just as well deposit it. She'll be asking me again on Thursday."

Once when young gentlemen callers were encroaching against the rule that forbade beaux on Sunday forenoons, Barney was stationed at the K-Leona gate, with orders to admit no man but the minister. Three young men got off the car. To the first swain, Barney recited his orders, firm against pleas. The second swain: no sir, his orders was his orders, not to let no man in but the minister. The third man: no sir, ye can't come in—nobody but the minister.

"But you see, I *am* the minister." And in he went. A young man descended from the next car and stated his case. Barney was annoyed: "Ye can't pull that gag on me. I already let the minister in half an hour ago." And, of course, the fourth man really was the minister.

When the friezes for the hall of the library came (copies of reliefs from Athens), Barney, unpacking them, was pained at their bad condition. "Half of 'em with their arms broke or their noses. The man that made 'em, or the railroad, or somebody ought to up and be told right out that they just can't work off any damaged goods on Mills College."

When her will was probated, those who knew her best could say once more, "That's just like her." For Susan Mills gave away twice as much as her estate came to. It was appraised at a little under $19,000. Her will (drawn in March before she died) provided a monthly pension of $200 for sister Jane—but Jane had died in April; a small pension for the widow of an adoptive nephew; legacies ranging from $250 to $1,000 each for ten of her husband's kindred; two legacies of $1,000 and one of $500 to three women who had been nearest to her for many years; one of $1,500 (the largest) for her maid; seven of $100 each to men and women employees, and $1,000 to Michael Herlihy. The rest went to the college, but I suspect there was no "rest." She and her husband had given half a million to the school—about ninety-eight percent of their estate.

Notes upon Source Material

CHAPTER ONE

I have depended mainly upon the *History of the Town of Dorchester, Massachusetts,* by a Committee of the Dorchester Antiquarian and Historical Society (1859); *Dorchester Town Records* [being the Fourth Report of the Record Commissioners of the City of Boston] (1880); and *Records of the First Church at Dorchester in New England, 1636–1734,* by S. J. Barrows and W. B. Trask (1891). All three books have the solid virtue of documentation. After studying these I went like the crab, backward, to James Blake's *Annals,* and understood why the authors of the first and third books had enjoyed and quoted him. *Captain Clap's Memoirs* has been reprinted several times and "improved" by later editors, but I prefer Captain Clap unimproved, as in Blake's edition (1731). However, it was Deacon Samuel Tolman's homely account, written in 1830, that started me back to Dorchester. Among Mrs. Mills' papers there were three copies of the Deacon's story, all of which had had the wrinkles pressed out by well-intentioned secretaries; but through the kindness of Miss Julia Tolman Lee I was given an unironed early copy. Family traditions, passed down orally through two centuries, nearly always become encrusted with myth, but I have found only one error—and that a very slight one—in Deacon Samuel's story. The wills and probate inventories of Dorchester men are in the Suffolk County probate records in Boston. For the interwoven genealogies of Susan Tolman's Dorchester ancestors I have, of course, depended upon the Dorchester Vital Records. The vital records of Desire Tolman's family after he removed from Dorchester (*c.* 1787) were gathered and verified by Miss Mary M. Tolman, a granddaughter of Samuel Howe Tolman (*q. v.*).

For the backgrounds of the Boutelle ancestors I have used Alonzo Lewis' *The History of Lynn* (1829); Lilley Eaton's *Genealogical History of the Town of Reading, Massachusetts* (1874); and David Wilder's *History of Leominster from 1701 to 1852* (1853). But even Eaton's mainly accurate work betrays some errors, and I have depended upon the vital records of Lynn, Ipswich, Reading, Sudbury, Bolton, and Leominster. The will of James Boutelle II is in the probate records of Middlesex County, in Cambridge; wills and probate records of the Leominster men are in Worcester. The persistent teacher habit impels me to urge any reader who may undertake research in New England family records to go if possible to the excellent

library of the New England Historical-Genealogical Society in Boston. Derived books are often amateurish; there is disciplinary virtue in the vital
records.

The story of Ephraim Adams and of the way in which a branch of the
Boutelle and Nichols families moved to Enosburg is in the *Vermont Historical
Gazeteer*, Volume 2, Part 1, pages 132 to 165.

CHAPTER TWO

My limited data upon Deacon Desire Tolman's activities in Winchendon
are derived at second hand from Hurd's *Worcester County*, Hyde's *History
of Winchendon*, and Mannis' *History of Winchendon*. All else pertaining to
Desire Tolman and his family I have from original family records, gathered
and verified by his great-granddaughter, Mary M. Tolman. College attendance
of the several descendants I have verified with the recorders of Dartmouth
and Mount Holyoke.

Data regarding John Tolman and his family and his business in New
Ipswich came from the church clerk, Mrs. Arlo Balch, who was most gracious
in sending church records and in locating and describing (with photographs)
the site of Tolman's tannery.

Similar data regarding the Tolman, Nichols, and Boutelle families at
Enosburg came from the well-kept church records furnished by Mrs. Lloyd
Chaffee and from family records supplied by George L. Nichols. Both were
liberal with maps and photographs. Mrs. Mills' own account of her school
days in Enosburg is among her papers in the Mills College Library.

I used Arthur Chase's excellent *History of Ware, Massachusetts* (1911),
supplementing this with information about the East Church, furnished by the
Rev. Roland D. Sawyer, and with other information furnished by Mrs. Ruth
Miller (Mount Holyoke, '30). Besides, I visited Ware.

My account of the ministers whom Susan Tolman knew at Ware is derived
mainly from Calvin Durfee's *Annals of Williams College*, one of the richest
source books I have had the good fortune to find.

CHAPTER THREE

Arthur C. Cole's *A Hundred Years of Mount Holyoke College* (1940),
with its encyclopediac details, is the standard source book. I have used these
biographies of Mary Lyon: Edward Hitchcok's *The Power of Christian
Benevolence Illustrated in the Life and Labors of Mary Lyon* (1851); Fidelia
Fiske's *Recollections of Mary Lyon* (1866); Beth Bradford Gilchrist's *Life*

of *Mary Lyon* (1910) ; a chapter in Gamaliel Bradford's *Portraits of American Women* (1919), and one in M. A. DeWolfe Howe's *Classic Shades* (1928). The first two are funereal; Miss Gilchrist's is the best; Bradford's chapter is as laconic as dried beef, and his quoting of Mary Lyon's aphorisms will save time for the reader who lacks the energy to look them up in Miss Gilchrist's and Miss Fiske's ampler quotations. If you read Miss Bradford, note that the account beginning on page 400 was written by Mrs. Mills. One of the best portrait characterizations of Mary Lyon is in George F. Whicher's *This was a Poet*. For the story of Erastus Smith and his son Byron, I am indebted to the Rev. Jesse Gilman Nichols' article on "The Smith-Dwight Family" in the *Mount Holyoke Alumnae Quarterly*, October 1924, and to my colleague, Mrs. Herman Owen.

But the most revealing parts of Susan Tolman's life at Mount Holyoke came from her notebook and the missionary newsletter which she wrote. (The first is in the Mills College Library; the second is in the Mount Holyoke archives, and a copy is now in the Mills College Library.) To trace the persons named, I learned to depend upon the alumnae archives at Mount Holyoke and the unfailing carefulness of the custodian, Miss Bertha E. Blakeley. Other stories of those friends were developed by many letters to their living descendants—a file too long to be listed here. Mount Holyoke catalogues for Susan Tolman's period are, of course, rich in material. The letters of Susan Tolman to Martha Grant and Abby Allen are in Miss Blakeley's files. Since Chapter 3 was written, George F. Whicher has published young William Gardiner Hammond's *Remembrance of Amherst, an Undergraduate's Diary, 1846–1848*, from which I was allowed to quote before its publication.

CHAPTER FOUR

The main source materials, Susan Tolman's notebook and missionary journal, were identified in the notes on Chapter 3. Louise Porter Thomas's *Seminary Militant* (1937) has a value far above its modest tone and size in presenting the subject of missionary zeal at Mount Holyoke. Miss Lyon's letter of recommendation is in the "Candidates' Letters" file in the missionary archives, in the Houghton Library at Harvard.

CHAPTER FIVE

The meager information about Cyrus Mills' parents and his early life came from his letters in the "Candidates' Letters" in the missionary archives. This was supplemented by the biographical sketch of David Mills in the alumni records of Princeton Theological Seminary, and by a letter written some twenty years ago by Mrs. Adeline Mills Titus, a daughter of Giles Mills. Material relating to Paris and Lenox was derived mainly from Pomroy Jones' *Annals and Recollections of Oneida County* (1851), and L. M. Hammond's *History of Madison County* (1872). Information about the Lenox Church as of 1837 was derived from Minutes of the General Assembly of the Presbyterian Church.

The richest source of information about Williams College men is Calvin Durfee's *Annals of Williams College*, supplemented by the later register of alumni. And as the stories of Susan Tolman's friends had to be developed through many letters, the stories of Cyrus Mills' friends at Williams and at Union Theological Seminary grew by following clues in the alumni registers on through missionary archives and, in the case of his California friends, through the exceptionally rich material in the Bancroft Library at the University of California. There is no source book on this subject; the work has been a matter of collecting and integrating material from many sources. Miss Ethel Richmond, reference librarian in Williams College, has been most helpful in furnishing letters by, or relating to, Cyrus Mills, and references to him in the successive records of the reunions of his class. Horace Davis' "Williams College in 1845" is in *The University of California Chronicle*, Volume XIV, No. 1, January 1912.

CHAPTER SIX

Material relating to the Hallock family is derived from the usual printed biographical sources, supplemented by Durfee, but more particularly from descendants of Leavitt Hallock, Jr. Mills College traditions are sprinkled with Hallock stories. Mrs. Mills' version of The Courtin' comes through the memory of Dr. Mariana Bertola. Cyrus Mills' activities during the year 1847–48 are related in his letters in the missionary archives.

CHAPTERS SEVEN AND EIGHT

Preliminary sources for these two chapters were the files of the *Missionary Herald*, supplemented by W. W. Howland's *Historical Sketch of the Ceylon Mission* (1865), and *Brief Sketch of the American Ceylon Mission* (1849). But the main sources are, of course, the letters and other records in the archives of the American Board of Commissioners for Foreign Missions, now preserved in the Houghton Library at Harvard University. (Copies of all letters and excerpts which I have utilized are now on file in the Mills College Library.) Biographical data concerning some of the missionaries came from reserve files of the American Board, through the unfailing courtesy of Dr. Enoch F. Bell, librarian and historian of the Board (now retired), and his successor, Mrs. Mary Uline Dunlap. Mrs. Mills' own account of the voyage to Ceylon and of their arrival and early work there is among her papers in the Mills College archives; but characteristically she tells nothing of her long illness in Ceylon and the journeys to the mainland in search of health; that story is derived from her husband's letters and, even more, from the sympathetic letters of their colleagues. The story of Mrs. Mills' care for the baby daughter of W. W. Howland came from W. W. Howland II, son of the missionary. The map of the Ceylon Mission is a synthetic combination of several maps in the mission archives. I have used the spelling of names of the mission stations as used by the missionaries themselves in the early period; modern maps give a modern spelling of many of those names.

CHAPTER NINE

The main sources are still the letters in the missionary archives, which contain also copies of the reports of the Deputation. One sin of omission: I have not traced the War of the Deputation through the religious and family papers of the period; the tenor of letters and comments in those journals I have taken from letters in the archives. Reports of the meetings of the missionary society as given in the *Missionary Herald* are *ex parte* in tone.

Information regarding Cyrus Mills' two years as supply pastor at Berkshire and Richfield is severely limited, and I regret that I have been unable to find anything about his business venture at Ware.

CHAPTER TEN

A History of Hawaii (1926), by R. S. Kuykendall and H. E. Gregory, is good for general background.

The wealth of biographies and journals of missionaries makes this a rich reading sector, from which I have chosen for variety these books:

Titus Coan's *Life in Hawaii* (1882)—vigorous and vivid.

Laura Fish Judd's *Honolulu: Sketches of Life in the Hawaiian Islands*, etc. (1880), Lucy Goodale Thurston's *Life and Times*, etc. (1882). Both books are quaintly old-fashioned.

E. L. Wight's *The Memoirs of Elizabeth Kinau Wilder* (1909) supplements

264 The Story of Cyrus and Susan Mills

the books by Mrs. Thurston and Mrs. Judd in presenting the family life of the pioneer missionaries.

Frances Gulick Jewett's *Luther Halsey Gulick, Missionary in Hawaii, Micronesia, Japan, and China* (1895).

Addison Gulick's *Evolutionist and Missionary, John Thomas Gulick* (1932), an excellent account of research in science by sons of the missionaries.

Autobiographies of Amos Starr Cooke and Juliette Montague Cooke (1941), useful particularly for a view of the mission schools.

Three books by Ethel M. Damon:

Father Bond of Kohala (1927), a fine and thorough biography;

Komalu (1931), the story of the family of William Harrison Rice; and

The Stone Church of Kawaiahao (1945), which weaves more than a century of mission history into the story of one church.

Mary Dillingham Frear's *Lowell and Abigail* (1934), a tenderly sympathetic story of the author's grandparents, Lowell and Abigail Tenney Smith.

Mary Charlotte Alexander's *William Patterson Alexander* (1934), one of the best biographies in this field; also her unpublished biography of her other grandfather, Dwight Baldwin, which I have read in manuscript.

Arthur D. Baldwin's *A Memoir of Henry Perrine Baldwin* (1915), excellent for the transition period, the development of the great plantations.

The Missionary Album, enlarged edition, published in 1937 by the Hawaiian Mission Children's Society, an indispensable reference work.

Punahou, 1841–1941, by Mary Charlotte Alexander and Charlotte Peabody Dodge. Indispensable for the history of the school and, almost equally, for the story of the entire mission.

A General Catalogue . . . of Punahou School . . . for the Fortieth Anniversary (1881), a useful check list.

The letters of Cyrus Mills, of the Punahou trustees, and of Rufus Alexander are in the missionary archives in the Houghton Library. Letters of Punahou students to and about Mrs. Mills, and her several letters relating to the school are in the Mills College Library. Excerpts from *The Friend* and from other Honolulu papers were made by Mrs. James Murray (Elizabeth Shepherd, Mills '33). Names of ships, dates of arrival and departure, for the Mills' Pacific voyages have been checked with Customs House Records in San Francisco and shipping records in the *Alta Californian*; prosaic facts, but disciplinary.

CHAPTER ELEVEN

Nothing in this chapter came ready to hand. From clues in the alumni registers of Williams College, Union Theological Seminary, and Mount Holyoke College, I traced the Mills' friends in California through the almost inexhaustible material in the Bancroft Library at the University of California. The available file of catalogues of the Benicia Seminary, though incomplete, is, of course, most useful. Most of the information about other schools of the period came from files of San Francisco and Sacramento papers. Solano County records of the successive sales of the Benicia Seminary property, and of the probate records of Mary Atkins Lynch's estate, have been clarifying. The letters of Maria Rice Isenberg are in Miss Ethel M. Damon's *Komalu*. Biographies of Charles H. Pope and of Miss Mary Snell are derived from Bowdoin College records and from obituaries of Miss Snell in Oakland and Berkeley papers. The diary of Mary Atkins' voyage to China was printed by the Eucalyptus Press in 1937. References to her state of mind and her activities in 1866 are based upon her diary for 1866 and upon letters to her kinsfolk, unpublished. *The Mary Atkins Book* (c. 1921), a collection of transcribed letters from Benicia Seminary alumnae, has some value but needs to be cross-checked for accuracy. The reunion letters of the class of 1844, in the files at Williams College, have been useful. Israel E. Dwinell's account of Cyrus Mills is contained in a pamphlet, *Mills Seminary*, published by the school in 1885.

CHAPTER TWELVE

The main sources are self-explanatory: Catalogues of Mills Seminary, files of the short-lived *Brooklyn Home Journal*, early volumes of the *Mills Quarterly*, and land records in Alameda County. Details concerning the cost of land, acreage, grantors, etc., I have taken directly from county records. Items concerning the general cost of the school plant, the donations, the debt and the interest paid, I have taken from the careful statements of Israel E. Dwinell and Robert Simson, the two trustees who wrote the historical sketch of the Seminary in the pamphlet, *Mills Seminary*, cited in notes for Chapter 11. I have also cross-checked this pamphlet with various newspaper accounts. Robert Simson's part in the Audubon expedition was derived from Jeanne Skinner Van Nostrand's monograph, *Audubon's Ill-Fated Western Journey*; other material relating to Simson came from various items of local biographies in the Bancroft Library, and from the land records in Alameda County. Some of the anecdotes were derived from *The Susan Lincoln Mills Memory*

Book, which Miss Clara K. Wittenmeyer compiled in 1915—a source from which other material in the last chapter and the final appendix came. From this chapter forward, other items have been derived from personal interviews and letters, which are on file in the Mills College Library.

CHAPTER THIRTEEN

Catalogues of Mills Seminary; the account by Dwinell and Simson in *Mills Seminary* (1885), which was, so far as can be proved by cross-checking, scrupulously accurate and not a piece of promotional literature. Shortly after the death of Cyrus Mills the school published a small volume, *In Memoriam,* which is mainly a compilation of addresses made at the time of his funeral and of accounts of him in newspapers and in denominational and other journals. This little volume has the many demerits usually found in obituaries, some innocent mistakes of fact such as are bound to occur in hastily prepared material; but it has a considerable value. Dr. Wythe's account of the nature of Mills' last illness has been cross-checked with current accounts in the *Oakland Tribune.* I have studied all of the real estate purchases and sales made by Cyrus Mills in Alameda County—only a few of which appear in this story; but I have not gone to the land records covering his investments in Los Angeles and other counties; these I have noted only in the inventory of his estate in the probate records.

Biographical data concerning the early trustees have been derived mainly from material furnished by their living descendants and by the usual local biographies in the Bancroft Library.

CHAPTER FOURTEEN

The pamphlet "Exercises of Inauguration of Homer Baxter Sprague, President of Mills College," is in the college archives. His pamphlet, "To my Friends," is in the Bancroft Library; the trustees' pamphlet of rejoinder is in the California State Library, Sacramento; a photostat is in the Mills College Library. Marion L. Phillips, alumni registrar of Yale, kindly sent a copy of Sprague's biographical data. M. Beatrice Johnstone, of the University of North Dakota Correspondence Study Division, sent her personal recollection of Dr. Sprague, and Donald J. Robertson, assistant to the president of the university, lent me the *University Quarterly Journal,* Volume 18, No. 3, May 1928, which gave a sketch of Dr. Sprague's life in that university. (I quoted from this article the estimate of Dr. Sprague's rank as an orator.)

A pamphlet containing the addresses at Stratton's inauguration is in the

Mills archives. Mr. (now President) Robert E. Burns, of the College of the
Pacific, kindly sent me extensive material upon the life of C. C. Stratton.
The main part of the material explains its own sources.

CHAPTER FIFTEEN

Keith, Old Master of California, by Brother Cornelius of St. Mary's College, contains authoritative information about the Lyon Street Swedenborgian Church, and especially Mary C. Richardson.

Rosalind A. Keep's *Fourscore Years: A History of Mills College,* Oakland,
1931, is so much a part of our campus tradition that a foreknowledge of it, on
the part of Mills readers, is assumed. I have had a copy close at hand throughout the preparation of this manuscript.

Index